SATIRE IN AN AGE
OF REALISM

AARON MATZ

CAMBRIDGE
UNIVERSITY PRESS

CAMBRIDGE UNIVERSITY PRESS
Cambridge, New York, Melbourne, Madrid, Cape Town,
Singapore, São Paulo, Delhi, Mexico City

Cambridge University Press
The Edinburgh Building, Cambridge CB2 8RU, UK

Published in the United States of America by Cambridge University Press, New York

www.cambridge.org
Information on this title: www.cambridge.org/9781107691230

First published 2010
First paperback edition 2013

A catalogue record for this publication is available from the British Library

Library of Congress Cataloguing in Publication Data
Matz, Aaron, 1975–
Satire in an age of realism / Aaron Matz.
p.   cm. – (Cambridge studies in nineteenth-century literature and culture)
Includes bibliographical references and index.
ISBN 978-0-521-19738-0 (Hardback)
1. English fiction–19th century–History and criticism.   2. Realism in literature.
3. Satire–History and criticism.   4. Eliot, George, 1819–1880–Criticism and interpretation.
5. Hardy, Thomas, 1840–1928–Criticism and interpretation.   6. Gissing, George, 1857–1903–
Criticism and interpretation.   7. Conrad, Joseph, 1857–1924–Criticism and interpretation.
8. Ibsen, Henrik, 1828–1906–Appreciation–England.   I. Title.   II. Series.
PR878.R4M38 2010
823'.80917–dc22

2010011210

ISBN 978-0-521-19738-0 Hardback
ISBN 978-1-107-69123-0 Paperback

For Elaine Blair

... to know, and to search, and to seek out wisdom,
and the reason of things,
and to know the wickedness of folly ...
Ecclesiastes 7:25

Contents

Preface

This book is about the antagonistic tendencies of realist representation. My focus is on the period commonly regarded as the pivotal era of realism in literature, the second half of the nineteenth century. But the book aspires to something larger too: a new understanding of genre, in which two modes normally considered discrete are instead seen to be interpenetrating.

Satire exists to isolate a condition or a sector of human life and hold it up for ridicule. Realism, in its nineteenth-century literary sense, is a method or an attitude seeking to represent experience, especially everyday experience, without implausibility. But toward the end of the Victorian period these two modes blurred into one another beyond easy division. The fiction and criticism of the era imply that to describe the world in starkly realist detail – to pursue and to represent facts and conditions without euphemism – *is* to expose this same world's essential folly and error. Realism cannot help being satirical, since its method of exposure is also a mode of attack; but satire must also be realistic, for it must persuade us that our failings are so entrenched in everyday life, and so extreme, that they need no embellishment or fantasy when transmuted into fiction. The result is something I name *satirical realism*, in which human beings are portrayed with nuance – and yet are objects of ridicule simply for being there.

We usually think of satire as a decidedly non-realistic kind of literary expression. Aristophanes's chorus of frogs, Rabelais's bawdy giants, Swift's talking horses: these all seem very far from the painstaking efforts in persuasive detail that we associate with *Middlemarch* or *Madame Bovary*. Such mockery does not seek verisimilitude; it is representational, but we cannot say that it represents what is recognizable, that it tries to evoke common experience. We usually think of realism, meanwhile, as a fundamentally non-satiric tradition in the history of literature, and in the history of nineteenth-century fiction in particular. George Eliot's scenes of modest life encourage us to understand her characters and to forgive them, not to scorn them. Realism in this view must be aligned not with satire but with sympathy, satire's opposite.

That division is wrong. This book aspires to correct what I see as a general critical reluctance to face the true polemical and censorious quality of nineteenth-century realism. In this great era of the liberal and tolerant novel, the most forceful energies of the satiric tradition were in fact transmitted through realist channels. As the novel developed in audacity and frankness, it could take up the great tasks of pre-novelistic satire but carry them out even more rigorously. The exposure of folly and the disparagement of human error were no longer the province of the fantastical or boisterous style of Rabelais, or the elegant neoclassical forms of Molière; they were now subject to the more austere method of Gissing and Ibsen. It was realism, with its harsher, blunter, and ultimately more credible procedures and vocabulary, that finally assumed the mantle of the satiric heritage. Irreverent condemnation, scornful and profoundly angry censure: these could now be lodged much more effectively, for they were now disguised as representations of the world as it really was. And in a sense they were far more alarming this way, since their equation of the ridiculous and the real made it hard to imagine a sphere different from the one represented. When fiction demonstrates realistically, and convincingly, that all is indeed vanity, then it denies us the succor that we might otherwise wish that it would provide.

I am writing about several things: satire's longstanding kinship with what I call realism; satire's realist form in the nineteenth century; realism's tendency toward censure and aggression in the late Victorian years. This third subject is my main one. My aim is to write a history of realism, not of satire; I am concentrating on the nineteenth century and especially its later phases, not (for example) on the eighteenth century and its already much-studied satiric tradition. But the pursuit of realism in literary criticism presents a kind of Zeno's paradox: as you inch closer and closer the thing seems to remain always just out of reach. Realism is better understood as an aspiration or elusive promise than as a fixed point: the study of representation is like the problem of closing a narrowing but stubborn gap. The very belief in literature's mimetic quality is one you hold or reject; if you hold it, that conviction is an act of faith that propels your reading and interpretation. Surely this is a major reason for the vastness of the scholarship on literary realism. We write about literature and the real because we believe in the fundamental union of the two, but since it can never be proven we hope our criticism will corroborate its very existence on the horizon.

This vastness looms over every study of realism. First, there is the question of period: can we limit a book about literary realism to the nineteenth century, or should we look back at least to the 1700s, as Ian Watt does, and maybe forward to the present day? Second, of course, is the problem of what we mean by realism – if our emphasis should fall on the visual, the procedural, the literary-historical, the world-historical, the political, the sociological, or maybe something else altogether.

I am following many other critics in concentrating on the second half of the nineteenth century. But in doing so I do not want to take for granted that the fiction of these years, in retrospect, seems somehow more realistic than that of any other sequence of a few decades of literary history. Instead I am insisting, throughout the book, on the question of realism as it existed *as* a question in the late Victorian period. This is why my focus is on the 1880s and especially the 1890s – these were the years when this idea or movement or school had the greatest dominion over English fiction and criticism, and when the term itself was in such constant currency. Every chapter that follows is informed by my concern for what "realism" meant to the writers in question: why Hardy went so far out of his way to reject it as "an unfortunate, an ambiguous word"; why Gissing returned constantly and anxiously to what he called "the place of realism in fiction"; why English critics clashed for years over whether Ibsen's plays were "realistic"; why Conrad was wary of being faithful to any "dogmas of realism" though sometimes seemed rather intrigued by them. This consideration of late Victorian views of realism, however, is only half of a two-part process. How – for these writers – "realism" became intertwined with something more accurately called "satire": this theme then shapes every chapter of this book. And every one of these chapters considers how the *critics* of the era, struggling to interpret such an intrepid and aggressive form of representation, relied so heavily on the two ambiguous words that together provide the title of this book.

My emphasis on the 1880s and 1890s means that I largely avoid those Victorian novelists most often understood to be satirists: Dickens, Thackeray, and Trollope (to say nothing of the earlier, and in many ways foundational, satirical novelist Austen). In part this is a choice informed by past criticism: the satiric quality of those novelists has been widely studied before. But it's a choice also fueled by my particular focus on the realism inherent in satire, and the notably dark kind of fiction I associate with Hardy and Gissing but not with Dickens and Trollope. Satirical realism – a kind of writing that is satirical precisely *because* it is relentlessly realist – conceives reality as a sphere that is uniformly subject to censure, not selectively, as in Dickens or Trollope. Satirical realism is a mode of austerity, not of Dickens's boisterousness or Trollope's lively panoramas. It is a tragic and not a comic mode. "The way we live now" is a fine phrase for satirical realism, but *The Way We Live Now* is not a work of satirical realism as I describe it in the following chapters.

Thackeray is a more difficult case, and he surfaces in my chapters on Hardy and Gissing, but it is exactly my point to begin my history after his death – once "realism" became something novelists could not ignore or circumvent – and, in particular, after Dickens's career was mostly over. Despite the proto-realist sensibility of some Dickens novels, and despite his fiction's residence in the same working-class spheres we find again in Hardy and Gissing (and which are so important in my evaluation of their realism), my writers were forging an art that set itself apart from Dickensian narrative and characterization, even when they were indebted to his example. I acknowledge this simultaneous debt and distance; and in the chapters that follow, especially those on Gissing and Conrad, I evaluate Dickens as a foil, a kind of contrapuntal figure, who only throws into greater relief the satirical realism of the writers in question. In a sense Dickens is one of the central figures of this book, but only as a shadowy counterexample. As will be clear throughout the book, there is an essential reason for my focus on the late nineteenth century, the era after Thackeray and Dickens: my point is that novelistic realism had by this point reached a phase that it *understood* to be late; it had traveled far enough along its own arc to blur into satire.

A related subject is the question of historical analysis. I am tracing a shift in the tenor and character of realism; to what extent can that shift be explained by social and political circumstances in Victorian England? This is an especially difficult question for my study of the hybrid mode *satirical realism* in particular. *Realism* I usually associate with the specific and the local, while I typically argue that *satire* – at least the wide-ranging and essential satire that I am examining – is a fundamentally ahistorical, context-resistant mode of writing. Satire tells us the same, continuous truth about mankind's folly; realism articulates it in new ways. This book is therefore historically aware without being historically determined. Specific extra-literary Victorian topics – especially population, poverty, and urbanism – are pivotal themes throughout these chapters; and I have benefited from the work of such historically focused critics as Catherine Gallagher and Patrick Brantlinger. But I also believe that satire's caustic energies usually resist historicizing, and that the satirical realism of the writers in question – particularly Hardy, Gissing, and Conrad – is precisely what connects them to the tragic satirical tradition that preexisted the Victorian era. Many studies of nineteenth-century realism have focused on its interest in social reform; none has really taken up its later surrender to the inevitable truth of human error, its relinquishing of a reformist ideal. Satirical realism, as I argue throughout this book, is a non-corrective, a post-corrective, form of satire. And so the key is to keep one eye alert to the historical circumstances that give rise to despair or censure, all the while keeping the other focused on the long view, on how satire seizes upon present conditions only to articulate a much broader and shared human situation: on how it zooms out from the local to the universal.

The problem of period, and periodization, also brings with it the question of international scope. A very similar book could be written about the same subject in French literature. That study would surely center on Balzac and especially Flaubert; it might culminate in the antagonistic quality of Zola's naturalism and ultimately the satirical realism of Céline, who is *sui generis.* Most stages in this French study would be moved a few decades earlier than the points on my arc here. But I have decided to write a history of English realism in particular, infused though it is with the strong presence of the consummate satirical realist Flaubert. My chapter on Ibsen focuses on the Norwegian's reception and interpretation in England, and as part of the specifically late Victorian debates about the workings and purposes of realism in literature. The dual, interpenetrating subjects of this study are, for now, too immense to confront beyond the margins of the English tradition.

Second, the problem of what we mean by realism. This, of course, is what I am trying to address on every page of this book. But I can begin by providing some orientation here, and by explaining where my energies are, and are not, directed. There are a few main strands in the scholarship on realism, several major ways of approaching the subject. The first is the study of realism's relation to the visual. The very term "realism" (to refer to creative representation, rather than scholastic philosophy) comes from nineteenth-century art criticism, and some of the most penetrating studies of literary realism have focused on its connection to the visual arts. The art-historical scholarship of E.H. Gombrich and Linda Nochlin, among others, has been very influential in literary studies; two of my own mentors, Peter Brooks and Ruth Bernard Yeazell, have recently written about the relations between literature and painting. I have benefited from scholars who have examined certain interconnections between realism and the visual (Kate Flint) or related questions of perspective (Elizabeth Deeds Ermarth). A second major line in the tradition stresses the political dimensions of realism: this line begins with the Marxist theory of Georg Lukács, passes through his critics Bertolt Brecht and Theodor Adorno, and continues through the recent work of scholars like Terry Lovell and Harry E. Shaw. A very closely related sequence is the tradition we inherit largely from Raymond Williams, and which has passed through Patrick Brantlinger and Franco Moretti, among others: the study of nineteenth-century literature through the lens of sociology, the sociology of literary forms, often taking the shape of cultural studies. (Ian Watt's work may be said to inaugurate another generous strand of this tradition.) Williams, especially, figures prominently here. Another central approach to realism emphasizes its connections to science; Gillian Beer and George Levine are the key writers in this tradition. Finally, there is the largely formalist line that descends from Erich Auerbach, and which informs so many contemporary studies of literary realism.

I am indebted to all these critics and traditions, and in the chapters that follow I often address the visual-optical, the sociological, the scientific, the formalist, and especially the political dimensions of realism. But if there is a single term to describe my approach to the subject it is undoubtedly *moral*, as long as we understand this word in its negative sense: I am evaluating the tendency of realist literature to be a strangely tragic protest literature, to represent people and things and conditions in a lifelike manner in order to expose their profound errors and failings. I am interested in the way a novel or play can seem at once detached and quite angry, neutral and yet partisan, objective but derisive, realistic and satirical. Satirical realism is a fundamentally moral kind of literature relying on a detachment or coolness that adroitly gives the impression of verisimilitude. It is dissent and description simultaneously. But satirical realism does not dissent in order to correct: it judges existing reality against a standard that reality can never achieve, and so it relinquishes any hope of correction. If it has been a virtually ignored tendency in the work of many of the greatest writers of the late nineteenth century, then I intend this book as a sort of corrective in its own right.

All translations from the French are my own. Other citations in translation – notably of Ibsen – are attributed in the text.

Acknowledgments

I owe my first thanks to the first two people who read this book. I began this project as a dissertation under the guidance of Peter Brooks and Ruth Bernard Yeazell, and years later it is still indebted to their influence. For their dedication to this book, their vast knowledge of nineteenth-century fiction, and the example they set as teachers and writers: for all these things I am infinitely grateful. At Yale I also want to thank Alexander Welsh for everything I've learned from him about the Victorian novel; Claude Rawson for teaching me most of what I know about satire; and Pericles Lewis for our many conversations about fiction, modernism, teaching, and publishing. Sandy, Claude, and Pericles all read parts of this book in its earlier stages. So did Tanya Agathocleous and Barry McCrea: thanks to both for their very helpful response to it.

At Cambridge University Press my thanks go first to Linda Bree for her guidance of the manuscript from the beginning, and to Gillian Beer for including the book in Cambridge's nineteenth-century series. Thanks to Elizabeth Hanlon for her editorial expertise and support, and to the two anonymous readers for their extensive commentary and valuable advice about the manuscript.

For financial support I'm grateful to Yale University, the Mrs. Giles Whiting Foundation, the Paul Mellon Centre/Yale Center for British Art, the Beinecke Rare Book and Manuscript Library, and Scripps College. Thanks also to my colleagues at Scripps for their support of my teaching and scholarship.

Chapters 2 and 3 appeared (in earlier versions) in *ELH* and *Nineteenth-Century Literature* and are reprinted by permission of The Johns Hopkins University Press and the University of California Press respectively.

I can't adequately thank my closest friends, but I'll try: thanks to Stephen Weiss and Adam Willens; thanks in particular to three friends who read parts of the manuscript: Jess Row, John Delury, and Ethan Leib. My longest-standing thanks and love I give to my brothers, Jeremy Matz and Jonathan Matz, and above all to Dr. Jane Balkin Matz and the Honorable A. Howard Matz, my parents and first teachers of French and English literature. My newest I give to my daughter Anya.

This book is dedicated with love and ardor to my wife Elaine Blair, my best reader.

CHAPTER I

Augustan satire and Victorian realism

In the last years of the nineteenth century, English critics found themselves reaching a tentative consensus: the school of fiction called "realism"
was finally coming to an end. Imported mostly from France, later propa-
gated by disciples of Zola and French naturalism, debated endlessly in the
British press, so-called realism had – in the span of only ten or twenty
years – conquered the landscape of English fiction and become the
dominant mode. But it was now in decline, the victim of its own excesses.

Edmund Gosse, omnipresent critic of the era, ascribed this decline to
"The Limits of Realism in Fiction": this was the title of his 1890 essay,
later published in the 1893 collection *Questions at Issue*. Realism to Gosse
largely meant Zolaesque naturalism and its progeny, full of rules and
dogma: "it is to be contemporary; it is to be founded on and limited
by actual experience ... to paint men as they are, not as you think they
should be." But as Gosse's title announced, and as he reiterated throughout
the essay, this kind of writing had hit a wall. "There are limits to realism,
and they seem to have been readily discovered by the realists themselves ...
in trying to draw life evenly and draw it whole, they have introduced
such a brutal want of tone as to render the portrait a caricature ... in their
sombre, grimy, and dreary studies in pathology, clinical bulletins of a soul
dying of atrophy, we may see what the limits of realism are."[1] Gosse was
wariest of those novelists adhering most closely to the rigid edicts of
doctrinaire naturalism, but he was also voicing skepticism about all the
fin-de-siècle fiction that trafficked in the grimy, destitute, ugly quarters
of contemporary life. These quarters had now been occupied, subjugated.
Realism of this sort had nowhere further to go.

Gosse was not alone in expressing such misgivings. The more dismis-
sive Oscar Wilde, who had always enjoyed flaunting his sneering distaste
for realism, cheered the movement's demise. In the 1891 "Critic as Artist,"

Wilde wrote sarcastically of realism as of a day whose sun had finally set: "Yesterday it was Realism that charmed one. One gained from it that *nouveau frisson* which it was its aim to produce. One analysed it, explained it and wearied of it." In "The Critic as Artist" Wilde called his bugbear "tedious realism," in *The Picture of Dorian Gray* "vulgar realism."[2] For Wilde the limits of realism had been reached from the start. But even observers more sympathetic to the idea of realist fiction worried about its abuses and dissipations. In "Reticence in Literature," published in *The Yellow Book* in 1894, Arthur Waugh praised "the realistic movement in English literature" and championed "the duty of the man of letters to speak out, to be fearless, to be frank." But he cautioned that "we ought, too, to be able to arrive instinctively at a sense of the limits of art, and to appreciate the point at which frankness becomes violence, in that it has degenerated into mere brawling, animated neither by purpose nor idea."[3] Waugh was sounding a familiar anxiety, heard throughout English criticism of the period: realism had grown so frank that it had turned aggressive, so blunt as to become destructively bleak.

This book is concerned with endings: with the end of the Victorian novel, and along with it the end of its governing paradigms of realism. My view of realism depends on a certain theory of direction or sequence. On the far side of realism, in this view, lies satire, just as on the far side of satire we are likely to find realism. Satire and realism are two ways of understanding literature's relationship with the world it represents. The first has to do with a moral attitude toward that world: satire isolates conditions or truths in order to chastise the mankind responsible for them. Realism has generally been understood as an expository or demonstrative stance – or posture, or method, or (like satire) attitude – that is interested in those same truths, in those same conditions, without necessarily operating on the assumption that it has set forth to mock them.[4] But when realism blurs into satire, its expository method becomes indistinguishable from its censorious essence. This blurring marks an extremity in the development of realism, in that realism marches toward satire but finds in it its own outermost boundary of representational possibility. In the following chapter I call Hardy's *Jude the Obscure* "terminal," but in truth virtually all works of satirical realism, especially those under examination here, are terminal as well.

My central premise is that nineteenth-century realism developed into satire and thereby engendered its own decline. But this is not to say that the fusion of these two modes was a fact of late Victorian literature alone. On the contrary, satire and realism have always existed in close proximity:

indeed, each has always been embedded in the other. Some of the earliest works of Western satire – Juvenal's, for instance – depended on an intense verisimilitude in representation and a realist directness in transmission; while English novelistic realism, as Ronald Paulson and others have demonstrated, emerged in large part out of a tradition of satire and satiric conventions in the eighteenth century.[5] And so my opening chapter has two main tasks. One is to examine these longstanding affinities of satire and realism, from Juvenal to the nineteenth century, in order to understand how late Victorian satirical realism was, in fact, a decisive fusion of two modes that had always been in such close proximity. The second task is to examine the more direct roots of late nineteenth-century satirical realism in the fiction of mid-century, notably in the work of George Eliot. But I tackle these two things together, rather than sequentially, since an examination of Eliot's fiction leads naturally to the long ancestry of satirical realism that stands in the background of her writing.

The subject of the interconnections between satire and realism has been mostly ignored in the history of literary criticism. One fine exception is a short 1955 essay by John Lawlor, "Radical Satire and the Realistic Novel." Lawlor begins with English Augustan satire and focuses on Swift, whose writings seem to reject what might once have been, in the hands of Horace or Dryden, one of the principal assumptions of satire: that it could serve a corrective purpose. Some kinds of satire exposed a folly in order to instruct the reader that it was a vice – and that it should be avoided. But from Swift, according to Lawlor, we can no longer expect such comforts:

We have an explanation of our insensibility and incapacity to alter. It is an answer that takes us beyond correction. The satire becomes radical, for it brings into the light the comfortable assumption that we can see our folly, let alone amend it. The inquiry is now to ask what is man's nature, in light of the evidence, including the evidence of satire itself? In *Gulliver's Travels* Swift writes a satire that at once ensures that we shall inescapably see ourselves, and is at the same time a satire to end all notions of "correction" ... What blindly resists the assaults of corrective satire unfolds to the radical inquiry: and if we pass beyond contempt into objective appraisal, a new territory is decisively entered. We move from satire to what may be called, with suitable qualifications, Realism.[6]

In a very rapid two pages, Lawlor then pursues his logic to Flaubert and *Madame Bovary*. Flaubert's fiction is something beyond satire: a diagnosis of an "unchanging condition," with no possibility for the correction native to earlier forms of satirical writing. Satire's telos lies in the realist novel, which depends on an expository method but dismisses the flat expectation that the depiction of human life can teach any cohesive or coherent lesson.[7]

Lawlor's argument is appealing and persuasive. And his emphasis on Swift and Flaubert is particularly apposite to my canvas here: these are the two writers who stand most prominently in the historical background of this book.[8] But Lawlor's scope is frustratingly narrow. It stops with Flaubert, as if the question of realism and satire somehow ended with *Madame Bovary*. What this brief overview does not take into account is the abiding coexistence of these two kinds of literature, and especially the increasing intimacy of this coexistence during the later years of the nineteenth century. Realist fiction can indeed be understood as the heir to the satiric tradition. When satire's corrective order begins to wane, we can recognize its enduring energies in the rather less rigid forms of the nineteenth-century novel. But it is no less true that realist fiction also seems to have its terminus, and that we might identify this point as something better named satire. A hyperrealism becomes satirical just as a radical satire becomes realistic. If this kind of logic seems vertiginous, it is only proof of the profound kinship of these two traditions – and of Alvin Kernan's reminder, in *The Plot of Satire*, that "we should not think that a genre distinction is an airtight category."[9] Indeed such porousness becomes only more marked over time. Genres emerge and blur into one another, especially upon the fading of other genres, and upon the expiration of earlier paradigms. Satire and realism are both genres of lateness: they come necessarily *after* other modes and traditions have been exhausted, and in some sense they are expressing the impossibility of writing in that earlier way – in the case of satire, epic; in the case of realism, fantasy or high romanticism – any longer.[10]

My history therefore concentrates on the final decades of the nineteenth century, and embodies a theory of limits and finality.[11] But no study of satire and realism in late Victorian literature can avoid English realism's central, archetypal figure: it must pass through the fiction of George Eliot. This chapter will largely focus on her writing as an exemplary prism through which we can study some of the tendencies and problems of Victorian realist representation – especially realism's connection to satire. It is her fiction that helps connect the Augustan satiric tradition to the realism of the fin de siècle. In many ways her writing prefigures the fiction of Hardy and Gissing and Conrad: novelists who could not forge a realism impervious to the censorious forces of satire. Like them, she was often ruled by a satirical temper that the past century of criticism has overlooked or misunderstood.

THE HUMAN COMPLEXION

Satire and realism are both fundamentally representational modes: both depend on the connection between what they describe and the referents of those things or persons or situations that we know from the world we inhabit. From satire we expect that the transmogrification of the referent into the description will be an act of judgment. Something in the world is to be scorned; the negative form it takes in satire will be confirmation of the attitude we should hold toward that thing. From realism we typically expect some kind of satisfactory verisimilitude or plausibility. If the represented form veers too far from what we know it to look like, or be like, in our experience, we will deem it to be non-realist or even anti-realist. Both satire and realism therefore put extraordinary pressure on the detail, on the shape and precision of the representation in its particularity, whether as a clue toward judgment in satire (the first thing we learn about Candide is that he has a gentle countenance; therefore he is a naïve fool), or as an index of lifelikeness or familiarity in realism (Anna Karenina's shining grey eyes, in her first appearance, evoke an erotic intensity that we are meant to recognize from experience). Detail and texture, especially the detail or texture of the visible, is the crucible of representation in each mode. Specificity in description is not the mere ornamentation of something else but a focus in itself, a guide and a gauge.

We praise George Eliot for precisely this kind of richly imagined and deftly executed detail in portraiture and representation: the crisp and bleak precision of the avenue of limes outside Dorothea's window in *Middlemarch*, for example, or the meticulous narrative camera that zooms in and out from the hands and eyes of the people around the gambling table in the opening scene of *Daniel Deronda*. When we talk about George Eliot's "realism" we can mean many things: her sympathetic imagination for ordinary people, her creation of a vast panorama of society. But we mean this too, that she sees objects and textures with a subtle and thorough vision, and that her fiction manages to evoke the grain of ocular and palpable experience in a way superior to most other writers.

Frequently Eliot is quite self-conscious about this kind of descriptive rigor and realism, nowhere more than in the famous chapter 17 of *Adam Bede*. Nowhere is her position on novelistic practice and attitude more comprehensively articulated; and, of course, no passage from her fiction has therefore attracted so much attention from scholars interpreting Eliot's own theory of realist representation.[12] The chapter later evolves into a discussion of Mr. Irwine and Adam, but at first it announces itself as an autonomous statement of purpose, an apologia that could be slotted anywhere in *Adam Bede* – and indeed just about anywhere in Eliot's fiction.

The chapter revolves around Eliot's comparison of her fiction to Dutch genre painting. Like the Dutch painters, she wants to redeem and reclaim the kind of people that other writers might deem unworthy of representation: the "more or less ugly, stupid, inconsistent people" leading a "monotonous, homely existence." The narrator mockingly imagines an "idealistic friend" who would object to paying any attention to this sphere of existence: "what a low phase of life! – what clumsy, ugly people!" the friend might say. But Eliot insists on training her eye on the ugly, "without trying to make things seem better than they were."

But, bless us, things may be lovable that are not altogether handsome, I hope? I am not at all sure that the majority of the human race have not been ugly, and even among those 'lords of their kind,' the British, squat figures, ill-shapen nostrils, and dingy complexions are not startling exceptions.

Her lesson seems clear. George Eliot's fiction, like the canvases of those seventeenth-century painters, will not paint such people for the purpose of scorning them. Ugliness does not equal loathsomeness; these pages are very plain in specifying that "these fellow-mortals, every one, must be accepted as they are: you can neither straighten their noses, nor brighten their wit, nor rectify their dispositions."[13]

And yet it is hard to ignore, at this critical moment in *Adam Bede*, how much Eliot lingers on all this ugliness, on all the unsightly things about the human form. These "irregular noses and lips," these "rounded backs and stupid weather-beaten faces" clearly hold a certain fascination for her, even beyond their ostensible purpose of directing us toward the faculty of sympathy. Above all Eliot seems drawn to the unpleasant color and texture of the human complexion. Those "dingy complexions," as she reminds us here, are not startling exceptions. They are a shared human trait – and indeed she will return again and again, throughout the cycle of novels that *Adam Bede* inaugurates, to the basic facts of surface reality, as represented by our common skin. The image appears even earlier than *Adam Bede*, in brief glimpses in *Scenes of Clerical Life*, where the Baronet's complexion in "Mr Gilfil's Love Story" "looked dull and withered," and where a Welshman in "Janet's Repentance" is defined by his "globose figure and unctuous complexion."[14] In the later fiction, complexion develops from an occasional image into a wider theme. *The Mill on the Floss*, for example, makes a point of the divide between Maggie's dark skin – which is distasteful to her mother – and the fairer Dodson complexion. The opening chapter of *Felix Holt* presents Mrs. Transome gazing at herself in the mirror, where she sees "the dried-up complexion, and the deep lines of bitter discontent about the mouth" and immediately thinks, "I am a hag!"[5] And in *Middlemarch* the ugly pallor and unevenness of Casaubon's skin serves as a warning of the repugnant person beneath it. In the novel's second chapter, Dorothea and Celia argue about the man who has just visited the Brooke house, and who will soon woo the elder sister.

When the two girls were alone in the drawing-room alone, Celia said—
  'How very ugly Mr Casaubon is!'
  'Celia! He is one of the most distinguished-looking men I ever saw. He is remarkably like the portrait of Locke. He has the same deep eye-sockets.'
  'Had Locke those two white moles with hairs on them?'
  'Oh, I dare say! when people of a certain sort looked at him,' said Dorothea, walking away a little.
  'Mr Casaubon is so sallow.'
  'All the better. I suppose you admire a man with the complexion of a *cochon de lait.*'[6]

In the end, of course, it is *Celia* who is right. Eliot is not teaching us here the error of judging someone on the basis of his skin: she is indicating a repulsive personality, to be revealed gradually, by a repulsive complexion, which can be detected immediately. Indeed Casaubon's complexion turns up repeatedly in *Middlemarch*, always a source of nausea for Celia but a subject of great interest to the author. In the following chapter, we are reminded that the younger sister "did not like the company of Mr Casaubon's moles and sallowness" (23). And in a famous passage much later in the novel, after Casaubon and Dorothea have come back from their honeymoon, Eliot returns once again to her persistent theme:

One morning some weeks after her arrival at Lowick, Dorothea – but why always Dorothea? Was her point of view the only possible one with regard to marriage? I protest against all our interest, all our effort at understanding being given to the young skins that look blooming in spite of trouble; for these too will get faded, and will know the older and more eating griefs which we are helping to neglect. In spite of the blinking eyes and white moles objectionable to Celia, and the want of muscular curve which was morally painful to Sir James, Mr Casaubon had an intense consciousness within him, and was spiritually a-hungered like the rest of us. (271–2)

As so often happens in George Eliot's fiction, the ground here shifts quite suddenly beneath the reader. We have been trained not to like Casaubon very much; his ugly moles and sallow complexion have been reliable emblems of his generally distasteful character. But for the moment the narrator seems to undercut this very equation – all young skins will grow old; and anyway we can hold out hope that even a mole-spotted complexion might mask an intense consciousness. The human skin appears to serve as some kind of terrain upon which a conflict of realism is to be waged. Nothing is more plainly superficial: skin is pure surface, the perfect subject for a realist description of straightforward, physical fact. And yet Eliot is ambiguous about its interpretive or symbolic value. At times complexion points the way to a kind of satire, where moles are meant to provoke our distaste; at others we are warned not to let it obstruct our path to sympathy. But as the ars poetica in *Adam Bede* suggests, and as the familiar, sustained imagery of the larger oeuvre seems to corroborate, our shared complexion – greasy, dingy, pallid – is none-theless quite significant in our basic processes of perception. And it is, evidently, essential to fiction's lifelike and credible representation of ordinary human life.

Not everyone in George Eliot's fiction looks exactly like this, of course. Most of her heroines have clear skin; in *Daniel Deronda*, Gwendolen Harleth's complexion is supposed to be particularly attractive. Nor does Eliot's focus on complexion – ugly or otherwise – make her unique in the tradition of the Victorian novel. Dickens, for instance, might also note the quality of his characters' skin: Uriah Heep's sweaty hands are the most memorable example. But we do not get the sense with Dickens, as we do with Eliot, that the representation of complexion figures so prominently in the machinery of realist technique and method – that it is suggested to be so fundamental a component of how we see, and how a novelist controls what we see. To encounter this kind of vision so often in Eliot's fiction is to discover a certain descriptive logic. She will show people in their everyday reality and therefore describe what they look like; she will be faithful in this description and therefore acknowledge that these people often have ugly skin. This novelist so renowned for the complex psychology of her characters, for the great moral ordeals of Hetty Sorrel and Dorothea Brooke and Gwendolen Harleth, is also committed to the comprehensive and credible delineation of surface. And if that surface is exposed to be prosaically ugly, some readers are likely to object. Ruskin's 1881 view of *The Mill on the Floss* is instructive in this respect. Eliot's novel was "perhaps the most striking instance extant of this study of cutaneous disease," Ruskin claimed, referring to the kind of fiction that depicted "the blotches, burrs and pimples" of vulgar daily life.[17]

A descriptive fixation like this can evoke the close-ups of Flaubert: Emma's shoulders at the beginning of *Madame Bovary*, for example, glistening with a few drops of sweat; or the reverse image of her corpse at the end of the novel, where her eyelashes are sprinkled with a sort of white powder and a viscous pallor covers her eyes.[18] But Eliot's persistent focus on the human skin has a strange tendency to recall a less likely forebear: Jonathan Swift. Swift cannot be said to enlist the precision of detail as a tool in a larger quest for verisimilitude in representation. And yet certain moments in *Gulliver's Travels* are eerily prescient of nineteenth-century realism's focus on the individual complexion. Gulliver's voyage to Brobdingnag provides the perfect scenario for Swift's oddly proto-realist visions: Gulliver, suddenly tiny, finds himself looking at immense humanoid figures; he can therefore see detail as never before. And just as George Eliot says that an authentic look at the "majority of the human race" yields the reality of "dingy complexions," so Swift tells us that Gulliver's microscopic vision will expose that same ugliness. This is a major theme of part II of *Gulliver's Travels* from its opening pages. Soon after Gulliver arrives on the island, and is taken in by a farmer, he witnesses the family's baby suckling at a nurse's breast. The incident yields one of the book's most harrowing visions.

I must confess no Object ever disgusted me so much as the Sight of her monstrous Breast, which I cannot tell what to compare with, so as to give the curious Reader an Idea of its Bulk, Shape and Colour. It stood prominent six Foot, and could not be less than sixteen in Circumference. The Nipple was about Half the Bigness of my Head, and the Hue both of that and the Dug so varified with Spots, Pimples and Freckles, that nothing could appear more nauseous: For I had a near Sight of her, she sitting down the more conveniently to give Suck, and I standing on the Table. This made me reflect upon the fair Skins of our *English* Ladies, who appear so beautiful to us, only because they are of our own Size, and their Defects not to be seen but through a magnifying Glass, where we find by Experiment that the smoothest and whitest Skins look rough and coarse, and ill coloured.

I remember when I was at *Lilliput*, the Complexions of those diminutive People appeared to me the fairest in the World: And talking upon this Subject with a Person of Learning there, who was an intimate Friend of mine; he said, that my Face appeared much fairer and smoother when he looked on me from the Ground, than it did upon a nearer View when I took him up in my Hand, and brought him close; which he confessed was at first a very shocking Sight. He said, he could discover great Holes in my Skin; that the Stumps of my Beard were ten Times stronger than the Bristles of a Boar; and my Complexion made up of several Colours altogether disagreeable: Although I must beg Leave to say for my self, that I am as fair as most of my Sex and Country, and very little Sunburnt by all my Travels.[19]

This is one of Swift's favorite devices: to expose an ugly truth by altering perspective. (It is the kind of distortion that Alvin Kernan identifies as the "magnifying tendency" of satire, or what Erich Auerbach, referring to Voltaire's method, calls "the searchlight device.")[20] Throughout Gulliver's stay in Brobdingnag, we are constantly reminded how ugly things are when seen from up close. A glimpse of the Queen eating is for Gulliver "a very nauseous Sight," since all the food is so grotesquely amplified; he is overwhelmed by the excrement of flies, visible to him but not to the natives, whose "large Opticks were not so acute as mine in viewing smaller Objects" (90–3).[21]

But nothing is as loathsome to Gulliver as the skin of the Brobding-nagians. Soon he comes across a sight similar to the child nursing at the breast: "There was a Woman with a Cancer in her Breast, swelled to a monstrous Size, full of Holes, in two or three of which I could have easily crept, and covered my whole Body. There was a Fellow with a Wen in his Neck, larger than five Woolpacks; and another with a couple of wooden Legs, each about twenty Foot high" (96–7). The fundamental horror of Brobdingnag is the horror of having to look too closely at the giants' complexion – and therefore the horror of having to contemplate our own. "Their Skins appeared so coarse and uneven," Gulliver remarks again later, "so variously coloured when I saw them near, with a Mole here and there as broad as a Trencher, and Hairs hanging from it thicker than Pack-threads; to say nothing further concerning the rest of their Persons" (103). To see in detail, says Swift, is to see the ugliness of the real. This is the lesson of the second part of *Gulliver's Travels*.

But this cutaneous disgust is not restricted to Gulliver's voyage to Brobdingnag. It marks the later sections of the book as well, such that the human complexion ends up exemplifying Swift's much more univer-sal misanthropy. In the voyage to Laputa, for example, Gulliver's educa-tion in the history of mankind evokes a despair expressed in altogether familiar terms:

it gave me melancholy Reflections to observe how much the Race of human Kind was degenerate among us, within these Hundred Years past. How the Pox under all its Consequences and Denominations had altered every Lineament of an *English* Countenance: shortened the Size of Bodies, unbraced the Nerves, relaxed the Sinews and Muscles, introduced a sallow Complexion, and rendered the Flesh loose and *rancid*. (185)

And in the darkest section of *Gulliver's Travels*, the concluding voyage to the Houyhnhnms, it is the flesh of the Yahoos that embodies their repulsive existence – and that produces some of the bleakest revelations of the Swiftian imagination. The Yahoos, Gulliver is shocked to discover, have human faces. Approaching them generates the same kind of revulsion at proximity that defined the voyage to Brobdingnag: "the more I came near them, the more hateful they grew" (214). Gulliver is ashamed to be seen without his entire body covered, lest the Houyhnhnms observe that he has the same hide as the Yahoos. He tries to explain that in England people cover their bodies with "the Hairs of certain Animals" (220); the Houyhnhnms, meanwhile, are perplexed that Gulliver resembles the Yahoos but seems to have a fairer complexion and less hair on his body.

Gradually the antipathy to the human skin gives way to a total condemnation of the ugly human form. Gulliver's feeble and ambivalent defenses of the English persuade neither the Houyhnhnms nor himself. The problem of skin keeps getting in the way. Complexion is, among other things, a prime indication of basic human hypocrisy and stupidity, since those who have the worst skin are the highest-born gentry: "a weak diseased Body, a meager Countenance, and sallow Complexion, are the true Marks of *noble Blood*; and a healthy robust Appearance is so disgraceful in a Man of Quality, that the World concludes his real Father to have been a Groom or a Coachman" (241). Meanwhile it is only when Gulliver pulls up his sleeves, revealing the flesh of human arms, that the Yahoos recognize him as the same species. This marks one of the most horrifying moments in the whole of *Gulliver's Travels*. From this point on, the skin of Gulliver and the skin of the Yahoos become intertwined in a morbid cycle of revulsion and recognition. Suddenly under threat from the Houyhnhnms, Gulliver uses the skins of Yahoos to fashion the canoe that will lead him back to Europe. And finally, toward the end of the book – after he has left the island of the Houyhnhnms – he is rescued by Portuguese sailors unable at first to understand what kind of creature he is. It is his skin that gives him away: "they admired to hear me answer them in their own Tongue, and saw by my Complection I must be an European" (269). By this point in Swift's book, of course, we can no longer think of the European complexion as anything to esteem.

For Swift the confrontation with man, and all that man embodies, begins on the surface, with the skin. The skin is where humor and horror meet and fuse beyond division, into that disquieting state of recognition that is Swiftian satire. The human skin appears not only in *Gulliver's Travels* but throughout his writings: in *A Tale of a Tub*, for instance, with its notorious line "last week I saw a Woman *flay'd*, and you will hardly believe, how much it altered her Person for the worse"; or in *A Modest Proposal*, where the skin of the child carcasses "artificially dressed, will make admirable *Gloves for Ladies*, and *Summer Boots for fine Gentlemen*."[22] Swift is not concerned with describing human beings "realistically," the way George Eliot might be: his fixation on human flesh and complexion is not a technique in the service of portraying individual people in all their physical idiosyncrasy. But the texture of skin nevertheless seems essential to his investigations of mankind. Swift cannot imagine or depict the human sphere without it, and because the ugliness of complexion is such an unfaltering index of the corruptness and nastiness of man, skin becomes a central ingredient, a defining trope, of his satire. Given its role as the focus of an ocular imagination, and its position as a marker of value and meaning, its relation to Swiftian satire is analogous to its relation to George Eliot's realism. Skin is both the essence of the visual and the means of making sense of the visual, as Steven Connor writes in *The Book of Skin*: "the skin figures. It is what we see and know of others and ourselves. We show ourselves in and on our skins, and our skins figure out the things we are and mean ... it has become the proof of our exposure to visibility itself." Connor's "historical poetics of the skin" does not focus on either Swift or Eliot specifically, but in its emphasis on inscription – on the skin in writing and on writing on human skin – it reveals a similar fixation on the skin as a signifying screen, a surface of meaning, a "borderline between form and substance."[23]

Swift's controlling image is, in fact, a recurring one not only in his writing but throughout English Augustan satire. Alexander Pope relies frequently on the motif and idea of the human skin. In book IV of the 1742 *Dunciad*, for instance, Pope writes that "the critic Eye, that microscope of Wit,/ Sees hairs and pores, examines bit by bit:/ How parts relate to parts, or they to whole."[24] Seeing microscopically is an essential idea in *The Dunciad*, where the poet pledges to "tell the naked fact without disguise" (line 433). *An Essay on Man* returns to the same theme and image:

> Why has not Man a microscopic eye?
> For this plain reason, Man is not a Fly.
> Say what the use, were finer optics giv'n.
> T'inspect a mite, not comprehend the heav'n?
> Or touch, if tremblingly alive all o'er,
> To smart and agonize at ev'ry Pore?[25]

To see in great detail has its perils: it can obstruct our wider view. But Pope, like his Scriblerian friend Swift, knows the temptation of gazing into the pores of man: he knows the appeal of the microscopic vision. That vision promises an insight and knowledge fundamental to Augustan satire, with its natively supercilious posture and supreme wisdom concerning the innate follies of mankind. Perhaps Swift's and Pope's shared fixation is particularly representative of eighteenth-century literature: Henry Fielding, in *Joseph Andrews* and *Tom Jones*, will often introduce a character through description of his or her skin, pimples and all. But maybe the human complexion is actually a basic and fundamental ingredient throughout all the satiric tradition. It appears frequently in Rabelais, from the first chapter of *Pantagruel* and its descriptions of the blistered and pimply noses of certain races of man.[26] And it turns up in the foundational works of Roman satire: in Horace, for example, who reminds us that "on a handsome body you might notice a few moles."[27] Swift and Pope would surely agree – if they could bring themselves to find a human body handsome in the first place.

Augustan satire and Victorian realism appear to have very different aims: the first wants to ridicule man, the second seems to want to portray him with sympathy. But both want to expose him. And both know that some important element of human essence is located in human surface: both know that to pursue the real, they need to confront the skin. Satire and realism are both low genres that are – unlike epic, unlike tragedy – allowed to traffic in the prosaic and worldly facts of physical matters. And if reality is often construed to mean what is visible or tactile, then perception promises to yield some kind of comprehension. Hence the recurrence of the human skin: a convenient metaphor, perhaps, but ultimately an inescapable fact. The way we typically describe satire is instructive in this respect: satire is an unmasking; it shows us the naked truth. In *An Essay on Comedy*, George Meredith writes that Molière's satire "strips Folly to the skin, displays the imposture of the creature."[28] All that satire needs to do, in its mission to detect the ridiculous or the corrupt, is remove the garments that cloak the most basic truths. But this kind of detection, this discovery of the cutaneous reality, is equally native to realist fiction and its exposure and description of everyday fact. *A la recherche du temps perdu* provides the perfect example of this kind of indoctrination into the world of the real. Marcel's first glimpse of the Duchesse de Guermantes forces him to abandon the images of her he had once entertained in his fantasies ("the others that I arbitrarily created") for the rather uglier truth: he sees right away that she has a "little pimple flaring up in the corner of her nose."[29] Proust's image is altogether Flaubertian – and even reminiscent of George Eliot. The most basic experiences of cognition, says Proust, are profoundly disillusioning. They reveal to us the true blotches and blemishes of the human skin.

Certainly to privilege the surface – or even to fetishize it – is a practice that belongs equally to the traditions of satire and realism. In *A Tale of a Tub* Swift returns again and again to what his hack narrator calls "the *Superficies* of Things"; his imagery of the flesh of giants and Yahoos and Irish babies is only the most sustained pattern in a larger, ambivalent preoccupation with visible and tactile detail.[30] A twentieth-century heir to this tradition, Wyndham Lewis, abhorred the modernist novelists who venerated the psychological; he himself trusted only the surface. Writing of his novel *The Apes of God* in his great critical compendium *Men Without Art*, Lewis exalted his own "*external* approach to things" and wrote that in his fiction "*the eye* has been the organ in the ascendant ... *The Apes of God* is a book made out of the outside of things."[31]

But, of course, it is Flaubert, consummate satirical realist, who embodies this fixation most completely. The "surface des choses" that captivates Frédéric Moreau in *L'Éducation sentimentale*, and which makes him think of becoming a painter, is the same plane, the same visual field, that controls so much of the Flaubertian vision.[32] (Naturally Flaubert is the main figure in Roland Barthes's essay "The Reality Effect," which lingers on the seemingly inert barometer in *Un coeur simple*: the object is seen but does not make clear what it really *means*.)[33] One of Flaubert's most resolute and revealing pronouncements is an 1852 observation to Louise Colet: "all that remains for us is the exterior of man."[34] This kind of fetishization of surface is either Flaubert's distinctive genius or his principal failing, depending on the reader. Henry James, evaluating Flaubert in 1876, emphasized his realism of the exterior: "Flaubert's theory as a novelist, briefly expressed, is to begin on the outside. Human life, he says, is before all things a spectacle, a thing to be looked at, seen, apprehended, enjoyed with the eyes."[35] But James did not mean this as an endorsement. His hesitation was largely moral, since Flaubert's microscopic vision was not just a tool for realist technique; it was also a conduit for satirical disgust. The exacting concentration that Flaubert directed at surfaces would reveal Emma Bovary's lovely shoulder – but it would also expose the viscous pallor of her corpse.

And yet for Augustan satirists and Victorian realists alike, the ocular intelligence does not merely mean a fetish of the surface. Both modes are proposing to see things with an amplified and even exceptional clairvoyance. And, of course, such insight does not just stop at the superficies; it exploits this visual power to claim a certain superior and essential knowledge. Gulliver's preternatural ability to see detail bestows a kind of acumen that penetrates the skin; in *Middlemarch*, despite the narrator's occasional interventions, Casaubon's sallow complexion does rather reliably indicate a distasteful character. Still, the comparison of George Eliot to Swift or Pope can be difficult to maintain; for many readers it may even seem counterintuitive. In the English tradition the one is considered the defender of sympathy, the others the most eloquent voices of disdain. But under closer scrutiny this divide begins to dissolve – for it fails to account for the authentic and sustained satirical temper of so much of Eliot's writing. And it ignores, in particular, how for the Victorian, as for the Augustans, it is precisely the heightened power of vision that can lead to disparagement. Seeing clearly in George Eliot does not only enable forgiveness: it can often lead to scorn instead.

In one peculiar but revealing moment in her fiction, Eliot even seems to address precisely the question that Pope had asked in *An Essay on Man*: "Why has not Man a microscopic eye?" Her 1859 story "The Lifted Veil" rather literalizes Pope's idea. It is a first-person account of a man, Latimer, "cursed with an exceptional mental character": he can look into the minds of others, and he can foresee the moment of his own death.[36] This rather supernatural power of clairvoyance allows him to see things in a detail so vivid, and so revelatory, that he compares it to "the growing distinctness of the landscape as the sun lifts up the veil of the morning mist" (10). A reader familiar with the George Eliot only of *Adam Bede* or *Middlemarch* might expect this supreme faculty of insight to show Latimer the inherent decency of his fellow man. But, of course, Latimer's experiences prove the opposite. He is overwhelmed by the corruption and duplicity that he sees in his wife Bertha's soul: "its barren worldliness, its scorching hate ... I saw all round the narrow room of this woman's soul; saw petty artifice and mere negation where I had delighted to believe in coy sensibilities" (19–20, 32). What he sees in Bertha is essentially what he sees across the spectrum of human life, especially among the people directly around him:

this superadded consciousness, wearying and annoying enough when it urged on me the trivial experience of indifferent people, became an intense pain and grief when it seemed to be opening to me the souls of those who were in a close relation to me – when the rational talk, the graceful attentions, the wittily-turned phrases, and the kindly deeds, which used to make the web of their characters, were seen as if thrust asunder by a microscopic vision, that showed all the intermediate frivolities, all the suppressed egoism, all the struggling chaos of puerilities, meanness, vague capricious memories, and indolent, make-shift thoughts, from which human words and deeds emerge like leaflets covering a fermenting heap. (14)

What is most remarkable here is the echo of Pope's "microscopic Eye" in Latimer's phrase "microscopic vision." The lesson of "The Lifted Veil" is alarmingly similar to the persuasions of Augustan satire. To look closely, says George Eliot in this tale, is to see the inherent ugliness of human life. Absent are the hesitant consolations of *Adam Bede*, where an ugly and dingy complexion may be the norm, but where it could still mask a lovable creature. In "The Lifted Veil" the human complexion is no longer even the problem; the horrid truths now lie underneath. Consequently it becomes hard not to sense, in Eliot's portrayal of Latimer, a sneaking analogy to the figure of the novelist. Indeed, ever since Sandra Gilbert and Susan Gubar's excellent and, in many ways, definitive discussion of the story in *The Madwoman in the Attic*, much recent criticism on "The Lifted Veil" has concluded that Latimer is some kind of representation of Eliot herself.[37] To be all-seeing, to know how things will turn out, to be able to pierce every consciousness: these are exactly the faculties and priorities that the author of *Middlemarch* and *Daniel Deronda* would esteem and promote. "The Lifted Veil" begins to read like George Eliot's allegory of realism. In a sense it is one of her least realist narratives: supernatural, melodramatic, even somewhat ridiculous. But its apparent moral, even if rendered in such a strange way, is that the most brilliant vision reveals the most terrible truth.

In this sense the extensive critical attention to "The Lifted Veil" in recent decades has tended to neglect one thing: if Latimer is a version of Eliot, it must be said that this is an Eliot who takes her cue from a particular tradition – satire. Latimer is a Gulliver figure set loose in the fiction of George Eliot: endowed with capacities of sight that overturn everything he had previously thought about mankind, and that set him at odds with all the human world. Clairvoyance is not a blessing; it is, in the closing words of the story, the rather Swiftian or Popeian "curse of insight" (42). "The Lifted Veil" ends with a final growl of misanthropy and execration, just as *Gulliver's Travels* does.[38]

We cannot say that the story's dark sensibility is very typical of Eliot's fiction. She wrote "The Lifted Veil" during a particularly despondent period in her life: she was depressed after the death of her sister Chrissey, consumed with questions concerning authorship of her novels, and saddened by the sudden coolness of her friend Herbert Spencer. Perhaps the mood and theme of the tale should be understood as a reaction to her circumstances in 1859.[39] Indeed the story was not even published under the name "George Eliot," and critics have long remarked its unusual and even *sui generis* place in Eliot's writing. U.C. Knoepflmacher wonders if it yielded "a nihilistic vision which its author would never have expressed as relentlessly in her acknowledged fiction."[40] But "The Lifted Veil" should not be dismissed as a mere curio in George Eliot's oeuvre. In her career it marks one of the major phases of interest in the possibilities of satire. Specifically, and despite the notable congruence with Pope in her phrase and theme "microscopic vision," it marks Eliot's primary debt to Swift: according to George Henry Lewes's diary, she was reading *A Tale of a Tub* during the composition of the tale.[41] On the second page of the story itself, she even cites Swift's famous epitaph: "*ubi sæva indignatio ulterius cor lacerare nequit.*" This is an astonishingly revealing allusion – neglected by even the most insightful critics of "The Lifted Veil" – for it ultimately confesses the tale's true satirical ancestry. Like Swift, Latimer will be free only when he is dead from the inescapable knowledge of man's corruption that will otherwise haunt him in life.[42] In the final analysis, the human complexion stands for a problem that exists far deeper than just on the skin. In both Augustan satire and Victorian realism it promises to reveal something essential about the human, and about the form that the human will take in fictional representation. For Swift and George Eliot alike it marks a much larger pattern and condition: a source of that underlying *sæva indignatio*; a fuller kind of truth; a clarity of detail that alone can yield the ugliness of the real.

SCORNING TO INFINITY

Every reader of George Eliot has noticed the occasional satirical tone in her fiction: the sardonic attitude toward Casaubon and his "Key to All Mythologies" in *Middlemarch*, for example, or the ironic distance between the narrator and Gwendolen Harleth in the first half of *Daniel Deronda*. Fewer readers have remarked the more persistent satire that reverberates throughout her writing. One exception is Christopher Lane, whose 2004 *Hatred and Civility* helps restore to the study of Victorian literature the period's very real and sustained expressions of misanthropy and odium.[43] Too often such expressions are obscured by the critical emphasis on the munificence of the Dickensian imagination, or on Eliot's sympathetic philosophy. But Lane stresses the less savory moods of Victorian prose and poetry, from Edward Bulwer-Lytton to Robert Browning, and in a chapter on George Eliot writes that "enmity not only haunts her work but also undermines her fictional endings and thrives at the expense of her moral philosophy" (109). Lane cites many contemporary reviewers who were taken aback by the suggestions of hatred and malice in the novels.

And he remembers that the narrator of *Middlemarch* cites a line from Goethe that would surprise many readers of Eliot: "the poet must know how to hate."[44]

Our usual focus on the processes of forgiveness and reconciliation in George Eliot is not misplaced. These are central themes almost everywhere in her fiction. But a powerful sympathetic imagination does not preclude a strong and concurrent inclination toward satire, as I will argue throughout my evaluations of Hardy, Gissing, Ibsen, and Conrad. In Eliot's fiction this inclination can be more than incidental; it can be, as in "The Lifted Veil," controlling and quite dark. If that 1859 story marks one notable phase of satirical interest during her career, the other comes just before her death, with the 1879 *Impressions of Theophrastus Such*. This strange last work – a combination of essay and fable, disjointed commentary and sustained polemic – includes Eliot's widest-ranging expressions of satirical temper and purpose. If "The Lifted Veil," a parable of seeing in extraordinary detail, focuses on the close-up, then *Impressions of Theophrastus Such* might be said to prefer the satirical long view: it is less interested in the hidden souls of individual people than in the widespread blunders and failings of humankind.

The book's epigraph immediately launches *Theophrastus Such*'s main satirical theme. Eliot cites the prologue to book III of Phaedrus's *Fabulae*, with its careful explanation that the speaker will not make the mistake of castigating specific enemies: "For I have no mind to brand any individual person,/ But rather to show life itself and the habits of men."[45] Chastisement in *Theophrastus Such* will not be ad hominem; it will not be petty or personal. Instead it has a much grander aim; the epigraph's vow to "show life itself" is even vaguely reminiscent of Rousseau's "je sens mon cœur et je connois les hommes," which inaugurates the *Confessions*.[46] Like Rousseau – whom she mentions only three pages later – George Eliot is invoking private observation and impression to express a much wider-ranging attitude toward human experience. To spend time branding individual people would mean to forfeit a certain moral authority. Throughout Eliot's writings there is a remarkable continuity in this line of thought. She voiced this exact sentiment when she was only 29 years old, writing in 1849 to her half-sister Fanny: "we may satirise character and qualities in the abstract without injury to our moral nature, but persons hardly ever."[47]

The difference between ridiculing individual people and scorning mankind in general will be one of my central themes in this study of satire and realism. All the writers in question faced the problem of determining how widely they should cast their satire: they understood that satire's scope is inseparable from its essence. Hardy, Gissing, Ibsen, and Conrad all struggled with some version of this same quandary in representation. Realist literature is above all the province of the idiosyncratic and pinpointable person: each differentiated from the rest of the field of representation by name, by personal history and narrated experience, by particularity. A hero is different from a villain and an orphan from an aristocrat; the protagonist is accorded a different kind of space and focus within the fiction from that of a minor character.[48] The very word *character* comes from the Greek term for the engraver's individualized mark etched into the surface. And in general it is this kind of individuation that yields understanding and clemency. We are predisposed to forgive the individual: this indeed is one of our inherited lessons regarding the fiction of George Eliot.

But satire, at least the essential and wide-ranging satire that I am discussing here, is typically in the hunt for shared folly, for mankind's collective error, and is therefore more interested in people than in the person. As novels like Gissing's *New Grub Street* and Conrad's *The Secret Agent* make clear, the larger category of "mankind" is hazier than any individual, less likely to gain the benefit of our doubt, and more liable to be a target for the satirist. As usual it is Swift who stands in the background of this problem, nowhere more explicitly than in his famous 1725 letter to Pope:

I have ever hated all Nations professions and Communityes and all my love is towards individuals for instance I hate the tribe of Lawyers, but I love Councellor such a one, Judge such a one for so with Physicians (I will not Speak of my own Trade) Soldiers, English, Scotch, French; and the rest but principally I hate and detest that animal called man, although I hartily love John, Peter, Thomas and so forth.[49]

Swift's satire, of course, usually accommodates this love for John, Peter, and Thomas by leaving them out altogether. Gulliver is not a character but a vessel or a void; the hack of *A Tale of a Tub* and the proposer of *A Modest Proposal* are voices or personae, not the kind of individualized representations we might expect from Victorian realism.

Satirical realism, that hybrid mode, consequently embodies a representational dilemma – a dilemma of person and people. It wants to depict the individualized human person in all her idiosyncrasy; and yet it wants to scorn all mankind. *Impressions of Theophrastus Such* marks an early instance of an approach to this problem: the later satirical realists will tackle it with much greater rigor. But there are many similarities. George Eliot here has no interest in the specific mockery of individual people that is so common elsewhere in her fiction. The entire work is, in a sense, devoted to developing the long view, to formulating a series of interconnected theories about man without getting very involved in the description of particular men and women. The only figure who plays any role in each of the chapters, accordingly, is Theophrastus himself. Our narrator is of indeterminate ancestry and unclear status: a middle-aged bachelor, an apparently amateur scholar and eloquent moralist. He is not George Eliot, exactly – and yet he is much more notably not *not* George Eliot. His aphorisms and observations bear a striking similarity to the narrative voice of the novels, especially of *Middlemarch* and *Daniel Deronda*, and also recall the skeptical pitch of much of Eliot's private correspondence. If we are meant to allow for some distance between Theophrastus Such and his creator, we are certainly not meant to over-estimate that distance. The satirical tenor of this book is not an oddity, but rather the most fully realized expression of an often latent mood.

Theophrastus's elusiveness – as narrator and as character – is not incidental. It allows Eliot to make use of him as a slippery entity who becomes harder and harder to dissociate from the mankind that he sets forth to scorn. Theophrastus himself makes a point of this very theme right from the opening pages. At the beginning of the first chapter, "Looking Inward," our narrator wonders how giving "an account to myself of the characters I meet with" relates to giving "any true account of my own." He decides immediately that he cannot exclude himself in his chastisement of others.

Thus if I laugh at you, O fellow-men! if I trace with curious interest your labyrinthine self-delusions, note the inconsistencies in your zealous adhesions, and smile at your helpless endeavours in a rashly chosen part, it is not that I feel myself aloof from you: the more intimately I seem to discern your weaknesses, the stronger to me is the proof that I share them. How otherwise could I get the discernment? – for even what we are averse to, what we vow not to entertain, must have shaped or shadowed itself within us as a possibility before we can think of exorcising it. No man can know his brother simply as a spectator. Dear blunderers, I am one of you. I wince at the fact, but I am not ignorant of it, that I too am laughable on unsuspected occasions; nay, in the very tempest and whirlwind of my anger, I include myself under my own indignation. (4)

This assurance sounds quite like the George Eliot of the earlier novels. Theophrastus will mock us – but far from remaining aloof, he will include himself in such wide-ranging censure. There are echoes here of the *Adam Bede* narrator, who speaks about the ugliness of the majority of the human race but exhorts us to acknowledge our kinship; or the narrator of *Middlemarch*, who closes that novel with the lesson that in all lives, great feeling will be always intertwined with error. The satirical sensibility of *Impressions of Theophrastus Such* is not that of Wyndham Lewis, who ridiculed everyone else in order to elevate himself, or even of Pope, who hardly included himself among the dunces. The sensibility here is more self-incriminating: it makes clear that the writer-figure inhabits the very sphere of folly and error he is writing about. In this respect the fundamental stance of Theophrastus is not altogether different from the underlying narrative attitude of the novels of Hardy and Gissing as I examine them in the chapters that follow. It makes little difference that *Impressions of Theophrastus Such* is not a work of narrative fiction, at least not in any conventional sense. In novels like *Jude the Obscure* or *New Grub Street*, the perspective of realist omniscience and representation generates a very similar self-incrimination: narrator, character, and reader are all conjoined in the same zone of censure.

These introductory words of "Looking Inward" are echoed throughout *Theophrastus Such*. That opening section ends much as it begins, with Theophrastus reiterating that "in noting the weaknesses of my acquaintances I am conscious of my fellowship with them"; for we must hold "the mirror and the scourge for our own pettiness as well as our neighbours'" (13). He revisits the theme several times, most notably in the thirteenth chapter, "How We Come to Give Ourselves False Testimonials, and Believe in Them." That chapter begins with Theophrastus's plain assertion, "It is my way when I observe any instance of folly, any queer habit, any absurd illusion, straightway to look for something of the same type in myself" (104). No other section of the book reads more like Montaigne. The spirit seems liberal, the stated aim "the natural history of my inward self." Our narrator is cautious: reluctant to apply the lash too readily to others, or indeed to conceive of himself differently from the way he regards them. "To judge of others by oneself," he writes, "is in its most innocent meaning the briefest expression for our only method of knowing mankind" (105).[50]

But *Theophrastus Such*'s apparently inclusive mood does not mean the book is usually very generous about the mankind that its narrator has set forth to know. In that same section of chapter 13, Theophrastus praises "the energies of indignation and scorn, which are the proper scourges of wrong-doing and meanness"; "I respect the horsewhip," he clarifies, "when applied to the back of Cruelty." The scourge is the crucial instrument of George Eliot's final work. In "Looking Inward" Theophrastus makes clear that his commitment to self-scrutiny will not inhibit any censorious energy: "Though not averse to finding fault with myself, and conscious of deserving lashes, I like to keep the scourge in my own discriminating hand" (6). Any reading of *Theophrastus Such* is a terrible misreading if it does not recognize the very real pleasure inherent in the book's satirical enterprise. There are certainly shades of difference between George Eliot and Theophrastus Such; this is not an autobiography. But the prose of *Impressions of Theophrastus Such* was an authentic channel for the intense satirical energies Eliot often restrained elsewhere in her writings. And because it was her last work, written in the bleak months of George Henry Lewes's fatal sickness, and with the wide panoramas of *Middlemarch* and *Daniel Deronda* just behind her, it is even tempting to think of it as a dark corrective to those luminous and compassionate masterpieces.

In one sense it is foolish even to compare *Theophrastus Such* to Eliot's greatest novels: in their compass and complexity, they simply dwarf their successor. But even if the late work's scope is much smaller, its ambitions are substantial. Its satirical program is expansive, aimed not only at self and other, but at all places and indeed all eras. In this respect one of the most instructive chapters is the second. Entitled "Looking Backward," it is a sort of response to the previous "Looking Inward." Here Theophrastus takes his comprehensive satirical thinking to its logical end.

Except on the ground of a primitive golden age and continuous degeneracy, I see no rational footing for scorning the whole present population of the globe, unless I scorn every previous generation from whom they have inherited their diseases of mind and body, and by consequence scorn my own scorn, which is equally an inheritance of mixed ideas and feelings concocted for me in the boiling caldron of this universally contemptible life, and so on – scorning to infinity. (17)

There is an echo of Juvenal's fourteenth satire in Theophrastus's emphasis on our legacy of corruption:

So avoid what should be condemned. There's at least one compelling
motive for doing so – to stop the next generation
from imitating our crimes, since we're all more than willing
to take models from vice and depravity.[51]

Nor, taken straight, is Theophrastus's calculus altogether different from Philip Larkin's proposition in "This Be the Verse" – your mum and dad fuck you up, man hands on misery to man: such is our common inheritance.[52] Eliot is hardly as bleak as Juvenal or Larkin, but Theophrastus's logic is an effective reminder of satire's inexorable bequeathing of the whip to every generation, its insistence on our endlessly self-reproducing folly. If we should not ridicule our neighbors without also ridiculing ourselves, then it follows that surely we should not castigate our times without also castigating all the eras that came before. There is, of course, more than a touch of cautious irony in Theophrastus's statement. Satire – Juvenal's, for instance – is often nostalgic for a better past, a time of virtue to which the degraded present is unflatteringly compared. But for Theophrastus the widespread chastisement of his present age is too suspiciously tempting and easy: certainly the previous ages were just as intrinsically corrupt, and anyway we essentially inherited our condition from them in the first place.[53]

"Scorning to infinity" is, then, both a flawed enterprise and a necessary one. Theophrastus knows the allure of scorning: he sees Folly everywhere around him, and he feels a genuine need to lash out at it. But he also understands that there is no logical endpoint to this kind of undertaking. He is wary of scorning; and yet he indulges himself.

This quandary lies at the heart of *Impressions of Theophrastus Such* – and it represents one of the great themes of satirical realism. In the chapters that follow I will return frequently to what I call "absolute satire": a kind of satire that refuses to distinguish between different kinds of people or spheres of life, that seems to include everything in the name of being exhaustive, and that therefore shares with realism the terrain of quasi-omniscient perspective and totality.[54]

But in these same chapters I will also examine how sympathy, oddly, so often seems to exist alongside such all-encompassing satire. If everything and everyone is to be scorned, then maybe everyone and everything deserves to be pitied. This is why my history of Victorian realism has begun just after Dickens, whose satire typically zeroes in on a particular segment of society: Chancery in *Bleak House*, the Circumlocution Office in *Little Dorrit*, the provincial schoolhouse in *Hard Times*. Dickens generally sequesters his satire – however broad it may sometimes seem – such that certain zones of life are held up for ridicule while others are spared that ridicule, and indeed are often sentimentalized. Satirical realism levels the field, such that satire and sympathy are always interpenetrating. It says: this is our world, and we should be both faulted for creating it and pitied for inhabiting it. Consequently, satirical realism is at once an aggressive and a tragic mode. It proposes to seek and then indict widespread folly and injustice; and yet, finding these things, it wonders despondently whether there can be any way out of such a terrible reality.

George Eliot's vision in *Impressions of Theophrastus Such* is not nearly as bleak as Hardy's in *Jude the Obscure,* or Gissing's in *New Grub Street,* or Ibsen's in *Ghosts,* or Conrad's in *The Secret Agent.* She seems in her last book to be tempted by some of the same satirical vigor that animates those works – but her rather lighter spirit, even here, works to restrain what can develop in those later novels and plays into a more austere and thorough aggression. Where Gissing or Conrad may punish, Eliot here steps back. In what is probably *Theophrastus Such*'s most essential chapter, "Debasing the Moral Currency," she articulates, through a Theophrastus who is for the moment her very equivalent, a doctrine of satire that could well be the clearest statement of satirical attitude anywhere in her writing:

The world seems to me well supplied with what is genuinely ridiculous: wit and humour may play as harmlessly or beneficently round the changing facets of egoism, absurdity, and vice, as the sunshine over the rippling sea or the dewy meadows. Why should we make our delicious sense of the ludicrous, with its invigorating shocks of laughter and its irrepressible smiles which are the outglow of an inward radiation as gentle and cheering as the warmth of morning, flourish like a brigand on the robbery of our mental wealth? – or let it take its exercise as a madman might, if allowed a free nightly promenade, by drawing the populace with bonfires which leave some venerable structure a blackened ruin or send a scorching smoke across the portraits of the past, at which we once looked with a loving recognition of fellowship, and disfigure them into butts of mockery? (83–4)

The later realists will feel far less compunction in lighting those bonfires, in blackening their structures into ruins. George Eliot, like Theophrastus, sees clearly that the world is well supplied with the ridiculous: "egoism, absurdity, and vice" take form throughout her fiction. But even here, in her most explicitly satirical work, she will not allow the identification of the ludicrous to degenerate into destructive censure. In "Debasing the Moral Currency," Theophrastus favors what he calls "wit" over the more unruly tendencies of wild derision: following La Bruyère, he only likes the kind of satire that might "give sympathetic insight."[55] In the end, this passage from "Debasing the Moral Currency" is an ars poetica not altogether different from *Adam Bede*'s famous defense of its modest realism. Once again George Eliot voices the need to find some balance between satire's temptations and sympathy's responsibilities. Once again she sets out to measure the true ugliness of the human race, or to decide how genuinely ridiculous the world really is. Her ambiguous final work is nothing less than an effort to determine the proper place and shape of satire in an age of realism.

RIDICULE IS THE TEST OF TRUTH

Theophrastus's remark that "the world seems to me well supplied with what is genuinely ridiculous" at first seems fairly straightforward. In fact it is a remarkably instructive statement about satire. What he is saying, in essence, is that the satirist merely observes what is actually out there in the world – and that in its most elementary form satire is a kind of empiricism, a realistic chronicle of the texture and truth of everyday life.

A very similar kind of logic underlies much of George Eliot's writing. In chapter 17 of *Adam Bede*, for example, Eliot's narrator describes herself as someone "obliged to creep servilely after nature and fact"; she is not a "clever" sort of novelist, a writer of fantasies, who would be able to "represent things as they never have been and never will be."[56] This emphasis on "facts" then yields, as Eliot sets the stage for her invocation of Dutch genre painting, to something she calls "truth":

So I am content to tell my simple story, without trying to make things seem better than they were; dreading nothing, indeed, but falsity, which, in spite of one's best efforts, there is reason to dread. Falsehood is so easy, truth so difficult. The pencil is conscious of a delightful facility in drawing a griffin – the longer the claws, and the larger the wings, the better; but that marvelous facility which we mistook for genius, is apt to forsake us when we want to draw a real unexaggerated lion. (166)

Eliot's most explicit defense of what has come to be called her "realism" sounds notably similar to her views on satire in *Impressions of Theophrastus Such*. Realist fiction and the proper kind of satire both demand a fundamentally accurate view of the world; falsity is the enemy of each, and truth their shared ideal and obligation. This obligation is a moral one for both modes. Devoting one's attention only to griffins is a distracting amusement or worse; ignoring the genuinely foolish in pursuit of chimeras is a travesty of the writer's real concentration. Life has an inexhaustible supply of real folly and error, and any novelist who disregards them is disregarding Truth itself.

For many people "satire" will always evoke the unreal and the fantastical: Rabelais's giants, Swift's talking horses, Orwell's tyrannical pigs. But the idea that a certain realism exists inherently in satire dates as far back as satire does. For proof we need look no further than Juvenal's first satire, with its famous exasperated axiom "difficile est saturam non scribere." It would indeed be difficult for Juvenal *not* to write satire, given the sheer cascade of appalling facts facing him on the opening pages alone.

Rome is a "monstrous city" filled with terrible writers, shyster lawyers, thugs, and informers. When Juvenal wonders why, in light of such present vice and inanity, he would ever use his pen to write mythology instead – "Why rehash Hercules's labours, or what/ Diomedes did, all that bellowing in the Labyrinth, or the legend/ Of the flying craftsman" – he sounds very prescient of the George Eliot who refuses to write about griffins. The evidence of Roman corruption is all around him; he writes satire because he has no other choice.[57] For Juvenal the *sæva indignatio* is a consequence of the basic experience of seeing:

> Don't you want to cram whole notebooks with scribbled invective
> when you stand at the corner and see some forger carried past
> exposed to view on all sides, in an all-but-open litter,
> on the necks of six porters, lounging back with the air
> of Maecenas himself? A will, a mere scrap of paper,
> a counterfeit seal – these brought him wealth and honour.
> Do you see that distinguished lady? She has the perfect dose
> for her husband – old wine with a dash of parching toad's blood.[58]

There is a remarkable proto-realism in these lines. Juvenal's satirist-figure, standing on a Roman street corner and watching the city's nauseating follies go by, is an ancestor of Gissing's narrator in *The Nether World* or *New Grub Street*, who registers the grime and vice of late Victorian London. Juvenal asks if we see that distinguished lady, and then goes on to describe her; Flaubert or Conrad might establish a scene in a similar fashion, in order then to expose the ludicrousness beneath the posture. Juvenal's first satire might well be the first work of satirical realism. Its lesson is not only that it would be hard not to write satire, but also that any other kind of writing would simply be pointless or irrelevant. In this prophetic opening salvo Juvenal equates what is repellent in Rome with what is real – and thereby looks ahead to Flaubert's Yonville l'Abbaye, Gissing's Farringdon Street, and Conrad's Greenwich Park.

Juvenal's first satire merely sets the stage; this intensely pictorial, vivid, lifelike sensibility defines all his writing. For two thousand years, readers have looked to these satires not only for their rhetorical force but also for what they can tell us about life in Rome in the second century AD. Epigrammatic as he can sometimes be, Juvenal never veers from the coarse detail of everyday reality. He is a satirist because he is an observer. In this respect many later satirists can be said to follow his example. Swift and Pope's focus on the "microscopic eye" is an English Augustan literalization of this idea, but even stronger echoes can be heard in a different eighteenth-century satirist, Henry Fielding. In the preface to *Joseph*

Andrews, Fielding distinguishes between the "Ridiculous" and the "Burlesque," claiming that only the former "falls within my Province in the present Work." The burlesque is "monstrous and unnatural," far removed from the actual flaws and vices of mankind. The other category, however, is essential: "life every where furnishes an accurate Observer with the Ridiculous." Fielding's phrase is, of course, remarkably similar to the lesson of both Juvenal and the George Eliot of *Theophrastus Such* (the world is "well supplied with what is genuinely ridiculous"): the detection of the ridiculous is inseparable from the basic act of perception and observation. The key is simply vigilance and accuracy. It is this same logic that informs the recent political protest slogan: *if you are not outraged, you are not paying attention*. It inspires us to reverse the old French adage *tout comprendre, c'est tout pardonner* by writing in its place: *tout comprendre, c'est ne rien pardonner*.

Fielding's preface makes clear that this pursuit of the empirically ridiculous will indeed be the driving motor behind *Joseph Andrews*: what lies behind the ridiculous is "Affectation," and affectation is the enemy of the book.[59] A similar conviction animates *Tom Jones* as well, where Fielding never ceases to remind us that "it is our province to relate facts"; that "it is our business to relate facts as they are"; and that unlike the Arabians and the Persians, who could write their tales from the genii and the fairies, "to natural means alone are we confined."[60] There is a certain irony in these lines – they are typically invoked at the height of Fielding's rambling and digressive asides – but that does not mean they are untrue. *Joseph Andrews* and *Tom Jones* depend fundamentally on the "natural" details of the everyday for their social, moral, and satirical authenticity.

This will be one of the main themes in my study of satire and realism: both modes claim a superior knowledge of the real and an exceptional method of representing it. The finest theorists of satire have always insisted on its supreme awareness and trenchant discernment of present conditions. William Hazlitt, as if echoing Fielding, argued in *Lectures on the English Comic Writers* that "ridicule is necessarily built on certain supposed facts."[61] For Hazlitt, as for Juvenal and George Eliot and virtually all the writers in question, "facts" lead invariably to something grander, something more commonly named "truth." Hazlitt believed that satirical truth is allied with "common sense," and that absurdity needs only to be exposed to "common apprehension" in order to be properly disparaged. His idea of truth is not so rigorously experiential as Juvenal's, not so dependent on the squalid facts that generate censure. But the essential and decisive maxim that Hazlitt cites here – *ridicule is the test of truth* – is a dictum inspired by the same realist spirit. If satirical realism were a political movement it could easily adopt this maxim as its slogan, its rallying cry.[62] Ridicule is exposure, a pathway to the real. The axiom would meet with no argument from Juvenal himself – or from a satirical realist like Conrad, whose *Secret Agent* remorselessly treads the blurred line between the two foci he calls "truth" and "caricature."

The history of commentary on satire is littered with such axioms. Indeed satire can be described as that mode of literature which identifies folly in order to declare accuracy, which believes that ridicule is the test of truth. Goethe, to take one example, praised Molière for "chastising mankind by drawing it as it truly is."[63] Trollope believed that satire must restrict itself to attacking what is genuinely wrong: "Satire, though it may exaggerate the vice it lashes, is not justified in creating it in order that it may be lashed."[64] Adorno made a similar criticism of Brecht's *The Resistible Rise of Arturo Ui*, objecting to the play's "unrealistic device" of having a mere band of imaginary criminals stand for Fascism: "This invalidates the caricature and makes it seem idiotic even in its own terms ... Satire which fails to stay on the level of its subject lacks spice."[65] Wyndham Lewis, never one to understate his case, claimed (in an essay about himself) that "satire in reality often is nothing else but *the truth* – the truth, in fact, of Natural Science."[66] And Thackeray, in his 1852 lecture "Charity and Humour," defended his censorious fiction in similar terms, frank and profoundly moral. "I cannot help telling the truth as I view it, and describing what I see," he wrote. "To describe it otherwise than it seems to me would be falsehood in that calling in which it has pleased Heaven to place me; treason to that conscience which says that men are weak; that truth must be told; that fault must be owned."[67] Charlotte Brontë's oft-quoted judgment of Thackeray – he was "the legitimate high priest of Truth" – spoke for many Victorians. As George Levine notes in *The Realistic Imagination*, Elizabeth Rigby believed *Vanity Fair* to be "a literal photograph of the manners and habits of the nineteenth century"; Thackeray's obituary memorialized him as a writer "sternly, ruthlessly real."[68]

These are only a few instances of a longstanding literary-critical habit.[69] But even these isolated observations bring with them their own kind of representational logic. If folly and truth are effectively two words for the same thing, that is, then the purest and most authentic kind of satire is the one that is most thorough, most comprehensive in its representation of the world. I wrote earlier, in relation to Theophrastus Such's idea of "scorning to infinity," that I would return frequently to the question of "absolute satire": that mode of ridicule which, in the name of being exhaustive, threatens to make everything a target for its scourge – and so shares with omniscient realism an ambition for a totality of perspective. Scorning to infinity is therefore the natural endpoint for a ridicule that seeks to be the test of truth. Satirical realism is the most ambitious kind of satire. It takes its cue from Juvenal's pledge in his first satire: "All human endeavours, men's prayers, fears, angers, pleasures,/ joys and pursuits, make up the mixed mash of my book" (5, lines 85–6). We should remember here that *satire* comes not from *satyr* but from *satura*: a medley, a combination of things. Juvenal promises nothing less than a complete treatment of his world. If it is human, if it belongs to real experience, then it is grist for satire and for the mixed mash of his book. We make a mistake when we are selective, when we exempt anything that might deserve the lash. "*Everyone* should be laughed at," writes Wyndham Lewis, "or else *no one* should be laughed at."[70]

As usual it is Flaubert who stands at the fulcrum of these ideas and convictions. Certain readers take for granted that Flaubert's enemy was what he tended to call the *bourgeois*: that his lash was reserved for petty figures like Homais in *Madame Bovary*. But while his hatred for such people was obviously fierce, we are naïve to think his satire stopped there. Some of the most revealing pages of the *Correspondance* are those where he articulates what he means by the *bourgeois*. In an 1852 letter to Louise Colet, Flaubert spoke of "the bourgeois (that is, all of humanity now, including the people)"; nine years later he predicted to Ernest Feydeau that *Salammbô* would anger "the bourgeois, that is, everybody."[71] Flaubert's essential odium was not simply a function of class, of course; but nor was it just a question of philistinism, as Nabokov always argued.[72] Flaubert hated widely and often indiscriminately, and much of his writing – both epistolary and novelistic – implies that his misanthropy was like a liquid that would take the shape of whatever vessel it encountered. Peter Gay writes of Flaubert: "he was persuaded that the Enemy – the bourgeois of his time – was so awesome in his stupidity and self-absorption that ridiculing him would be an exercise in redundancy. An objective portrayal would be enough to damn him without appeal."[73] Flaubert took such logic to his own extreme: in his final work, *Bouvard et Pécuchet* (with its companion *Dictionnaire des idées reçues*), he tested the possibility of professed non-interference in his fiction. He would merely reproduce the ludicrous words of other people; his last book would be a sort of perverse documentary masquerading as a novel.

With Flaubert – and, later, with Céline – it is hard not to wonder whether misanthropy and objectivity might be coexistent and indeed interpenetrating.[74] If we are all so clearly foolish and corrupt, then satire needs no embellishment or ornamentation; it suffices simply to show us as we are. And though it is clear that Flaubert's loathing of the bourgeois transcends the boundaries of class, it is also true that the bourgeois nineteenth century was the ideal breeding ground for this kind of antipathy. Literature's angry confrontation with a swelling middle-class society – a key idea in Peter Gay's volumes on nineteenth-century European culture – is a theme that will appear in this book too. The rise of the bourgeoisie, with its attendant hypocrisies and complacencies, is a recurring problem in Ibsen's and Conrad's polemical dissections of society, and even in Gissing's explorations of a rather poorer sphere, whether in his "working-class" fiction of the 1880s or his more "middle-class" novels of the mid- and late 1890s. All these writers were effectively contending with the problem George Meredith described in 1897: "you see Folly perpetually sliding into new shapes in a society possessed of wealth and leisure, with many whims, many strange ailments and strange doctors."[75] Meredith's own satires on such folly were relatively demure and gentle; in the hands of Flaubert and Ibsen and Conrad a more aggressive satirical realism declared a much more ruthless war.

BEYOND CORRECTION

What Meredith suggested about satire is also true of realism. Theorists of the novel have almost always located the foundations of realism in bourgeois culture and society – just as they have typically attributed its flourishing to a bourgeois world of readers. Ian Watt traced the emergence of novelistic realism in the eighteenth-century English novel to the "increasingly prosperous and numerous social groups concerned with commerce and manufacture" and the "great power and self-confidence of the middle class as a whole"; Georg Lukács saw Balzac's nineteenth-century Paris as the archetype for the realist representation of life in a society determined by the forces of capitalism.[76] In the work of Lukács and those who engaged him directly, we consequently find the most sustained and the most significant grappling with the political implications of realism. Lukács's strain of Marxism was, as his antagonists always pointed out, an unusual kind of Marxism, at least in the earlier half of his career: a sort of leftist-humanism, with old-fashioned tendencies that such antagonists would always condemn as retrograde. His canonization of Balzac and Tolstoy – and his corresponding antipathy to both naturalism (in the personage of Zola especially) and the avant-gardes of modernism – connect to his central idea that after 1848 most forms of literature succumbed either to mere reification (naturalism) or to solipsistic formalism (modernism).[77] Lukács's opposition to naturalism – for which he rebuked not only Zola but Flaubert too – was not altogether different from the position of novelists like Hardy, Conrad, and even Gissing, who would all object, often despite themselves, to certain moods of late Victorian realism, infused as it was with what Hardy called its "spasmodic inventory of items." Lukács would similarly identify such fiction as a surrender to reification, since those items had come to determine human relations: Flaubert and Maupassant and Zola contented themselves with a detached description of the material and objective world, and "description is the writer's substitute for the epic significance that has been lost."[78] Balzac and Tolstoy, on the other hand, practiced the true realism: a realism of types rather than averages, focused on "human beings in action," committed to penetrating and exposing the "driving forces" of life under capitalism and "the laws governing objective reality."[79]

Lukács's most significant antagonists were also Marxists, and indeed their criticism was mostly directed at his essentially conservative and fussy tastes, so apparently anathema to the revolutionary aspirations of twentieth-century Communism. Brecht, most prominently, could without much difficulty parody Lukács's prescription for a literature that would be of use to Marxists: "Writers just have to keep to the Old Masters, produce a rich life of the spirit, hold back the pace of events by a slow narrative, bring the individual back to the centre of the stage, and so on."[80] Much of Brecht's resentment stemmed from Lukács's hostility to expressionism, of course, but in a larger sense it was born from a refusal to understand "realism" in such a calcified way: as a kind of literature that reached its peak with Balzac and Tolstoy, finding ongoing life only, perhaps, in the work of Gorky and Mann. Brecht, too, understood realism in political terms, even if those terms – or the forms they could take – differed from Lukács's, because they could still be sculpted anew: "We must not derive realism as such from particular existing works, but we shall use every means, old and new, tried and untried, derived from art and derived from other sources, to render reality to men in a form they can master" (81). Brecht shared Lukács's aversion to naturalism, but they could find little common ground when it came to defining realism or promoting its true Marxist identity.

Lukács's other most prominent adversary, Adorno, was no less astringent in disputing his narrow view of realism and dismissal of modernism.

Lukács's notion of realism, according to Adorno, was ignorant regarding questions of form, naïve about the singular mimesis of nineteenth-century fiction, and wrong to "transfer to the realm of art categories which refer to the relationship of consciousness to the actual world, as if there were no difference between them. Art exists in the real world and has a function in it ... Nevertheless, as art it remains the antithesis of that which is the case." Lukács erred in assuming that art could "provide knowledge of reality by reflecting it photographically"; art instead reveals what lies under the veil of reality, by virtue of its autonomy.[81] Adorno was notably skeptical – as many postwar critics were – of any claim that the nineteenth-century novel held any special status as realistic: despite Lukács's veneration, those novels "are by no means as realistic as all that" (163).

But it is important to remember that these criticisms of Lukács's theory of realism are waged on political grounds too. The dispute between Lukács and Brecht essentially revolved around the political value of two different forms of art: on the one hand, nineteenth-century realism; on the other, twentieth-century expressionism and the avant-garde. Both writers naturally believed their own version of "realism" to be the suitable and useful one politically; Brecht's epic theater was nothing if not a literature of desired utility. Even Adorno's darker view of art and politics was a Marxist one: his valuation of the autonomous work of art over the committed one did not mean it lacked any radical possibility. But I am interested in all three theorists precisely because none of them in the end associates realism with a loss of faith in progress, and that loss is the central fact of satirical realism as I conceive it in this book. Despite their differences, Lukács and Brecht aligned realism with a Marxist teleology of progress, a politics that was fundamentally historical. In this respect later Marxist critics like Raymond Williams viewed realism in similar terms.

But satirical realism has a complicated and ambivalent relation to politics. Indeed this is one of the essential points I am making in this book. In my chapter on Gissing, for example, I follow Orwell's point that the author of *New Grub Street* and *The Nether World* was disabused of any conviction of the prospect of amelioration, whatever his apparent politics might have been. In my chapter on *The Secret Agent*, I am notably interested in Conrad's absolute satire of the world of politics, and in the novel's unsettlingly serene confidence in the impossibility of salvaging or redeeming mankind, whether in a political or any other sense. Satire and realism have both long been understood to be by nature political: realism by theorists from Lukács to Terry Lovell, who come usually from the left; satire by critics from Ronald Paulson to Christopher Yu, traditionally (but not always) with the assumption that its politics are conservative.[82] But what I am suggesting is that when realism and satire merge they cease to be political, at least in any recognizable way, because they arrive at a recognition that politics is no longer an option.

This recognition is, of course, the same recognition I alluded to earlier, with regard to "radical satire." Politics suggests progress, and progress suggests correction. But satirical realism is the art of absolute disillusion-ment: it surveys the terrain that exists beyond correction. Surely this is a major reason that the writers I am interested in here – Swift, Flaubert, Hardy, Gissing, Ibsen, Conrad – have always been especially difficult to interpret or assimilate politically. We invariably hit up against a certain apolitical conservatism in their work, a distressing sense that reality is an unchanging sphere of folly. At first glance it might seem that Lukács's interest in underlying "driving forces" might be able to accommodate the dark suspicions native to satirical realism. But any critic who writes that the "practical road to a solution for the writer lies in an ardent love of the people ... together with an unshakable faith in the march of mankind and their own people toward a better future," or that realism "enables readers to clarify their own experiences and understanding of life and to broaden their own horizons" is entirely antithetical to the essence of a realism that is satirical.[83] If Lukács's lodestars are Balzac and Tolstoy, mine is Flaubert, whose realism was always a fundamentally censorious one. As for Brecht, who would never put the ideology of realism in quite this way, and whose plays, of course, had their own satiric tendencies, his representational politics were also grounded in an ideology of correction, even if this was a correction through *Verfremdung* rather than Lukács's more conventional or established forms. Adorno perhaps comes closer to an understanding of a non-corrective art: his native pessimism is more hospitable to the interpretation of novels like *New Grub Street* or *The Secret Agent*, and his aphorism that "art is the negative knowledge of the actual world" is infused with a similar sensibility or even ideology (160). Satirical realism is congruent in the sense that it could be said to exist in a dialectical tension with reality, even if my theory affords literature a somewhat more direct relation to the represented sphere than Adorno would allow. But to say that fiction can know the world is not to concede that it can correct it. And to say that ridicule is the test of truth is not to consent to a political understanding of truth – not a conventionally political one, anyway.

I am making a political point when I say that satirical realism exists beyond correction, but it is not a political point alone. To identify a mode of representation that is non- or post-corrective is also to acknowledge that it resists the persuasions of nineteenth-century positivism, for example. In the chapters that follow, notably the chapter on Ibsen, I argue that satirical realism is a realism that refuses the curative or restorative promises of science; it is therefore a kind of representation that cannot be assimilated to the scholarship, dominant in recent decades, that examines Victorian literature through the lens of nineteenth-century science. Most important, satirical realism is non-corrective because it rejects the comic principle of correction that we instinctively expect from satire generally. Satire very often seems to promise us that it will cure us through laughter. Comic satire – from many of Horace's formal satires to Molière's farces to Shaw's intellectual comedies – holds forth this promise. But satirical realism either produces a very dark comedy whose laughter fails to be curative, or else it forbids us from laughing at all.

Zola, a novelist not generally celebrated for his great humor, seems to have had this very idea in mind in his 1866 article "Mes haines" ("My Hatreds"), first published in *Le Figaro* and later collected in *Mes haines, causeries littéraires et artistiques.* The essay (betraying Flaubert's strong influence on Zola in these years) begins with a panegyric to hatred, which Zola calls "holy ... It is the indignation of strong and powerful hearts, the militant disdain of those who are angered by mediocrity and stupidity." Then, sounding just like the Juvenal who only needs to walk outside to be confronted by folly, or the Flaubert who cannot avoid the despicable reality everywhere around him, Zola writes: "I can't take two steps in life without meeting three imbeciles, and that's why I'm sad."[84]

Zola's last clause here is extraordinarily revealing. For many writers the presence of imbeciles would be a source of great humor: Rabelais or Molière or Shakespeare, in certain moods, might portray fools or foolishness in order to make us laugh. But satirical realism discovers imbecility and becomes despondent instead. Zola's own fiction actually embodies this tendency less than the work of those authors I am examining: for Hardy, Gissing, Ibsen, and Conrad, the uncovering of folly is a profoundly tragic experience. This is one of the essential qualities of the satirical realism that marked the second half of the nineteenth century. After Thackeray, after Dickens, once the gap between satiric and realist treatment had narrowed, comedy was displaced by a far bleaker and more heartrending form of representation. The works under inspection here are therefore rarely very funny; a work like *Jude the Obscure* goes so far as to dare us to laugh at its austerity and desolation.

And so perhaps satire needs to be redefined: no longer exclusively that literature which relies on wit in order to expose folly, but more broadly that literature which holds up conditions and realities for attack and ridicule, even if that process is not inherently funny. In his book on Shaw, G.K. Chesterton writes that there are two kinds of humorists: those who love to see a man absurd (Rabelais, Dickens) and those who hate to see him so (Swift, Shaw).[85] The satirical realists found little comfort or delight in man's absurdity. And the kind of fiction and drama they forged rarely moves us to laughter. Theirs was – in Flaubert's phrase, explaining to Louise Colet the thing he most aspired to accomplish as a writer – "le comique arrivé à l'extrême, le comique qui ne fait pas rire." Satirical realism is exactly that extreme comedy: the comedy that does not make us laugh. It is the mode of writing that follows Wyndham Lewis's conviction: "there is laughter and laughter. That of true satire is as it were *tragic* laughter."[86]

This non- or even anti-comic satire means also that the very form of fiction, in satirical realism, would be different. Typically we associate satire with *satura*, with the boisterous, teeming, all-inclusive, or even encyclopedic kind of representation native especially to Menippean satire but characteristic of many of the central works in the satiric tradition. Mikhail Bakhtin's theory of Menippean satire, as formulated in his book on Dostoevsky, stresses characteristics of the genre that are antithetical to the kind of satire I am interested in here. The Menippean novel is founded on a polyphony of voices; it is open-ended; it thereby grants a certain freedom to its characters. Menippean satire incorporates all forms and genres into itself, including – and especially – the fantastic.[87] Satirical realism, on the other hand, is monologic; its represented sphere is a closed one; it confines rather than liberates the humans it imagines into being. Its realism prohibits any suggestion of the fantastic: indeed that is the point. Nor is satirical realism at all like Bakhtin's idea of "grotesque realism" as developed in his book on Rabelais. Grotesque realism has a "positive assertive character"; it is based on "fertility, growth, and a brimming-over abundance"; it is remarkable precisely for its "gay and festive character." Its principle of degradation is always a restorative and regenerating one, and its carnivalesque laughter purifies.[88] The satirical realism of Hardy, Gissing, and Conrad, on the other hand, is defined by its negativity, its dismissal of any kind of regeneration. There is nothing festive (and therefore, by implication, corrective) in *Jude the Obscure*, in *New Grub Street*, in *The Secret Agent*.

Nor does satirical realism tend to indulge in another habit of much satire, especially typical of satire's Menippean or encyclopedic forms.

Boisterous novelistic satire, that is to say, tends to be formally very self-referential, and indeed depends on such playful self-awareness for creating that comic mischievousness that makes us think of them as satirical. The eighteenth-century English novel of Fielding and Sterne is a fine example of this tendency; its self-awareness, as Bakhtin would maintain, comes out of the Rabelaisian tradition. *Gargantua* and *Pantagruel*, *Tom Jones*, *Tristram Shandy*, and indeed later fiction like *Vanity Fair* all rely heavily on the attention they call to their own artifice or authorial voice. They announce themselves; they tell us what is absurd and when to laugh; they often remind us that they are merely fabrications. Their descendants today are the novels that make up the genre James Wood calls "hysterical realism": the busy, rowdy, and wordy books typical of contemporary fiction, and whose main ancestor is Dickens.[89]

Satirical realism, on the other hand, refuses to make such gestures. Its austere discipline cannot admit any chortling. It incorporates its mockery into its sheer descriptive method and narrative perspective; it wastes no time poking fun at its inauthenticity or fictionality. Indeed it *depends* on such realism to keep its satire so focused and its censorious energy so controlled. Nineteenth-century satirical realism is defined not by boisterousness but by *austerity*: it is the mode not of Thackeray and Dickens but of Hardy and Gissing. Nor is it the mode of those late nineteenth-century English writers who more typically get called "satirists": writers like Wilde, Beerbohm, Beardsley. The 1890s were not only the years of whimsical satires like *The Importance of Being Earnest* and *The Happy Hypocrite*. They were also the years of the rigorous, severe, and realist satires *Jude the Obscure* and *New Grub Street*, and the pages ahead are the story of those years.

CHAPTER 2

Terminal satire and
Jude the Obscure

Two words haunted Thomas Hardy in the years he was plotting and composing *Jude the Obscure*. The first of these, *satire*, litters his notebooks and diaries of the era, and it appears with remarkable frequency in the finished novel itself. The word first surfaces when Jude receives his cousin Sue's letter stating her decision to marry his former schoolmaster Phillotson. The letter is brutally short; Sue is so formal that she signs her complete name. Hardy then shifts to Jude's reaction:

Jude staggered under the news; could eat no breakfast; and kept on drinking tea because his mouth was so dry. Then presently he went back to his work and laughed the usual bitter laugh of a man so confronted. Everything seemed turning to satire. And yet, what could the poor girl do? he asked himself: and felt worse than shedding tears.[1]

The sentence in question seems deliberately vague, as if Jude's paranoid sense of victimhood cannot place the source of the cruel joke to which he has been subjected. The satire is on Jude. But from what or from whom does this satire issue – from Sue, or Phillotson, or God? This question may be simply another useless effort to pursue the elusive riddle of *Jude the Obscure*, which is the problem of knowing why Jude Fawley must suffer so intensely and relentlessly. The satirist in question must be elusive. If the true cause of Jude's misery were known, he might be in the position of overcoming it, and such a promise is impossible amidst the bleakness of this novel. In this sense the agent of the satire on Jude is like the "President of the Immortals" who concludes his sport with the heroine at the close of *Tess of the d'Urbervilles*, or the "sinister intelligence bent on punishing" Henchard in *The Mayor of Casterbridge* – these abstractions are similarly beyond human reach, and equally cruel.[2]

But in *Jude the Obscure* this abstraction consistently takes the same name: Hardy insists on calling it *satire*. When things go wrong for Jude – when Sue causes him pain, or when he is denied a reprieve from the vicissitudes of Christminster – he routinely imagines his misfortune in the guise of an immense conspiracy of mockery. So when Jude receives a subsequent letter from Sue asking if he would give her away at the wedding, Hardy writes that "if Sue had written that in satire, he could hardly forgive her"; after Jude and Sue overhear two clergymen speaking in hushed tones outside their home, Jude cries "What a satire their talk is on our importance to the world!"; and even Sue herself begins to imagine things in the same terms, begging Jude in the midst of their deterioration, "Don't satirize me: it cuts like a knife!" or, pages later, "Don't crush all the life out of me by satire and argument!" (205, 424, 435).[3] *Satire* may not be the word most readers of this novel would expect at such moments; we observe the lashings endured by the blighted couple but struggle to find any humor behind them, as a satire might suggest. But the peculiar word keeps reappearing, and we start to wonder if it signals a larger pattern in the substructure of Hardy's final novel.

Jude the Obscure was the product of the early 1890s: the germ of the novel can be traced back to 1888, when Hardy recorded in his diary his plan for "a short story of a young man – 'who could not go to Oxford' – His struggles and ultimate failure," but he did not sit down to write it until the turn of the decade.[4] *The Early Life of Thomas Hardy* also testifies that in 1890, after finishing *Tess* and just before beginning *Jude*, Hardy immersed himself in a particular course of reading:

In the latter part of the year, having finished adapting *Tess of the d'Urbervilles* for the serial issue, he seems to have dipped into a good many books – mostly the satirists: including Horace, Martial, Lucian, "the Voltaire of Paganism", Voltaire himself, Cervantes, Le Sage, Molière, Dryden, Fielding, Smollett, Swift, Byron, Heine, Carlyle, Thackeray, *Satires and Profanities* by James Thomson, and Weismann's *Essays on Heredity*. (301)[5]

It can be dangerous to seek too much significance in a novelist's reading at a particular point in his career: those books will often have little to do with his own writing. But Hardy's immersion in "mostly the satirists" cannot be ignored in light of the furious book that was to emerge from these first years of the 1890s. The two volumes of *The Early Life* and *The Later Years* of Hardy – published under the name of his wife, but essentially from Hardy's own pen – are notable for their concision; there are few allusions that stray from the central project of charting the evolution of the artist's consciousness in chronological relation to his work. It is unlikely that a nod to "the satirists" would have found its way into the autobiography if it did not have some reason to be there. It is significant, too, that this is the only such instance of generic classification in *The Early Life* or *The Later Years*. When Hardy provides other catalogs of his readings, they are typically a farrago of classical literature, English verse and prose, and philosophy; nowhere else does he choose his books around a single tradition or mode. Hardy's own remark that he embarked on this reading just after completing *Tess* is no less noteworthy. These satirists seemed to arrive at a pivotal moment in his career; something would be quite different afterwards.

There is, in fact, evidence of Hardy's interest in satire throughout his private writings of this era. At the beginning of 1890, according to *The Early Life*, he was "looking over old *Punches*" and was "struck with the frequent wrong direction of satire ... when seen by the light of later days" (293). It seems that Hardy was far more impressed by Voltaire than by *Punch*. His *Literary Notebooks* from this same period contain jottings from two Voltaire-related works from the previous two decades: T.B. Macaulay's *Critical and Historical Essays* (1879), from which he excerpted passages about Voltaire and Frederick the Great; and John Morley's *Voltaire*, first published in 1872 and reprinted in 1886. From the first book Hardy fixated on Macaulay's titles for the French satirist: "*the great scoffer-mocker –* Voltaire"; "*the greatest puller-down,* both of bad & good – Voltaire."

From Morley's monograph, the future author of *Jude the Obscure* extracted longer passages for his notebooks, focusing mostly on Voltaire's attacks on Christianity. Hardy cited Morley's remarks on "the strange & sinister method of [Voltaire's] assault upon religion wh. we of a later day watch with wondering eyes" and noted his inclusion of Voltaire in the category of "persons with something of a vested interest in darkness."[6] For Morley – and for the Hardy who was reading him in 1890 – supreme among Voltaire's achievements was his role as truth-teller, freed from the constraints of polite society. "Such a liberation of the human mind as Voltairism" quotes Hardy from Morley; and it is hard to ignore, even in the fragmented extracts that make up the notebooks, Hardy's veneration for a writer he was coming to regard as an authentic literary ancestor.[7]

The immediate consequences of such reading and note-taking for *Jude the Obscure* may be obvious. The profound religious skepticism of Hardy's novel surely owes a great debt to Voltaire. Hardy even casts Sue in the position of religious freethinker in the French tradition – on two occasions Jude calls her by Voltaire's name. When Sue offers to create for Jude a "new New Testament" by cutting and pasting the Epistles and Gospels into their proper chronological order, Jude protests that she is "quite Voltairean"; two chapters later, when Sue declares her refusal to consider marriage a sacrament, he cries: "Sue, you are terribly cutting when you like to be – a perfect Voltaire!" (182, 199–200). If Jude complains elsewhere about the designs of an elusive satirist, some agent responsible for the miseries with which he is so relentlessly cursed, he also identifies his beloved cousin as a sort of satirist-in-miniature, a Voltaire figure as capable of cruelty as she is of blasphemy. The book's terror hovers between a grand satire from without, something cosmic acting upon Jude and Sue together, and a narrower satire from within, issuing most often from Sue, but which is no less ruthless in its grip on the title character. The first may seem rather fantastical, perhaps out of place within the bounds of normal realist fiction; the second, involving as it does the clash of a man and a woman within the confines of a narrow society, is positioned squarely in the tradition of the nineteenth-century realist novel.

I began this chapter by claiming that two words haunted Hardy in the era of *Jude the Obscure.* The other is *realism*, a term which on the surface seemed to vex him as much as *satire* intrigued him. According to *The Early Life*, in August 1890 – just as he was immersing himself in "mostly the satirists" – Hardy recorded these reflections in his journal:

Art is a disproportioning – (*i.e.*, distorting, throwing out of proportion) – of realities, to show more clearly the features that matter in those realities, which, if merely copied or reported inventorially, might possibly be observed, but would more probably be overlooked. Hence 'realism' is not Art. (299)

Hardy would not allow himself to belong to a movement that pretended to represent the world in documentary terms without – as he saw it – the mediation of a dominant poetic sensibility. The following year Hardy again voiced his objection to the word *realism* and the school that bore its name, this time in the essay "The Science of Fiction," which he contributed to a symposium in the April 1891 issue of the *New Review*:

Realism is an unfortunate, an ambiguous word, which has been taken up by literary society like a view-halloo, and has been assumed in some places to mean copyism, and in others pruriency, and has led to two classes of delineators being included in one condemnation.[8]

By the final decade of the century, Hardy understood that realism had come to dominate the debates in England about the methods and uses of fiction: this awareness is the source of his vehement opposition to the term. One participant in these debates whom Hardy read particularly closely was his friend John Addington Symonds, whose *Essays Speculative and Suggestive* (1890) are cited extensively in the notebooks; Hardy read them in May 1891. Symonds was as skeptical of the "realist" project as Hardy. The realist, according to Symonds – and in a passage later excerpted in Hardy's notebooks – "seeks to ignore the fact that art must aim at selection." The phrase could just as easily be Hardy's own. Symonds described realism, with considerable irony, as "truth to actual fact." This line also is cited in Hardy's notes from the period.[9]

But Symonds's writings of the era, like Hardy's, train one eye on the problem of realism while keeping the other focused on theories of satire. The chapter of *Essays Speculative and Suggestive* that provided Hardy with such reflections on realism was called "Realism and Idealism"; it considered both literature and painting. Only three chapters later came a sort of companion essay, "Caricature, The Fantastic, the Grotesque," in which Symonds studied literary characterization in relation to caricature, obscenity, and satire. Despite this division into discrete chapters, Symonds's collection retains the focus of a unified argument, and so he is careful to relate his discussion of satirical caricature back to his earlier theme, the question of realism:

The real aim of caricature is to depreciate its object by evoking contempt or stirring laughter, when the imaginative rendering of the person is an unmistakable portrait, but defects are brought into relief which might otherwise have escaped notice. Instead therefore of being realistic, this branch of art must be reckoned as essentially idealistic. (1: 242)

This central question of the relative realism of satirical art was to reverberate incessantly in *Jude the Obscure*. Hardy seemed to take away two major lessons from his reading of Symonds: a skeptical frustration with the concept of realism as it was understood in late Victorian England, and an increased attention to the relation of realist fiction to the tradition of satire – a tradition in which he had already been immersed for the previous year. In the same notebook pages as his citation of "*realism* – 'truth to actual fact,'" Hardy thus jotted these fragments from Symonds: "[Sometimes] characterization borders upon caricature. In all cases it implies a willing sacrifice of superfl. beauty for the sake of force & uncompromising veracity"; and, a few entries later, "For examples of satire = Archilochus & Aristophanes, Juv. & Persius, Rabelais, & Regnier, Cervantes & Swift, Dryden & Pope, Heine & V. Hugo" (2:37–8).

This catalog from 1891 is, of course, strikingly reminiscent of the "mostly the satirists" reading list from the previous year. These were the writers who occupied Hardy as he turned from *Tess of the d'Urbervilles* to *Jude the Obscure.*

It is no accident that this struggle with these two interpenetrating ideas – a struggle so exemplary of late Victorian literature – would define Thomas Hardy's last novel in particular. Despite his reluctance to accept realism as a name for his own fiction, it is hard to ignore that *Jude the Obscure* owes more than any of his previous works to that tradition. *Jude* does not fit easily into the pastoral mold of earlier fictions like *Under the Greenwood Tree* or *A Pair of Blue Eyes*; it does not share the comic lightness that characterizes *The Hand of Ethelberta* or much of *The Woodlanders*; it does not depend as heavily upon the improbable coincidences that fuel the plots of *The Return of the Native* and *The Mayor of Casterbridge.* More than any other Hardy novel it exposes both hero and reader to the brutal facts of real experience. *Jude* is mostly devoid of esoteric Wessex folklore; it leaves rustic life behind when Jude sets off for Christminster. In its arc of promise and disillusionment set against a backdrop that for Hardy is relatively urban, in its story of utter failure in love and vocation, it has a tendency to recall Balzac's *Illusions perdues* or Flaubert's *L'Éducation sentimentale* more closely than Hardy's earlier novels. But this realism coexists awkwardly with the strong influences of Swift, Voltaire, and *Satires and Profanities. Jude the Obscure* exists at the remote edge of Victorian realism, where the detachment of the novelist blurs into the scourge of the satirist, who forfeits any semblance of impartiality in the interest of fury and abuse. "There are limits to realism," Edmund Gosse wrote five years before *Jude* was published, "and they seem to have been readily discovered by the realists themselves."[10] *Jude the Obscure* is a testament to the accuracy of Gosse's judgment.

SATIRE FROM ABOVE

Hardy's novels typically begin on a grand scale, as if to suggest that the eye of the narrator represents a distinctly suprahuman position. *Two on a Tower* opens on an early winter afternoon "when the vegetable world was a weird multitude of skeletons through whose ribs the sun shone freely"; in *The Woodlanders* we are introduced to "the physiognomy of a deserted highway [which] bespeaks a tomb-like stillness more emphatic than that of glades and pools."[11] The finest example of this perspective is the first chapter of *The Return of the Native*, the famous landscape of Egdon

Heath, in which "the distant rims of the world and of the firmament seemed to be a division in time no less than a division in matter": there is not a single human character in these first four pages.[12] Hardy's wish for *Two on a Tower*, as expressed in his preface to that novel, was to "set the emotional history of two infinitesimal lives against the stupendous background of the stellar universe," and indeed in all his novels the individual is at some point overwhelmed by the sheer immensity of his environment. There is something in Hardy's relation to the human that seeks to be always above it or beyond it.[13]

In *Jude the Obscure* this perspective, so critical to the novel's own distance from its central characters, shapes much of the narrative, from the endless stretches of landscape and the immense bleak sky of the early chapters to similar moments later on, when various figures watch the protagonist from a skeptical distance. In the scene of the pig-killing, as Jude and Arabella ready the animal for slaughter, the narrator notes that "a robin peered down at the preparations from the nearest tree" before flying away in displeasure with the incident unfolding below (73). In a typical scene after his arrival in Christminster two chapters later, Jude, sitting alone, is startled by an unfamiliar voice: "It came from a policeman who had been observing Jude without the latter observing him" (94). These scenarios are characteristic of *Jude the Obscure*: the protagonist is under the regular surveillance of various suspecting eyes, but he is rarely aware that he is being watched. It is only in moments of pain that he senses and curses the existence of a satire from above.

The accumulation of such visions – from the geological and astronomical gestures that open the novels to the instances of detached observation on a smaller scale – encourages us to think of Hardy's narrators as occupying some kind of supreme position, a point of view that seeks at times to mimic God's.[14] Hardy literalizes the notion of the omniscient narrator. The eye of the narration must see penetratingly but must also evade any detection. In this sense the idea behind Hardy's project is similar to Flaubert's famous doctrine that "the author, in his work, must be like God in the universe: everywhere present and nowhere visible."[15] And yet Flaubert's analogy poses more of a problem than many readers realize. This is the paradox of assuming the position of God when the writer in question does not accept the presence of God. James Wood rephrases the scenario persuasively: "It is not really that Flaubert withdraws from his books to become God as such, for God does not exist. No, he withdraws only to the *place* God would occupy if He existed."[16]

This difference is not just semantic; it lies at the center of Flaubert's – and Hardy's – relation to a novel's characters, whether we define this relation as realistic or satirical. *Jude the Obscure* vacillates between suggesting that God is absent and declaring that God is unnervingly present, in the form of cruelty – and thus between presenting a narrator who fills the void that God has left and creating a narrator who mimics a satirical God (as at the end of *Tess of the d'Urbervilles*, with its sport-playing President of the Immortals). In this respect the consistent position of the novels, *Jude* included, is to partake equally of the two traditions: Hardy adopts techniques of ironic omnipresence native to so much realist fiction; and yet he consistently reminds us that such omnipresence, in the satirical harshness of its ironies, is not the same as neutrality. This stance is closer to a different formulation of Flaubert's: "When will someone write the facts from the point of view of a *superior joke*, that is to say, as God sees them, from above?"[7] Flaubert's *blague supérieure* – this supreme or cosmic joke – is probably the finest, the most essential, phrase for the literary mode I am calling satirical realism. It encompasses both the supreme wisdom of a George Eliot narrator and the cruel humor of a persona in Swift. It is the best metaphor for the point of view of *Jude the Obscure*, since the hero's own interpretations of why things happen depend upon both a feeling of the utter contingency of things *and* a paranoid conviction that he is the object of a very personal satire.

This series of interpretive dilemmas and quandaries naturally recalls the Book of Job, to which *Jude the Obscure* alludes extensively. The novel's crucial point in this respect is Jude's deathbed scene, where his whispered recitations from Job – "Let the day perish wherein I was born" – are interspersed with the cries from outside celebrating the boat races of Remembrance Day. Nowhere in the novel are Hardy's ironies harsher.[18] The fundamental similarity between the plights of Job and Jude Fawley is that they do not understand the origins of their suffering, or the reasons for it: their endurance of a "general drama of pain," as the finale of *The Mayor of Casterbridge* phrases it, means being unable to comprehend the motives behind the dramatist's designs.[19] The result of such consistent perplexity for Jude is that, no matter how much the novel may encourage our compassion and sympathy for his wretchedness, we are also kept at a considerable distance. Our identification with the suffering hero is mediated by our concurrent impulse to align our perspective with that of the narrator: watching Jude from the horizon of the long Wessex highways, from the trees above his reach, from down the street where a policeman is observing him warily. Our sole method of avoiding the trap of Jude's own miserable confusion is to view his trials with the detachment of the same elusive satirist he senses around him.

The novel begins with Jude wondering why the world does not want him; it ends after his deathbed invocation of the Book of Job produces no response besides the cries of "Hurrah!" outside his door. The "obscure" of the title certainly captures this vagueness and murkiness, Jude's invisibility in the world. But the book's more significant title in this respect is not the one Hardy finally settled upon, but rather the working title he had in mind during most of the novel's evolution: "The Simpletons."[20] This original title effectively destroys any theory that Jude and Sue were conceived in a conventionally heroic manner: a simpleton is not a tragic hero but a figure found in Pope or Voltaire or Waugh. This title mocks Jude and Sue; it emphasizes their ignorance by annulling any possibility that they can comprehend their own folly. Hardy never seemed to abandon this notion of Jude and Sue as "simpletons," not even after the novel was completed. In an 1895 letter to Edmund Gosse, he wrote of his title character as "my poor puppet": Hardy's phrase seems to signify something crueler than merely a puppet of the circumstances of the world.[21]

It can be difficult not to feel some disappointment when we are faced with such evidence – difficult not to wonder whether Hardy's view of Jude as a simpleton or puppet compromises the dignity of Jude's afflic- tion, or even the novelistic realism of the story itself. (The same feeling arises in light of the protagonist's last name, though Hardy scholars – focusing instead on the fact that the novelist's grandmother came from the village of Fawley – never remark the perfect homophone. Jude Fawley is also Jude *Folly*: his name evokes that perennial target in the history of satirical writing.)[22] But we may indeed be mistaken if we view Hardy's portrait of Jude solely from the vantage point of the main tradition of the Victorian novel, from which we often quarry such notions of sympathy and realism. The attitude implied by epithets such as "simpleton" or "puppet" may owe a greater debt to Hardy's readings in satire instead.[23] This is not to say that *Jude the Obscure* is a book like *Candide* or *Gulliver's Travels*, rather that the fact of suffering can get subsumed by the more intellectual problem of the generic and ironic representation of this suffering – and that this can align the reader uncomfortably with the narrator's cool and cruel detachment.

I have implied some continuity between several agents in this novel: Hardy, the narrator, the satirist-figure, God. There are significant differ- ences between these entities, but *Jude the Obscure* – as I suggested in

relation to Hardy's technique of adopting a perspective from above –
continually exhorts us to think of them as different versions of the same
thing. This method has a tendency to elide certain distinctions between
the human and the non-human: to make the narrator somewhat divine
while simultaneously personifying the Hardyan God. The anthropomorphous shape of Hardy's deity has long been a curiosity for critics of
his fiction. G.K. Chesterton wrote in 1913:

[The God] of Thomas Hardy is almost made personal by the intense feeling that
he is poisonous ... It has been said that if God had not existed it would have been
necessary to invent Him. But it is not often, as in Mr Hardy's case, that it is
necessary to invent Him in order to prove how unnecessary (and undesirable)
He is. But Mr Hardy is anthropomorphic out of sheer atheism.[24]

Chesterton disparaged Hardy more than any other writer in *The Victorian
Age in Literature*: it is here that he bestows upon the author of *Tess of the
d'Urbervilles* the notorious title of "village atheist brooding and blaspheming over the village idiot" (143). But Chesterton might have taken his
formulation about the anthropomorphism in Hardy's representations of
God straight from Hardy himself, who had written in *Jude the Obscure*,
shortly after the infanticide, "affliction makes opposing forces loom
anthropomorphous; and those ideas [of a benevolent God] were now
exchanged for a sense of Jude and [Sue] fleeing from a persecutor" (413).
And though Chesterton never alludes to a single Hardy work by name, his
observation can indeed apply to works across the corpus of prose and
verse. This is especially true of some of Hardy's most significant poems.
The central conceit of "God's Education," for example – from the 1909
collection *Time's Laughingstocks and Other Verses* – is a man's conversation
with God upon witnessing the gradual death of his lover. It is also the
structure of a better-known poem, "Channel Firing," in which the dead
carry on an exchange with a sarcastic God about the first rumblings of
war. Hardy's renderings of a satirical God can, in effect, take at least two
forms: the satirist can be a silent and unknowable figure beyond the grasp
of a human character; or else he can be an active and ironic interlocutor,
within the range of conversation but still cruelly mocking in tone.[25]

The question of satire in *Jude the Obscure* is therefore largely a question
of interpretation: terrible things happen to Jude, and both he and the
reader must try to determine whether they are accidental and meaningless,
or whether they are devised by some agent with a satirical intent. If the
latter is true, then the interpretive dilemma centers on a subsequent
question: whether the novelist seeks to reproduce the designs of a satirical

God or is, in fact, the satirical agent himself, engineering the mockery of his characters. The swirling together of these various hypotheses indicates the difficulty of examining the presence of satire within realist fiction. There is no persona boisterously exposing the folly of man; this role has been subsumed into a more self-effacing narration. This means that Hardy's characters must take certain occurrences in their lives and decipher them as signals.

It is not only in *Jude* that these characters come to the conclusion that such signals should be interpreted as satire. As the heroine of *Tess of the d'Urbervilles* waits longingly for the husband who has abandoned her, the narrator cites two lines from Wordsworth's "Ode: Intimations of Immortality" – "Not in utter nakedness/ But trailing clouds of glory do we come" – and writes that to Tess "there was ghastly satire in the poet's lines" (456).[26] We must remember that Wordsworth did not write these lines as ghastly satire; Hardy has ripped them out of context and slotted them ironically into his own story, where the phrasing does not change but the significance does, since they seem like satire and mockery directed at Tess amidst her misfortunes. This passage provides a valuable analogy for our own interpretation of a novel like *Jude the Obscure*. It represents a moment of reading. It is not necessarily clear that Tess Durbeyfield knows these lines from Wordsworth – she probably does not – and yet Hardy implies that their spirit is nevertheless familiar to her, except that she can only understand this spirit in reverse, as satire. Tess is thereby in the position of reading a sentiment but only comprehending it as a mockery of her situation. This is an attitude of suspicion that insists on understanding the self as a constant target.

There is one other viewpoint available in Hardy for the interpretation of why things happen. This is to see occurrence not as satire but as accident, to see God not as mocking but as absent or indifferent instead. It would seem that this is the true Hardy position, closer to steadfast atheism than manic paranoia. In 1865, when he was only 24, he wrote in his journal: "The world does not despise us; it only neglects us";[27] this also became the theme of his 1866 poem "Hap." He suspected from early in life that cosmic satirical readings could only be misreadings. Hardy would maintain this suspicion throughout his life, noting in 1917 that his new verse collection, *Moments of Vision and Miscellaneous Verses*, was designed "to mortify the human sense of self-importance by showing, or suggesting, that human beings are of no matter or appreciable value in this nonchalant universe."[28] Still, because *Jude the Obscure* aligns its expressions of satire with its invocations of religion, and because it so steadily posits the notion that satirical forces haunt Jude, it seems inadequate to call the novel a declaration of atheism. The novel cannot tell us how to read the workings of fate, nor can it tell us how to comprehend the workings of causality in novelistic art, precisely because it always offers two contrary philosophies. The realism of the novel pushes us to comprehend its universe in atheistic terms, while its satire urges us to accept the existence of a malevolent power who lashes the meek. This, in short, is how in Hardy the interpretation of literature as *genre* becomes inseparable from the novel's articulation of its metaphysics. Tess, in understanding Wordsworth's verses as satire, is bending the rules of genre in order to account for lived experience. *Jude the Obscure* asks us to do something quite similar. It presents – as I will argue later – implausible scenarios that strain any sense of verisimilitude, and yet it does so within the bounds of a mostly realistic narrative. The novel tells a story that, consistent with its author's 1890s quarrel with "realism," cannot be justified solely by the rules of that tradition. And so it trains us to read with two incompatible beliefs: in the utter contingency of things, and in the orchestrated malice of an agent who wields more force than we do.

The long and difficult critical reaction to *Jude* issues largely from this problem, from not knowing how "realistic" the novel should be assumed to be. In particular the tradition of calling the novel "blasphemous" assumes that its anti-religious expressions should be understood as a series of non-ironic statements by its author. Chesterton's famous 1913 epigram ("a sort of village atheist brooding and blaspheming over the village idiot") merely codified a widely shared impression from the first days of its publication that *Jude the Obscure* was a blasphemous book. Joss Marsh, in her study of blasphemy in Victorian England, devotes her final chapter to *Jude the Obscure*, which she rightly considers the culmination of the nineteenth-century novel's struggle with piety and irreverence.[29] Indeed, much of the scandal of *Jude* in 1895 and 1896 centered on the question of Hardy's perceived assaults on religion. These reactions ranged from the abusive, as in Mrs. Oliphant's notorious *Blackwood's Magazine's* censure of the novel, to generally sympathetic receptions that nevertheless labored to understand Hardy's rage. One example is Gosse's own 1896 review, in which he asked a rhetorical question that has since become a cliché: "What has Providence done to Mr Hardy that he should rise up in the arable land of Wessex and shake his fist at his Creator?"[30] This reaction would be commonplace in discussions of *Jude* through at least T.S. Eliot, who in *After Strange Gods* attacked Hardy in a chapter mostly about literature and blasphemy. But in Eliot's judgment Hardy is not, in fact, a blasphemer. Eliot's important point is that blasphemy is a favorable sign of a civilization, since it cannot be committed unless there is some modicum of belief in the first place: "no one can possibly blaspheme in any sense except that in which a parrot may be said to curse, unless he profoundly believes in that which he profanes."[31]

Marsh notes Eliot's qualification, a restriction that – despite expressing a skepticism about Hardy's novel similar to that of vociferous critics like Mrs. Oliphant – places the author of *Jude the Obscure* outside the category of blasphemers. What Marsh does not acknowledge is that this very definition of blasphemy had been formulated in a book that Hardy himself read while working on *Jude*: James Thomson's *Satires and Profanities*, which he included in his list of "mostly the satirists." The version Hardy read contained a preface by G.W. Foote celebrating the powers of satire, which "more than any other form of composition, rouses antipathy where it does not command applause; and the greater the satire, the more intense are the feelings it excites."[32] Foote continued: "Thomson's satire was always bitterest, or at any rate most trenchant, when it dealt with Religion, which he considered a disease of the mind, engendered by folly and fostered by ignorance and vanity." And indeed the fiercest satires in this collection were directed at Christianity, nowhere more explicitly than in the chapter "A Word on Blasphemy." Thomson writes:

For the Atheist, God is a figment, nothing; in blaspheming God he therefore blasphemes nothing. A man really blasphemes when he mocks, insults, pollutes, vilifies that which he really believes to be holy and awful ... Speaking philosophically, an honest Atheist can no more blaspheme God than an honest Republican can be disloyal to a King, than an unmarried man can be guilty of conjugal infidelity. (69)

Thomson anticipates both Hardy and Eliot: the assault can only be truly blasphemous if there is some trace of belief behind it. But, of course, Thomson's volume is not a sober, scholarly study of blasphemous satire; it is itself a prolonged exercise in satire. *Satires and Profanities* wields much of the same late Victorian aggression that would characterize *Jude* a decade later; Thomson, like Hardy, understands this antagonistic position as something called *satire*. His angry volume anticipates the way in which narrative, blasphemy, and satire would be interwoven in Hardy's final novel. *Jude the Obscure*, written with *Satires and Profanities* still on Hardy's shelf, adopts a narrative perspective that sometimes mimics an angry God, and might thus be labeled blasphemous; and at other times implies an entirely Godless universe, an attitude which by definition has to be called atheistic instead. According to Thomson or Eliot the two cannot coexist within a religious philosophy – but Hardy proves that they *can* coexist within the bounds of a single novel. *Jude the Obscure* has to be both agnostic and entirely pervaded by God. This is as much a requirement of genre as it is of belief, categories which for Hardy are interpenetrating rather than purely discrete. His readings in satire in the early 1890s, especially in Voltaire and James Thomson, testify that Hardy did not conceive of satire as separable from religion. To adopt the aggression and contrariness of the satirist was to write a fiction in which God is both impersonated and attacked, since the narrator would have to imitate his authority in order to question his existence. In this sense, the agnostic realism of *Jude the Obscure* is just as bleak, just as pitiless, as the novel's aggressive satire.

PREPOSITIONAL SATIRE

Nowhere in Hardy's fiction is the influence of satire – or the invocation of its name – more prominent than in *Jude the Obscure*. But *Jude* is, in fact, one of two focal points of satire in the larger Hardy corpus. The other is his verse cycle *Satires of Circumstance*, first published in 1911, his only work to name the genre in its title. In 1914 this was subsumed into a considerably larger collection, entitled *Satires of Circumstance, Lyrics and Reveries*, which featured no fewer than one hundred poems, among them "Channel Firing," "The Convergence of the Twain," and "God's Funeral": all in the first rank of his verse. In this larger collection the cycle *Satires of Circumstance* itself constitutes the final part. Each of its fifteen poems is short: between two and five stanzas. They all describe an ironic situation: some scenario in which a character does not know, or only learns too late, something that would change utterly his or her perspective on personal circumstances. In the second "satire," for example, a preacher mesmerizes his congregation from the pulpit, then retires to the vestry where he thinks no one can see him. One of his Bible students, hoping to speak with him, sees him behind the door he thought he had closed. But her "idol" is reenacting "Each pulpit gesture in deft dumb-show/ That had moved the congregation so": the seemingly authentic display of piety from the pulpit was merely a performance.[33] The first, fourth, fifth, and tenth satires all concern the harsh recognition that a man or woman has chosen the wrong spouse; the lurking presence of a different lover is an unforgiving reminder of an earlier mistake.

Three other satires take place at a grave. In the third poem, a girl tells her lover that her now-deceased aunt had been giving her money to pay for her headstone upon her death; the lovers decide to spend the money on a dance that night instead. The sixth satire tells the story of two women arguing over whose son is buried in a particular plot. Another voice – "the man of the cemetery" – tells us that the plot in question was removed long before to make way for a drain. And in the fourteenth satire the first and second wives of a dead man hold a conversation next to his grave; the first regrets that she divorced him simply because he loved the second.

These "satires" are all condensed tragedies of ignorance. In each case the circumstance is satirical because someone has been oblivious to a certain fact, or has never understood the true opinions or desires of someone else, or continues to be kept in the dark about the actions of another. The result of such ignorance is either a small cruelty – as with the dead aunt whose headstone money is being used for other purposes – or a belated recognition of extraordinary error, as in the plight of the miserable brides who have chosen the wrong man to marry. These are satires, says Hardy, but the satirist in question is never named. It is not even suggested that those who do something improper (the lovers who spend the headstone money) are the agents of satire. These are "satires of circumstance": though some cruelty defines each poem, its source is not identified.[34] The aphoristic or parable-like structure of the satires even implies that it would be a mistake to seek this source in the first place. In Hardy's equation the proximity of human to human – even the dead to the living – is enough to render every circumstance satirical. We find ourselves endlessly in laughably tragic scenarios.

Over the course of the last thirty-five years of his life Hardy created an immense body of verse; the most recent edition of *The Complete Poems* numbers 948 poems. But among these, *Satires of Circumstance* is the only major cycle unified by both theme and title. Apart from some war verse and a few short numbered poems, this is the only group of Hardy poems designated as belonging together or revolving around a central theme or genre. This unity is evident in the common ironic or satirical situations they narrate, of course; but it is equally clear in the titles of each poem. Each of the *Satires* is named for a situation expressed grammatically through a preposition: "At Tea"; "In Church"; "By Her Aunt's Grave"; "In the Cemetery"; "In the Nuptial Chamber"; "On the Death-Bed"; "Over the Coffin." These prepositional phrases are consistent with Hardy's vision of "circumstance": a circumstance is a position we find ourselves in, a scenario of the self in relation to its surroundings. But this chain of titles is strikingly reminiscent of another series in Hardy: the individual titles of each section of *Jude the Obscure*. That novel is divided into six parts, each centered on the scene of action, the place where Jude finds himself: "At Marygreen"; "At Christminster"; "At Melchester"; "At Shaston"; "At Aldbrickham and Elsewhere"; "At Christminster Again." This design is unique in Hardy's mature fiction. In certain of his other novels each section division is titled, but in *The Return of the Native* and *Tess of the d'Urbervilles* these titles bear no real or consistent thematic relation to one another.

This strange parallel encourages us to read *Satires of Circumstance* and *Jude the Obscure* side by side – to read *Jude* as a six-part satire of circumstance in prose. All these narratives are structured around the most basic statement of existence. The unstated verb that precedes each preposition is *to be*: the young girl is in church; the lovers are in the cemetery; Jude is at Marygreen, then at Christminster, then at Melchester, and at the end of the novel he is at Christminster again. The preposition is the most basic grammatical unit of Hardyan satire. To be located in some place, to take up space on a particular plot of land somewhere in Wessex, is already to fall into the error that draws the wrath of an elusive cosmic satire. Every "at" is a scourge and a curse. This is a major theme in Hardy's fiction, of course: the association of darkly comic absurdity with the stark reality of existing in this world. To find oneself in a particular place is the one unchanging circumstance that begins at birth; and to be born, says Hardy across his fiction, is the primal mistake. For Tess Durbeyfield "birth itself was an ordeal of degrading personal compulsion"; after her disastrous wedding night she realizes that "in some circumstances there was one thing better than to lead a good life, and that was to be saved from leading any life whatever," at which point she hears "a penal sentence in the fiat, 'You shall be born'" (456, 311). In *The Return of the Native* Eustacia Vye expresses "an agonising pity for myself that I ever was born"; Clym Yeobright later reaches a similar discovery that "he had been ill-used by fortune, so far as to say that to be born is a palpable dilemma, and that instead of men aiming to advance in life with glory they should calculate how to retreat out of it without shame" (232, 455). This nihilism finds its strongest expression in *Jude the Obscure*, where Father Time is said to represent "the coming universal wish not to live," and the hero, on his deathbed, recites the verses from the Book of Job: "Let the day perish wherein I was born" (406, 488). These are all different ways of rephrasing the quandary of Hardy's prepositional satire: to be born, and then to exist, is to fall into the trap of being satirized.

This extreme pessimism, the object of much study in Hardy criticism, would seem to be another word for what is often called the novelist's "tragic" sense. But Hardy's own formulation for the problem is not the "tragedy" of circumstance; it is the "satire" of circumstance. In Hardy's staging of circumstance, satire is what happens when a person becomes *aware* of his own tragedy.[35] Satire is a name for self-consciousness and recognition, even when this may be a false recognition. In that scene from the serial version of *Jude* to which I alluded earlier – when Jude overhears the conversation of some clergymen after the infanticide and cries, "What a satire their talk is on our importance to the world!" – the allegation of satire is the expression of a paranoid vision of reality. Jude hears other people and relates this conversation to himself; this magnifies his conception of the wretchedness of his situation; suddenly he sees himself as a victim and tragedy dissolves into satire. A scenario therefore becomes satirical precisely when the central character himself *feels* satirized, even if he cannot know the source of the attack.

As I claimed in relation to the lines from Wordsworth in *Tess of the d'Urbervilles*, satire in Hardy is a question of interpretation, of reading things as signs and reacting accordingly. In *Fiction and Repetition* J. Hillis Miller notes that Hardy's narrators "see things in figure" and call attention to repetitions that may not, in fact, be true likenesses. "The problem," writes Miller, "is not that there are no explanations proposed in the text, but that there are too many."[36] This observation applies to Hardy's characters no less than to his narrators. To see patterns in the world beyond ourselves, and then to seek total explanations for them despite the probability of mere contingency, and finally to connect them to ourselves: this is to see things in figure. This is to succumb to the temptation of personifying circumstance; and this is to take certain rules of the realist novel and reread them as satire.

Satire in Hardy must be vague to be prepositional; if it were too specific, we would be able to discern in too vivid detail the identity of the forces acting upon Jude Fawley. *Jude the Obscure* relies heavily on its hazy suspicion of "things": Jude and Sue's contemplation, late in the book, of "the direct antagonism of things" is exemplary of the novel's stance towards the vagueness of animosity (413). It is important to remember that there is no villain in this novel. This is true of many Hardy novels; Alec d'Urberville, if he should even be called a villain, is exceptional. In *Jude the Obscure* it is "things" that fill the void left by villainy. This is one reason for their anthropomorphism; antagonistic forces can only be understood when they are given a human shape. But if "things" are so often to blame, they are also the very essence of Hardy's stories and plots. In his explanatory note to the first edition of *Tess* he wrote that his purpose had been "to give artistic form to a true sequence of things" (xv). His novels – like most novels that belong to the realist tradition, broadly stated – are efforts to explain why things happen the way they do: in what sequence, and through what chain of cause and effect. But in *Jude* the very idea of sequence is left radically uncertain. Since Jude's fate is so often reduced to his simply being *at* a particular place, then finding himself somewhere else later, this chain is reduced to a series of brute statements of existence. The "true sequence of things" of *Tess* becomes the six-part satire of circumstance of *Jude*, which, as a result, pushes forward to the extreme boundary of the realist project. It represents the point at which realism, the generally meticulous effort to describe life as it is, can no longer be dissociated from a radical form of satire, in which human character is depicted in order to show how it is mocked simply for being there. This is the essence of prepositional satire, the starkest mode of realism. Nowhere is this idea of genre expressed more succinctly than in Hardy's own title for his later verse cycle. *Satires of Circumstance* seems on the surface to be a paradox: "circumstance" should be far too neutral a term to allow for the polemics and prejudices of satire. But in Hardy's equation the two are fused into one another; and in the end *satire* and *circumstance* sound so interchangeable that the phrase itself risks being redundant.

FARCE AND THE COMPARATIVELY UNREAL

Prepositional satire is the fate primarily of the title character in *Jude the Obscure*. But he is not the only figure in the novel to lament this basic condition of existence, or to locate its origin in the fact of having once been born. Jude's closing words – "Let the day perish wherein I was born" – are, in fact, an echo of an earlier proclamation by his son Father Time. Time, in his final conversation with Sue before hanging himself and his two half-siblings, bluntly declares: "I wish I hadn't been born!" (402). His ensuing suicide/infanticide seems on the surface to be the corrective to this blight of entering the world, a corrective that Jude himself can only attain through a much more protracted suffering, at the end of the novel. But Time's notorious act cannot be understood merely as a corrective to his own existence, or to that of the two other children he murders. In his conversation with Sue, just after proclaiming his wish never to have been born, he elaborates: "I think that whenever children be born that are not wanted they should be killed directly, before their souls come to'em, and not allowed to grow big and walk about!" There is an alarming universality in this statement, a total theory behind it, which transcends even the particular instance of the excruciating scene that follows. There is no alternative proposed in the novel for how to deal with children: after Time kills himself and his two half-siblings there are simply no other children left in the story. He has, effectively, accomplished his goal of a large-scale extermination.

If Father Time has always been a problem for readers of *Jude the Obscure*, it is largely this very universality that is to blame. Everything the child says and does bears such an extraordinary weight of significance, and his doctrines reach so far beyond the normal ken of a young boy, that it seems he cannot be accommodated within the realist contours of the novel. Many readers of Hardy therefore deem it impossible to accept the characterization of the boy in the same way we do the veracity of Jude or Arabella or Sue. D.H. Lawrence, who in his study of Hardy devoted many pages to the explication and analysis of Jude and Sue, also wrote that Father Time was "very badly suggested, exaggerated": the boy is not accorded anything like the seriousness Lawrence directs at the novel's other figures.[37] Irving Howe similarly complained about the "glaring falsity" of such scenes as the infanticide, which is a "botched incident"; he pronounces it "a failure of tact to burden [Father Time] with so much philosophical weight."[38] We can presume that if Father Time were simply a moody child who ended up killing himself – but without exemplifying "the coming universal wish not to live" – Howe and others might not object so viscerally to his inclusion in a novel so widely admired for the unforgiving precision of its realism. The strange personage of Father Time ultimately leads readers of *Jude* to seek divergent ways of explaining him; few can bring themselves to ignore him. Early vociferous critics of the novel rejected him altogether. Mrs. Oliphant, for example, writing in *Blackwood's*, called the infanticide "pure farce ... only too grotesque to be amusing."[39] An unsigned review in *The Illustrated London News* went into more detail:

Now, up to this point, woe has been heaped upon woe, and the reader has accepted it all, with some reservations, as a natural evolution of the circumstances. The tragedy of the children strains his belief to snapping point ... It is strange that Mr Hardy did not perceive how he had imperilled the whole fabric by a stroke which passes the border of burlesque.[40]

This anonymous critic's "burlesque" is similar to Mrs. Oliphant's "farce": both are registering the difficulty of assimilating the infanticide with the realism of the story. This was also the objection of Havelock Ellis, who in an otherwise reverential review in *The Savoy* – "*Jude the Obscure* seems to be the greatest novel written in England for many years" – singled out the infanticide as the novel's lone fiasco:

> Only at one point, it seems to me, is there a serious lapse in the art of the book, and that is when the door of the bedroom closet is sprung open on us to reveal the row of childish corpses. Up to that one admires the strength and sobriety of the narrative, its complete reliance on the interests that lie in common humanity. We feel that here are real human beings of the sort we all know, engaged in obscure struggles that are latent in the life we all know. But with the opening of that cupboard we are thrust out of the large field of common life into the small field of the police court or the lunatic asylum, among the things which for most of us are comparatively unreal.[41]

For all these 1890s readers, this scene at some basic level cannot be accepted as true: it is closer to farce or burlesque than to their idea of the novelistic, and so it is unreal.

Father Time's lurid achievement also has a tendency to remind us of Thomas Malthus, as Gillian Beer has noted, especially in the language of the infamous suicide note: "*Done because we are too menny*" (405).[42] The expressed universality of Father Time's project is indeed Malthusian: the slaughter of the young is in essence a drastic method to limit population on a small scale. It is an especially grotesque Malthus that *Jude the Obscure* invokes, so outrageous that it overflows any familiar boundaries of philosophy or discipline. In calling it "farcical," Mrs. Oliphant – for all her foolish opposition to the novel upon its publication – made an excellent judgment of the infanticide. The nineteenth-century novel is rife with examples of child-killings, real or alleged: in Walter Scott's *Heart of Midlothian* and Frances Trollope's *Jessie Phillips* the crime is presumed; in George Eliot's *Adam Bede* Hetty Sorrel does, in fact, kill her infant child. But in none of these novels is the killing of children related to the problem of overpopulation, grandly stated; and in none of them is the individual event asked explicitly to serve the exemplary role played by the catastrophe in *Jude the Obscure*. In *Jude* the vast design behind the event tugs its reader in two contrary directions. It asks us to believe its credibility by alluding to the possibility that there is, in fact, a problem of overpopulation; and yet it burdens the boy and the act with such overwhelming consequence that it strains all bounds of verisimilitude. It is a moment of such excess that it actually does approach the farcical.

Father Time's own stated philosophy – "I think that whenever children be born that are not wanted they should be killed directly" – has no real precedent in the Victorian novel. The vast scope of its potential application exceeds, for example, the specific tragedy of Hetty Sorrel's fatal abandoning of her child. In truth Father Time's proclamation owes much more to Swift's *Modest Proposal* than to any scene or statement in nineteenth-century literature. At the beginning of Swift's satire, before he has revealed the essence of the proposal, he writes that his intention

is very far from being confined to provide only for the Children of *professed Beggars*: It is of a much greater Extent, and shall take in the whole Number of Infants at a certain Age, who are born of Parents, in effect as little able to support them, as those who demand our Charity in the Streets.[43]

Father Time's oath sounds like an echo of the Modest Proposer's: it plays on the idea of taking in a vast portion of society, the "whole Number of Infants." In both cases the problem has to do with the danger of taking things too literally. The interest of the *Modest Proposal* lies not only in its rhetorical bravura but also in the unlikely but possible danger of a reader's absurdly literal interpretation.[44] For Father Time the tragedy can also be traced to a literal interpretation of things: when the boy asks Sue if it would be better for him and the other children to be "out o' the world than in it," she replies "it would almost, dear"; two pages later the three children are hanging from box-cords. Sue realizes just after the infanticide that "he took it literally" (408). We err when we read things by the letter, for – according to the novel's epigraph – "the letter killeth."

John Bayley has remarked that this "literalness" provides the shock-value for both Hardy and Swift, but he does not acknowledge that this shared effect may not be coincidental – that Hardy may have had Swift in mind when he decided to kill off the children in this way.[45] We should not forget that Swift was one of the "satirists" Hardy was reading as he turned from *Tess of the d'Urbervilles* to *Jude the Obscure*. Though Swift's name, unlike Voltaire's, does not appear in the novel itself, Hardy had a distinct interest in him throughout most of his career, and especially toward the end of the nineteenth century. *The Early Life* records that in 1880 Matthew Arnold had advised Hardy to study him: "The best man to read for style – narrative style – was Swift" (175). It is uncertain whether Hardy took up Swift in earnest before 1890, but by the final decade of the century the great satirist had become a central figure for Hardy's own self-image. An 1899 entry in *The Later Years of Thomas Hardy* makes this quite clear:

Hardy had a born sense of humour, even a too keen sense occasionally: but his poetry was sometimes placed by editors in the hands of reviewers deficient in that quality. Even if they were accustomed to Dickensian humour they were not to Swiftian. Hence it unfortunately happened that verses of a satirical, dry, caustic, or farcical cast were regarded by them with the deepest seriousness.[46]

By the turn of the century Hardy had devoted himself exclusively to poetry; the allusion here is to his verse in particular. But this affinity for Swift emerges no less forcefully in the novel published only four years earlier. If there is humor in *Jude the Obscure*, it is a perversely Swiftian humor: a radically ironic and misanthropic, perverse humor. It is revealing that Hardy instinctively opposes this kind of humor to the Dickensian variety, which was a much more familiar and available mode of satire within the idiom of the Victorian novel. Dickens's satire typically zeroed in on a particular segment of society: Chancery, the Circumlocution Office, the provincial schoolhouse. But Swift's was more pervasive and more essential: less compatible, it would seem, with the generous perspective of the Victorian novel. The apparent universality of Father Time's murderous proclamation may seem comical if we know to associate such grand suggestions of child exterminations only with proposals that must be satirical; it is when the boy enacts a small-scale version of it that we shudder to see implausible theory transformed into grotesque action. Such an awkward transition will inevitably baffle many readers of the novel. And so it is difficult not to associate Hardy's complaint above – that reviewers of his poetry could not appreciate its Swiftian satire – with his similar grievances a few years earlier, when other reviewers had greeted *Jude the Obscure* with such revulsion.[47]

As with so many other aspects of *Jude*, however, the infanticide hovers between its debt to satire and its concurrent gestures toward a certain realism. One might say it is satirical in design and realistic in execution. It is hard to think about the scene without recalling the vividness of its detail, the ruthless intensity of its visual sense. Here is our first vision of the hanging children, which we see through Jude's eyes:

He looked in bewilderment round the room. At the back of the door were fixed two hooks for hanging garments, and from these the forms of the two youngest children were suspended, by a piece of box-cord round each of their necks, while from a nail a few yards off the body of little Jude was hanging in a similar manner. An overturned chair was near the elder boy, and his glazed eyes were staring into the room; but those of the girl and the baby boy were closed. (404–5)

The entire scene depends upon the ocular, from the grotesque panorama we share with Jude to Father Time's own eyes, staring stubbornly at the follies of the world he has just renounced. Nowhere else in *Jude the Obscure* is the narration so matter-of-fact. It is disconcertingly calm, taking us patiently through every cruel detail in the room.[48] This exactness of detail marks Hardy's total mastery of the mercilessness lurking within so much late Victorian realism. But it also seems strangely at odds with the grandiosity of the boy's theory of child-killing only two pages earlier. It is as though the infanticide were a crucible of genre for Hardy: in this sequence of the novel, more than any other, he would have to vacillate between the implausible hyperboles of satirical suggestion and the rigorous methods of realist narrative.[49]

The specter of three children hanging from hooks and nails marks a terminus in the evolution of Victorian realism. The bleak rustic tragedy of *Adam Bede* or the urban poverty of such 1880s Gissing novels as *The Nether World* might have looked ahead to such a vision, but they could not predict its clear aim to bring a novelistic tradition to a point past which fiction could not go. And yet the novel itself *does* continue beyond this point. There are, in fact, nine subsequent chapters in *Jude the Obscure*, each bringing a new portion of misery and wretchedness to Jude and Sue. Even the end of the infanticide chapter allows no respite from the horrific. Most readers remember three dead children in this chapter – Father Time and the two others he has hanged alongside himself. But there is a fourth: in the chapter's final line, Jude learns that the pregnant Sue has gone into labor prematurely and that the child is stillborn. If Gosse's "limits of realism" had not been reached in the scene of the infanticide, surely they are attained here: at such a moment the plausibility of tragedy threatens to dissolve completely, leaving only the sour taste of an author intent on subjecting his reader to an absolute assault on the senses.

The final chapters of *Jude the Obscure* taunt us; they provoke our complete stupefaction that Hardy can push his narrative any further. These eighty pages are, more perhaps than any sequence in any other English novel, a prolonged exercise in excruciation – an excruciation of prolongment and protraction. The pattern is repeated throughout these late pages: Sue threatens to go back to Phillotson, and after more debate she finally does; Jude turns gravely ill, but two chapters from the end he recovers briefly, delaying the death that could finally bring the novel to a close; in the final chapter, when Arabella discovers his corpse, she chooses not to report his death immediately, but to go out to join the crowds at the boat race instead, and so the dead Jude must lie there, unattended, a little longer.

This perverse excruciation in *Jude the Obscure* signals a larger resistance in Hardy to the idea of continuation and the regular flow of events. In the most basic sense Hardy was profoundly suspicious of the normal evolution of time; this is an essential part of his deep-rooted conservatism. In 1888, according to *The Early Life*, he wrote: "It is the on-going – *i.e.* the 'becoming' – of the world that produces its sadness. If the world stood still at a felicitous moment there would be no sadness in it" (265). Elsewhere the same volume cites Hardy's opposition to nature's "blunder of overdoing" – the mistake of man's having evolved this far in history – and elaborates several pages later: "We [human beings] have reached a degree of intelligence which Nature never contemplated when framing her laws, and for which she consequently has provided no adequate satisfactions" (192, 213). This relates directly, of course, to the fierce ambivalence in *Jude the Obscure* toward the very idea of the propagation of the human species; these axioms are blatantly prophetic of Father Time's suicide note. But Hardy's resistance to the "on-going" of things also has a formal or novelistic interest for us. It suggests that such conservatism risks being fundamentally at odds with the structure of narrative art itself – which in any realist idiom traces the evolution of events, or what Hardy called in his prefatory note to *Tess of the d'Urbervilles* the "true sequence of things." But in *Jude* the "on-going" of the world no longer seems in harmony with that true sequence. This is not to say that Hardy completely reconceived his relationship to narrative after *Tess*, just that – as his plots revealed their debt to non-novelistic forms like satire – the continuation of narrative began to seem less like a natural progression of a particular story, and more like a lesson that on-going itself was the problem.

These late, post-infanticide chapters in *Jude the Obscure* suggest that if on-going is tragic or "sad," to use Hardy's own term, this sadness cannot be dissociated from a certain grotesque comedy. The pastoral sorrow of the first parts of the novel yields to a much more bizarre, carnivalesque wretchedness by the novel's end. The closing chapters ring with the inescapable sound of discordant laughter, a laughter which emanates primarily from Arabella.[50] A few chapters after the hanging we find her with her father, engaged in a conversation about the absurdity of her reuniting with Jude: "Arabella was suddenly seized with a fit of loud laughter, in which her father joined more moderately" (457). A short while later, as she flirts with the quack doctor Vilbert and brings him a drink, "Arabella began shaking with suppressed laughter" (485). Such awkward hilarity is exemplary of the garish tone that distorts the late sequences of *Jude the Obscure*. Jude seems particularly haunted by this laughter: in his final days he begins to hear the voices of the great minds of Christminster – Addison, Johnson, Arnold – and cries: "They seem laughing at me!" (474); in the same scene in the serial version he rails against the "great permanent sneer" of the university.[51] This, of course, recalls all the previous occasions of Jude's paranoid conviction that he is the object of a grand satire; but in these late scenes such laughter tolls even more cacophonously.

It may seem peculiar to record the sounds of laughter in Hardy's fiction, much as it first seems counterintuitive to trace the influences of satire. Hardy cannot be called a comic novelist in any ordinary sense. Father Time, in his first appearance in the novel, is said to bear an expression that says: "All laughing comes from misapprehension. Rightly looked at there is no laughable thing under the sun" (332). We are not supposed to understand this completely ironically; this grave suspicion of laughter is a genuine reflex in Hardy's view of things. In a letter to Symonds in 1889 – the year before the publication of Symonds's *Essays Speculative and Suggestive* – he wrote: "All comedy, is tragedy, if you only look deep enough into it."[52] (Hardy's maxim seems to be at once the contrary and the close pair of a dictum of Schopenhauer, who wrote that "the life of every individual, viewed as a whole and in general, and when only its most significant features are emphasized, is really a tragedy; but gone through in detail it has the character of a comedy.")[53] But such resistance to laughter and comedy does not mean that Hardy rejected the inclusion of either one in *Jude the Obscure*. It cannot be accidental that laughter emerges brashly in the late chapters of the novel, after so many forms of tragedy have already run their course. If all comedy is tragedy, then the arc of *Jude the Obscure* suggests that the reverse must also be true. When all the realistic manifestations of tragedy have been exhausted, there remains nothing else for us to do but laugh – if only for the terrible fact that for an excruciatingly long period, even after the elimination of the whole number of infants, the novel perversely refuses to end.

HARDY AND THE LIMITS OF GENRE

At a much earlier point in *Jude the Obscure*, only shortly after he has arrived at Christminster and met Sue, Jude receives a letter from T. Tetuphenay, master of Biblioll College. The letter recommends that

Jude abandon his effort to enter any of the colleges at Christminster. Jude, devastated, goes to a local bar and has two drinks, then continues on to an intersection called The Fourways, located in the middle of the city. "It had more history than the oldest college in the city," writes Hardy. "It was literally teeming, stratified, with the shades of human groups, who had met there for tragedy, comedy, farce; real enactments of the intensest kind." It is here that Jude realizes that his desire for an education at Christminster is futile, and that "town life was a book of humanity infinitely more palpitating, varied, and compendious than the gown life" (139). But The Fourways is also a natural metaphor for *Jude the Obscure* itself: a crossroads of genre, where "tragedy, comedy, farce" intersect to produce a hybrid form that yields a mode of a whole new intensity.

To pursue the contours and limits of genre in Hardy is only to trace a subject that consumed the novelist himself. Such remarks as "All comedy, is tragedy, if you only look deep enough into it" are echoed throughout his private writings, especially toward the end of the nineteenth century. In an 1888 journal entry, according to *The Early Life*, he wrote: "If you look beneath the surface of any farce you see a tragedy" (282); the lesson again is that a thorough examination of any ostensibly humorous human situation provides a revelation of its genuine sadness. But different genres could be theorized as distinct as well as fluid. In the "General Preface to the Novels and Poems," written for the 1912 Wessex Edition, Hardy advised novelists to orient themselves toward the mode or idiom for which they felt a natural affinity:

Differing natures find their tongue in the presence of differing spectacles. Some natures become vocal at tragedy, some are made more vocal at comedy, and it seems to me that to whichever of these aspects of life a writer's instinct for expression the more readily responds, to that he should allow it to respond.[54]

So although Hardy might have seen comedy slipping frequently into tragedy, he could nevertheless conceive of genre as a category that might retain certain immutable properties. Though it may seem paradoxical, this belief is no less typical of Hardy. He had, in the Balzacian tradition, a strong interest in classifying his own fiction. In the "General Preface" he laid out the categories in which each novel would fall: "The Wessex Novels," Hardy's own unified *Comédie humaine*, would be further grouped into "Novels of Character and Environment," "Romances and Fantasies," and "Novels of Ingenuity."[55] Such categories are indeed closer to Balzac's subject- and locale-based groupings than they are to the

Shakespearean classifications of the First Folio – "Comedies, Histories, & Tragedies" – but they are nevertheless proof of a novelist keen on the generic subdivision of his own body of fiction.

In fact Hardy was not the first to propose a system for classifying what would become the Wessex novels. In 1894, before even the arrival of *Jude the Obscure*, Lionel Johnson published *The Art of Thomas Hardy*, the first volume ever devoted to Hardy's fiction. Johnson immediately set about organizing the novels by genre:

> For clearness' sake, a classification of these fifteen volumes may be tried, according to the dominant tone and nature of the various groups, into which they fall with ease. There seem to be three such groups: the *Tragic*, the *Idyllic*, and a third; for which I can find no name, until one word be discovered to express in combination the *comic*, the *ironic*, the *satiric*, the *romantic*, the *extravagant*; a spirit of mocking audacity, and of serious laughter, animating a Pantagruel of Psychology.[56]

The first group included most of the major novels: *The Return of the Native, The Woodlanders, Tess of the d'Urbervilles, The Mayor of Caster-bridge*, and others; the second consisted of *Under the Greenwood Tree* and *The Trumpet Major*. But it is this third group that demonstrates the considerable difficulty that would await those inspired to classify Hardy's novels – even as early as 1894. Johnson placed in this third category *A Laodicean, The Hand of Ethelberta*, and *Two on a Tower*, then hastened to explain that such classification was "a little whimsical," since certain properties and sensibilities seeped from one group to another: "A touch of innocent joy does but deepen the prevailing tragedy; a stroke of grim tragedy does but add fresh zest to the sad laughter of the satirist."[57] Still, Johnson would return later in his study to the problem of this third category, represented primarily by novels written early in Hardy's career:

> His earlier extravagance is an extravagance, which delights in audacities of situation, and in exhibitions of temperament, rather startling than brilliant: a certain touch of unpleasantness, and taste of vulgarity, just felt by the distressed reader, went near to spoiling some stories, otherwise delightful. The satire seemed almost splenetic, the humour little else than bad nature: the cynic's wit was mordant, the jester's smile, a sardonic wrinkling of the lips ... something unkind, an uncanny sort of pleased and sly malevolence, looks out upon me from many a page, and stops the laughter. (54–5)

Johnson was wary of such early manifestations of Hardyan humor and satire; he goes on to compare these novels unfavorably with "Rabelais, Voltaire, Swift, Heine, Sterne" (55). Indeed, even though he never says this explicitly, his tripartite division of the novels amounts to a ranking in the quality of the books, with the "Tragic" category clearly at the top of the list. But these other novels of "splenetic" satire continued to puzzle Johnson. This perplexity is quite significant: the odd satiric strain in Hardy, Johnson understood in 1894, dated back to the earliest novels.

Hardy himself, though he would not declare his turn to the "satirists" until 1890, provides similar evidence of a youthful interest in the genre. In *The Early Life* he includes an unusually long anecdote about his effort to secure a publisher for his first novel, *The Poor Man and the Lady*. The tortuous route leads Hardy finally to the firm of Chapman and Hall and a mysterious "gentleman" who reads the manuscript – and who turns out to be George Meredith. Meredith first agrees to accept the novel, though he has strong reservations; he worries that it will be "attacked on all sides by the conventional reviewers" (81). *The Early Life* explains:

> The story was, in fact, a sweeping dramatic satire of the squirearchy and nobility, London society, the vulgarity of the middle class, modern Christianity, church restoration, and political and domestic morals in general, the author's views, in fact, being obviously those of a young man with a passion for reforming the world ... The satire was obviously pushed too far – as sometimes in Swift and Defoe themselves – and portions of the book, apparently taken in earnest by both his readers, had no foundation either in Hardy's beliefs or his experience. (81)

This anecdote, in Hardy's eventual rendering of it, takes on the status of a veritable foundation myth in the story of his emergence as a novelist. Some of the themes that would define his career – the threat of controversy, the attack on religion – are there in embryonic form. The genesis of the novelist is the same story as the birth of the satirist. And there is a remarkable escalation, a spiraling out of the satire, in this version of the story: it begins with the squirearchy and ends with political and domestic morals in general. In retrospect, this description of his own early fiction sounds overstated; "sweeping" satire – or Johnson's "splenetic" satire – sounds like a far better name for the later fury of *Jude the Obscure*. But Hardy clearly believed that the roots of such a mode lay in his earliest fiction, and that the identification of this satiric tendency was closely related to his own fixation on the generic classification of his novels.

In the debates over realism that would define English criticism in the late Victorian period, the main participants would often describe the school or movement in terms similar to those used by Hardy, Johnson, and others in their reports on novelistic satire. Gosse, in "The Limits of

Realism in Fiction," wrote of the wave of naturalism that began to leave its mark on English fiction in the 1880s: "It was to be the Revealer and Avenger. It was to display society as it is, and to wipe out all the hypocrisies of convention" (141). This is a curious pair of epithets: it encourages us to ask what exactly *revealing* has to do with *avenging*. To reveal seems the province of the realist; it is demonstrative and aspires to a certain objectivity. But to avenge is immediately to forfeit any semblance of objectivity or neutrality; it is to pick sides; and it marks an important blurring of realist narrative into something approaching satire.

The Thomas Hardy who wrote *Jude the Obscure*, and who throughout these years was so perplexed by the problems of genre in his own fiction, exemplified the uneasy simultaneity of these two endeavors. To reveal, proposed Hardy, *is* to avenge. In the same 1888 journal entry in which he laid out the first plan for *Jude* (the story of a young man "who could not go to Oxford"), Hardy went on to declare of this nascent project: "There is something [in this] the world ought to be shown, and I am the one to show it to them."[58] "Showing" was from this first moment a furiously moral act – an exigency and a responsibility. Though Gosse would not read *Jude the Obscure* until several years after he had written "The Limits of Realism in Fiction," Hardy's novel would mark such an affirmation of his prophecy that Gosse seems almost to have anticipated it. *Jude* marks that critical point at which immersion in bleak detail divulges a strong negative morality, where realism yields to satire. This is why Hardy's oft-repeated line from his poem "In Tenebris II" – "if way to the Better be, it exacts a full look at the Worst" – is so significant.[59] Hardy toys with the idea that an exhaustive look at misery or folly can point the way out of the morass of experience, even if in *Jude the Obscure* he effectively renounces such a hope.

Such declarations and confusions were the very terms of the debates over genre so common in these late Victorian years. In a later chapter I will focus on the prime example of these debates: the Ibsen controversy among British critics in the late 1880s and early 1890s, when Ibsen's plays were constantly called either "realistic" or "satirical." Hardy himself followed these debates closely. In 1890 he noted in his journal: "In an article on Ibsen in the *Fortnightly* the writer says that his manner is wrong. That the drama, like the novel, should not be for edification. In this I think the writer errs. It should be so, but the edified should not perceive the edification. Ibsen's edifying is too obvious."[60] Hardy seems always anxious to achieve such a concealment of edification, to bury his moralism deep within his narratives. In his 1892 preface to *Tess of the d'Urbervilles*, he declares that his aim was "to be neither didactic nor aggressive ... a novel is an impression, not an argument" (xviii); and at the end of *The Return of the Native* he writes sympathetically that Clym Yeobright's philosophical discourses were "sometimes secular, and sometimes religious, but never dogmatic" (484). If Hardy was drawn to satire, especially in the first half of the 1890s, he nevertheless obscured most of its traces in his fiction. For although he recognized that genres had a tendency to fuse into one another, he was intent on containing the moralizing force of satire within the predominantly realist contours of his fiction.

By 1895, however, realist representation had become too abrasive to hide its polemical tendencies, and the idea of genre could no longer be dissociated from the question of the moral implications of novelistic art. In the following year, more than six months after the publication of *Jude the Obscure*, Hardy wrote to an American journalist who had first excoriated the novel in the pages of the *New York World*, then asked him for an interview: "Those readers who, like yourself, could not see that 'Jude' (though a book quite without a 'purpose,' as it is called) makes for morality more than any other book I have written, are not likely to be made to do so by a newspaper article, even from your attractive pen."[61] And indeed, for all the enraged readers who considered *Jude* an immoral book, there were many others who complained of its excessive moralizing: few found it an amoral – and thus purely "realistic" – effort.[62] The "extravagant" satire that Lionel Johnson identified and objected to in Hardy's earlier novels had evolved into a far more essential and profoundly moral satire in the form of *Jude the Obscure*. There is perhaps no greater proof that Hardy's final novel blurred the boundaries of genre beyond recognition, and that it did so through the channels of its satiric heritage: it was no longer very easy to distinguish reckless immorality from the unbearable sobriety of deeply moral art.

TERMINAL SATIRE

The destructive energy of *Jude the Obscure* is aimed in many directions: at the oppressive Victorian strictures of marriage, at the exclusion of the universities, at a society in which the lot of the poor is so wretched. A less obvious but perhaps more fundamental object of the novel's vituperation is the existence of writing itself. The suspicion of books is an integral theme of Hardy's novel from its first pages. In an early scene, when the young Jude first tries to learn Latin and Greek and discovers the immense difficulty of that project, he is already starting to understand books as part of the larger problem: "He wished he had never seen a book, that he might never see another, that he had never been born" (31). The long defeat at Christminster is encompassed in this single line, for Jude already feels betrayed by the knowledge that will continually fail him. He expresses this enmity syntactically as a version of that essential curse of prepositional satire: he wishes he had never fallen under the spell of writing just as he wishes he had never been born.

Jude's oath against books is a prophecy of Hardy's own vow that he would abandon fiction after *Jude the Obscure*. In his letters Hardy implied that it was the abusive reaction to *Jude* that impelled him to renounce novels altogether – and for the most part the last century of Hardy criticism has taken this version of the story to be true.[63] But the 1897 section of *The Later Years* reminds us that it was a decision "to abandon at once a form of literary art he had long intended to abandon at some indefinite time," especially since in his estimation the novel was becoming merely "a spasmodic inventory of items" – an art form under the dominion of a tyrannical realism (65). It is a mistake to say that Hardy's renunciation of the novel was a decision he made in response to the aftermath of *Jude the Obscure*. It was, instead, something he had set out to do in the very writing of the book.

The renunciation of words and writing is a prominent enough theme in Hardy to constitute a veritable subgenre in itself. Bayley goes so far as to begin his monograph on Hardy by claiming that in the novels he "gives the impression of a man who would rather be silent than speak" (1). This impression is as central to Hardy's poetry as to his fiction. The final poem in his enormous body of verse is entitled "He Resolves to Say No More": though a statement from 1928, it can refer just as naturally to his momentous decision to renounce fiction in 1896. Miller is correct to say that this predisposition to reticence, though articulated most explicitly in this final poem, "has been covertly present in the tone of all his speech."[64] Although Hardy may at times be the great "Revealer," he is at other moments resistant to divulge anything at all; such that his final poem announces defiantly: "From now alway/ Till my last day/ What I discern I will not say."[65] Perhaps the best expression of this essentially Hardyan theme is to be found in his preface to the 1912 Wessex edition of *Tess of the d'Urbervilles*. Addressing the controversy that swirled around the book's subtitle – "A Pure Woman Faithfully Presented" – Hardy writes: "It was disputed more than anything else in the book. *Melius fuerat non scribere*" (xxi). Though Hardy may have been referring specifically to the problem of the subtitle, the grammar of the Latin is appropriately open-ended in the scope of its implications. In a sense, Hardy encourages us to understand, it would have been better not to write at all.

There is a point in much satirical writing when the satire turns into an attack on writing itself, an expression of exasperation at the endless production of words. This is one of the lessons of Swift's *Tale of a Tub*; an important theme in another late Victorian realist novel, Gissing's *New Grub Street*; and a central idea in such twentieth-century satirical apologias as Wyndham Lewis's *Men Without Art* and Louis-Ferdinand Céline's *Entretiens avec le professeur Y.* Ultimately Hardy's strange ambivalence about expression and writing cannot be understood apart from his lifelong interest in satire. And his great renunciation of a specific kind of writing – his repudiation of fiction after *Jude the Obscure* – cannot be divorced from his course in reading "mostly the satirists" in the 1890s. *Jude* is a novel that courses inexorably to its ending, and that makes the very idea of an ending a theme in itself. It is true that the post-infanticide chapters are excruciatingly protracted. But after these nine late chapters have at last run their course, the novel does necessarily come to an end. This conclusion is markedly different from the endings of so many Victorian novels: there is not only no marriage, but no *promise* of marriage, no suggestion of any kind of regeneration. In this sense it is different even from Hardy's earlier tragic novels. In *Tess of the d'Urbervilles*, for example, the weighty fact of the heroine's execution is mitigated partly by the suggestion that Angel Clare and Tess's sister, Liza-Lu, will provide some minimum futurity – and so the story continues despite Tess's death. The Victorian novel does not so much *end* as it gets displaced elsewhere, off the page. But this is not the case in *Jude the Obscure*. The novel ends with a conversation between Arabella and the Widow Edlin as they stand over Jude's coffin. This conversation turns mostly on the question of Sue, and whether she ever came to see Jude in his final days. Mrs. Edlin asks whether the dying Jude had ever asked for Sue to be sent; Arabella says that she offered to do so but that Jude refused. Arabella then has the final word of the novel: Sue has never found peace since she left Jude, and she never will find peace until she is dead, as Jude is.

This is the novel's final, perverse cruelty: it ends with Arabella and her bleak recognition. But in a larger sense it is also a glaring rejection of the conventions of the Victorian novel maintained even in a work as dark as *Tess*. Instead of providing a man and a woman, and the promise of regeneration that such a couple implies, it leaves us with the figure who most complicated the story of Jude and Sue in the first place. To conclude with the woman who laughs rather than the woman who cries – for in theory *Jude the Obscure* might have shifted to Sue in its closing scene – is to bestow one final reminder of the novel's great debt to the grotesque, the farcical, and the satirical. This ending offers no hint of what may come next. There is no suggestion of Sue's future life, or even Arabella's. There are no children to pin our hopes on – they have all been killed off. There is, rather, a sense that this ending seeks to be a *total* ending, the expression of an absolute silence. The arc of *Jude the Obscure* is an arc of noisy fury: it reaches its height in the brash sounds of Sue's convulsions upon seeing the hanging children, then in the dissonant noise of Arabella's laughter. But when this arc has reached its full distance, and when all this noise has been exhausted, there is nothing the novel can do but fall silent.[66] The book's destructive energy, having directed its own anger at so many institutions and circumstances, must in the end turn inward, on itself. By its final chapter, *Jude the Obscure* seems rendered hoarse from its own howls. And so it reaches an end that appears to be a true terminus, as if to say: *melius fuerat non scribere*.

I claimed earlier that this ending is entirely unlike anything in the Victorian novel. If there is a precedent for this way of concluding a narrative, it lies instead in the satirical tradition. This pattern of noise and silence is part of the fabric of such satires as *A Tale of a Tub*, in which Swift's Hack, exhausted by digression after digression, can only end by saying: "Therefore, I shall pause here awhile, till I find, by feeling the World's Pulse, and my own, that it will be of absolute Necessity for us both, to resume my Pen."[67] Or Hardy's novel is prescient of certain twentieth-century novels that fuse an intense hyperrealism with the fury of satire, novels like Céline's *Voyage au bout de la nuit*, which ends with the narrator on the banks of the Seine renouncing all desire to continue his narrative any further: "*qu'on n'en parle plus*."[68] This bleak statement – "let's speak no more of it" – could be just as easily the final line of *Jude the Obscure*. Hardy's final novel ends not like a recognizably realist novel, but in the mode of a terminal satire: after such a litany of protest and complaint it can do nothing else but end in exasperated and absolute silence. Hardy understood this, and by 1896 he had abandoned the novel for good.

CHAPTER 3

George Gissing's
ambivalent realism

THE PLACE OF REALISM IN FICTION

There are too many writers in George Gissing's *New Grub Street*: too many reviewers and aspiring novelists, too many critics and petty journalists, too many scribblers trying to eke out £50 a year from their unwanted prose. Nearly all exist on the margins of the London literary scene; only a very few manage to break through to success. Focal among the novelists is Edwin Reardon, the once somewhat successful but now blocked and deteriorating writer, who in the course of *New Grub Street* manages the notable feat of succumbing to twin states of degradation: aesthetic (he consents under duress to writing trash) and material (he surrenders to poverty and eventually dies in abjection). Foremost among the legion of essayists and occasional writers is the atrocious Jasper Milvain. Milvain is Reardon's opposite and complement: he is savvy, he is unscrupulous, and he is successful. He sees the London literary scene with total clarity, and he adapts dexterously to its warping demands. In the end he even marries the late Reardon's beautiful wife.

It is easy to remember *New Grub Street* as a novel oscillating between these two figures – the wretched loser and the cunning victor. Indeed, together, Reardon and Milvain could be said to embody two sides of Gissing himself: on the one hand, the writer he knew himself to be, the psychological novelist with exacting standards (but who really wants to be a classicist living in Greece); on the other, the figure he understood he needed in some way or another to become, the crafty player who knows what it takes to survive. For all Gissing's own struggles in the marketplace of fiction, he possessed a small portion of that Milvainian savvy; at minimum he knew he required it, and therefore the portrait of Milvain could be said at least to represent a part of the writer's desired identity despite himself. This bipolar view of the novel is tempting, but it neglects the very rich and crowded world of *New Grub Street*. There are many variations on attainment and ruin in Gissing's novel. There are figures who, like Milvain, meet with some success: the essayist Whelpdale, who becomes the nicely remunerated editor of *Chit-Chat* and marries Jasper's sister Dora. And there are figures who, like Reardon, know only failure and debasement: Alfred Yule, who writes a book that gets disparaged, fails in his quest for an editorship, and goes blind.

In this second category falls one of the most remarkable creations of *New Grub Street*. This is Harold Biffen, the indigent friend and confidant of Reardon, who spends the better part of Gissing's novel writing and desperately trying to publish his opus of realistic fiction, "Mr Bailey, Grocer." Biffen's all-but-quixotic effort is the reason for the nickname that follows him everywhere: both Gissing and the novel's other characters have a perverse inclination for calling him "the realist." The chronic nickname is one of *New Grub Street*'s cruelest ironies. He writes realist fiction, but there is nothing of the pragmatist in Biffen, who lives in a garret and, because of his devotion to "Mr Bailey, Grocer," forfeits any hope of life or indeed subsistence. But the name trails him anyway, like a leitmotiv he can never evade. In one early scene Reardon pays a visit to "the realist"; elsewhere Biffen is said to behave with deference to Reardon's wife: "the realist would never smoke in Amy's presence"; in the street one day "Reardon encountered his friend the realist"; when Reardon falls ill, Biffen is his only well-wisher: "the realist visited him once a week."[1] Biffen is "the realist" the way that Bradley Headstone is "Schoolmaster" in *Our Mutual Friend*: the epithet is both a literal truth and an ultimate curse.

Biffen's first appearance in the novel allows him to expound on his peculiar identity. In a long conversation with Reardon, the realist defends his platform and method, and sets forth his great ambition as a writer:

What I really aim at is an absolute realism in the sphere of the ignobly decent. The field, as I understand it, is a new one; I don't know any writer who has treated ordinary vulgar life with fidelity and seriousness. Zola writes deliberate tragedies; his vilest figures become heroic from the place they fill in a strongly imagined drama. I want to deal with the essentially unheroic, with the day-to-day life of that vast majority of people who are at the mercy of paltry circumstance ... Other men who deal with low-class life would perhaps have preferred idealising it – an absurdity. For my own part, I am going to reproduce it verbatim, without one single impertinent suggestion of any point of view save that of honest reporting. The result will be something unutterably tedious. Precisely. That is the stamp of the ignobly decent life. If it were anything *but* tedious it would be untrue. (144–5)

To describe with absolute precision the tone of this passage would be to determine where Gissing truly stands on the question of realism, and therefore to solve the great mystery of *New Grub Street*. Clearly much of the novel's attitude toward "realism" is ironic; such doctrines appear to provide the food for a large portion of Gissing's satire. The very title "Mr Bailey, Grocer" signals the laughable excesses of the realist project, the absurdity of a school of fiction dedicated to reproducing contemporary urban life in all the monotony of a grocery. Biffen's vow to Reardon – that only tedium points the way to truth – is no less ridiculous; and his unyielding commitment to finding a publisher for his book is perhaps the surest proof of such folly, since his crowning error is nothing less than the stubborn belief in the genuine value of his realist art. We might therefore take Reardon's own immediate response to Biffen's declaration of purpose to be entirely accurate. Biffen's realism, Reardon affirms, is "monstrously ludicrous."

But we cannot forget that Gissing was, surely more than any other English writer, at the center of the debates about realism in the 1880s and 1890s – and that he was often in the position of defending the school and its aims. He was the author of an 1895 article called "The Place of Realism in Fiction," in which he declined to cast off the term altogether; he was the subject of a review, published one year after *New Grub Street* in 1892, titled "Our One English Realist," which he cited proudly in one of his letters.[2] For many readers and critics George Gissing was the archetypal English writer of realist fiction. Henry James's 1897 evaluation of the author of *New Grub Street* – "he loves the real, he renders it" – is entirely typical of the critical response to Gissing's large body of work from the last two decades of the nineteenth century; upon Gissing's death H.G. Wells called him "the master and leader of the English realistic school."[3] The 1891 reviews of *New Grub Street* alone are a testament to the determination of Gissing's readers to assimilate his fiction to a school or an idea they called realism. An enthusiastic article in the *Whitehall Review* argued that the novel "is so sad because it is so real. Mr Gissing points out with a truthful and realistic force what every sensible person cannot fail to recognize – that it is not the man who aims nobly who succeeds"; while an *Athenaeum* review a month later, more guarded but still favorable, praised Gissing for the verisimilitude in his rendering of contemporary life: "His matter is of the moment, and his treatment and touch distinctly realistic."[4]

Indeed virtually no evaluation of *New Grub Street* failed to address his relation to realism. It is perhaps most remarkable that the critics could take up this theme but emerge with such contradictory conclusions – even within the pages of the same publication. The first, unsigned *Saturday Review* article about *New Grub Street* (on May 2, 1891) quarreled with Gissing's version of literary London, which it found implausible: "we cannot believe that all the parishioners are gloomy failures, conscientious *ratés* ... the entire population does not consist of worthy 'realistic' novelists, underpaid and overworked on one side, and of meanly selfish and treacherous, but successful, hacks on the other." But only one week later, a different anonymous reviewer in the same weekly instead praised the novel's veracity, citing the very characterizations that the *Saturday Review* had disparaged earlier: "all [Gissing's characters] are instinct with life, not the lay figures of the ordinary three-volumed novel. The book is almost terrible in its realism, and gives a picture, cruelly precise in every detail, of this commercial age."[5] A strikingly similar debate occupied the pages of the *Author*, in which its editor, Walter Besant, declared in the June 1891 issue that he recognized far too well the world of *New Grub Street* – "I can testify to its truth ... the fidelity of Mr Gissing's portraits makes me shudder" – but in which the following month Andrew Lang dissented, disputing "the burden of what is queerly called 'Realism.' One reads in reviews about Mr Gissing's 'poignant realism,' but is it real at all?"[6] This was the tenor of the reception of Gissing's great novel. Readers could disagree about the quality of *New Grub Street*, but none could resist the impulse to hold the book up to the principal standard of verisimilitude, especially in relation to its dominant gloominess. It was according to this criterion that Gissing's effort was ultimately to be judged.

To consider *New Grub Street* in relation to the journalistic criticism it inspired seems fair, even necessary, in a way not true of any other English novel. This is the very terrain that Gissing surveys so painstakingly in the narrative itself; indeed the novel can be said to anticipate every accolade and every disparagement that met it upon publication. And though *New Grub Street* overwhelms us with its grand vision of a teeming world of writers and journalists, it is the novel's strange immersion in the debates about realism in particular that makes it so clairvoyant. Gissing's stance with respect to the idea of realist fiction is awkward: the novel seems at once sympathetic and ruthlessly satirical. This is because *New Grub Street* curiously tackles the problem from both within and without. It addresses the problem of realism explicitly within the story, naming a prominent character "the realist" and giving him the platform to expound his theories; but it also exists as an austerely realist novel itself.

It refuses, among other things, the ornamentation of romance or the nostalgia of history; instead it dedicates itself to the depiction of the poor, the petty, and the unadorned conditions in which they all live. In this latter respect *New Grub Street* falls squarely in the sequence of Gissing's fiction, especially the novels of the working classes that occupied him in the 1880s: books like *Demos* and *The Nether World.*

But though these other novels might be considered as "realistic" as *New Grub Street,* none addresses the theme so directly within its pages. It is *New Grub Street's* dual stratagem that permits it such elasticity in its posture – that allows it to be both realistic and satirical when it talks about realism. To portray people in realistic conditions is likely to evoke the reader's pity, but to embed realism within realism is to encourage that reader to laugh at the whole ridiculous affair. Harold Biffen – with his dubious theories but very real suffering – might thus be said to embody Gissing's conflicted attitude toward realism as it was commonly understood in late Victorian England. Few novelists saw more clearly than Gissing that a steady immersion in bleak detail could provide such an odd synthesis of sympathetic characterization and biting satire.

In the previous chapter I noted that in 1891 Thomas Hardy expressed his strong resistance to the catchword of late Victorian fiction: "'realism' is an unfortunate, an ambiguous word, which has been taken up by literary society like a view-halloo."[7] Hardy was not the only nineteenth-century novelist to be called a realist but to reject the word as a description of his art. Flaubert, in an 1876 letter to George Sand, expressed an even greater frustration: "I loathe what has come to be called *realism,* even though I've been made one of its high priests."[8] "Realism" to these writers implied something unimaginative and indeed insipid, the mere duplication of everyday life.[9]

But Gissing never refused the label in quite so categorical a fashion. His best opportunity came in 1895, when he was one of ten contributors to a forum on "The Place of Realism in Fiction" in the *Humanitarian.* His essay began in the spirit of Flaubert and Hardy, with Gissing suggesting that "realism" might, in fact, have no place in fiction whatsoever:

One could wish, to begin with, that the words *realism* and *realist* might never again be used, save in their proper sense by writers on scholastic philosophy. In relation to the work of novelists they never had a satisfactory meaning, and are now become mere slang. Not long ago I read in a London newspaper, concerning some report of a miserable state of things among a certain class of work-folk, that 'this realistic description is absolutely truthful,' where by *realistic* the writer simply meant painful or revolting, with never a thought of tautology. When a word has been so grievously mauled, it should be allowed to drop from the ranks.

From this objection to the facile equation of realism and squalor Gissing goes on to voice a more general complaint. He argues against the premise that there could exist for novelists such a thing as objectivity in the first place: "a demand for objectivity in fiction is worse than meaningless, for apart from the personality of the workman no literary art can exist . . . There is no science of fiction."[10]

And yet Gissing's main objection, sustained as it is, is directed really at what he considers the lazy application and misapplication of the term: at those who want "realism" to mean either mere vulgarity or else the "laborious picturing of the dullest phases of life," tedious fiction in the manner of "Mr Bailey, Grocer." (In this respect his skepticism is similar to Lukács's antipathy to naturalism, or Hardy's distaste for the "spasmodic inventory of items.") Gissing is still quite careful to insist that the tradition of realism in the novel emerged from a spirit of upheaval: "realism, naturalism, and so on signified an attitude of revolt against insincerity in the art of fiction. Go to, let us picture things as they are" (14). He cannot hide his admiration for this spirit, even if so much of his essay objects to the misleading assumptions of late Victorian readers about the purposes of realist fiction. "It seems to me," he clarifies, "that no novel can possess the slightest value which has not been conceived, fashioned, elaborated, with a view to depicting some portion of human life as candidly and vividly as is in the author's power . . . Realism, then, signifies nothing more than artistic sincerity in the portrayal of contemporary life; it merely contrasts with the habit of mind which assumes that a novel is written 'to please people,' that disagreeable facts must always be kept out of sight" (15–16).

By the time he contributed this essay in 1895 Gissing had been called a "realist" too many times to count; the article was clearly written with some exasperation. He did not want to be regarded as a sociologist of the slums, or as a mere chronicler of his day; he did not seek the imprimatur of science that Zola had advocated and popularized in France, and which influenced such English disciples as George Moore.[11] But "The Place of Realism in Fiction," resilient though it is, cannot be said to refuse all associations with the movement in question. For Gissing there *was* an acceptable usage of the same word that proved such a bugbear to other novelists: "realism" could mean fearless sincerity, freedom from timid or easy storytelling. The novelist's duty to "show life its image as he beholds it" – these are the closing words of the essay – is not simply an aesthetic preference (16). It is nothing less than a moral imperative. In Gissing's estimation this is the necessary stance in any author's task of exposing the warts and failings of contemporary society. Realism does not have to be a synonym for objectivity; it can be another name for a writer's very personal, and even partisan, audacity.

One cannot overstate the importance of Gissing's specific phrasing in advocating "artistic sincerity in the portrayal of *contemporary* life." With only a few exceptions (minor novels like *A Life's Morning*, *Denzil Quarrier*, and *The Crown of Life*) Gissing set his fiction in his contemporary London. The reason that critics reacted so strongly to the "realism" of *New Grub Street* and Gissing's other novels of the period was that they recognized, or refused to recognize, the totems of an existing reality, the symptoms of a modern, urban condition that still defined them. Reliance on the contemporary is a common feature of two genres in particular – realism and satire, both of which know that to veer too far from the representation of the present-day is to risk losing much of their significance and intensity. It is no small thing, as Linda Nochlin reminds us, that "il faut être de son temps" became the battle-cry of the realist movement in France.[12]

New Grub Street is such an indispensable document in the history of late Victorian realism precisely because it operates so deep within the recognizable sphere of contemporary London. It occupies this sphere, it dramatizes it, and it satirizes it – much as it simultaneously inhabits and critiques the idea of realism itself. The novel is situated crucially at the mid-point of Gissing's own career, the point at which his craft has finally come into its own: as Q.D. Leavis and others are right to argue, this is surely Gissing's masterpiece.[13] By 1891 Gissing understood that he had fallen squarely in the middle of the realism debates. This awareness enabled him to render in fiction all the difficult ambivalence about a vexed theme that he would express in essay form four years later. Gissing "shows life its image" (in his phrase) through a method that he knows qualifies as realism, as approximating a detachment in the representation of everyday life; and yet on these same pages he insists on satirizing much of the premise behind that very project. Since he cannot resolve definitively where to stand in relation to "realism" this must be his hybrid position: he must simultaneously indulge in it and hold it at an ironic distance. The interest of *New Grub Street* lies in the strange fact that these two modes become so intertwined that we can no longer really keep them separate.

THE BUSINESS OF LITERATURE ABOLISHED

In the opening chapter of *New Grub Street*, Jasper Milvain, the scheming and generally unsavory literary journalist, says that Edwin Reardon "sells a manuscript as if he lived in Sam Johnson's Grub Street. But our Grub Street today is quite a different place" (9). This is only the first of Gissing's allusions to the Augustan phrase that lends the novel its title; it is repeated throughout the narrative by different characters aware that their contemporary London bears at least some resemblance to an eighteenth-century culture. In an 1891 letter to his regular correspondent Eduard Bertz, Gissing explained his choice of title for the novel about to be published:

Grub Street actually existed in London some hundred & fifty years ago. In Pope & his contemporaries the name has become synonymous for wretched-authordom ... Poverty & meanness of spirit being naturally associated, the street came to denote an abode, not merely of poor, but of insignificant, writers.

Gissing then goes on to cite the entry in Dr. Johnson's *Dictionary*: "originally the name of a street near Moorfield's in London, much inhabited by writers of small histories, dictionaries, & temporary poems; whence any mean production is called *grubstreet*."[14]

What is perhaps most remarkable about *New Grub Street*'s title is the sheer economy with which it expresses the synthesis of genres that so strongly defines the novel. "Grub Street" announces an Augustan precedent; "New" clarifies that the story will transpire in the present day. One might say that "Grub Street" bestows the satire and "New" provides the realism. But the juxtaposition within the title also reminds us that these two genres have much in common, and that there is likely more continuum than discordance in Gissing's phrase. Pat Rogers, in his authoritative study of the culture of Grub Street in Augustan satire, reminds us repeatedly that allusion to Grub Street, in Pope and others, depends always on the specificity of its attack, the precision of its ridicule. "The Scriblerian group kept a detailed file on their victims over a period of many years," Rogers explains. "Their final satiric references are chosen with pointed accuracy. Indeed, there is a malicious brand of specificity which marks out all Pope's practice." Rogers emphasizes the importance of such specificity in *The Dunciad* in particular – "the Dunces are indeed types; but types whose clarity of presentation and immediacy of character derive from a real individuality, amounting at times to idiosyncrasy ... the fictional lines of the poem have been in part laid down by the facts of real life" – but he also traces a similar pattern in Swift's poetry and in *A Tale of a Tub*:

It is not, of course, mere reportage; its social brightness and topicality are not those of the gossip column, and its realism is not to be confused with straight naturalism. Despite that reservation, it would be fair to say that Swift makes more *poetic* capital out of the raw material offered him by real life than any other writer of his time. If we take 'real life' to mean, for the moment, the daily round of eighteenth-century urban dwellers, then Swift, far more than Prior or Gay, is the poet of real life.[15]

Gissing's newer Grub Street and his brand of satirical realism operate in much the same way. His novel's title evokes a longstanding culture of miserable hacks, but it clarifies that his specific hacks will be rendered with the kind of uncomfortable detail that can only emerge from a real familiarity with the existing culture, with his own malicious brand of specificity. Indeed, some Gissing critics emphasize that specific characters in *New Grub Street* represent real figures of late Victorian literary London – William Heinemann, Hall Caine, even Andrew Lang, who criticized *New Grub Street* for its false realism in the *Author* – and, of course, the autobiographical elements in Gissing's portrait of Reardon might encourage others to read the novel as a *roman à clef.*[16] Such factual basis, though much lost on readers today, would only sharpen the satire for Gissing's own contemporaries. As with much satire, Gissing's method is to start with the local and extend to the universal. And so if he positions his novel within a larger sequence of English satire, it is only by passing through the particular late Victorian manifestations of a post-Popeian reality. One might call this tactic satire by realist means.

Gissing's title, distinctive as it is, is nevertheless quite representative of much of his fiction: it is a pseudo-topographical expression of a present condition. "New Grub Street" is not altogether different from "The Nether World" or "The Whirlpool," the titles of his novels of 1889 and 1897. They are all vaguely allegorical names for both a place (London) and a general state of contemporary existence (poverty, unhappiness, turmoil). And if it seems that "New Grub Street" is a rather more specific term than these others – alluding as it does to a certain profession, situated, at least in the eighteenth century, in a particular zone of the city – we should remember that this world of writers is, in effect, the only world of the novel. The Grub Street of *New Grub Street* is remarkably self-contained. There is a kind of barrier that isolates these legions of writers from all the other kinds of people we might expect in a novel set in nineteenth-century London, but who are absent in Gissing's. The world of this novel sometimes bears a greater resemblance instead to the phantasmagoria of *The Dunciad*, peopled by Dulness's "Grubstreet choir" and indeed "all the Grub-street Race": Gissing's crowds also begin to look like a miserable but unified tribe.[17] The report of Reardon's sad isolation midway through the narrative – "he lived in solitude, never seeing those of his acquaintances who were outside the literary world" – therefore seems like something of a tautology or non sequitur (159). In truth such acquaintances exist virtually nowhere in Gissing's novel.[18]

The consequence of such an enclosed novelistic world, of offering no real alternative to the abysmal sphere represented, is that Gissing's frequent satire on a particular segment of society risks becoming a more generalized, even an absolute satire. But for the literary world to stand in plausibly for the world, Gissing must make us believe, if only temporarily, in the total seriousness of this cosmos of writing, whether as a business by which these characters eke out their meager livelihood or even as a condition somehow representative of modern life. Most of the novel's expressions of protest, accordingly, become directed against writing itself. *New Grub Street* launches this line of attack as early as the second chapter. In one of the novel's essential scenes – in many ways the complement to the later chapter in which Biffen outlines his "realism" to Reardon – the brazen Jasper Milvain talks with the Yule brothers, Alfred and John, about the value of contemporary literature. The conversation (here between Milvain and John) quickly turns to the problem of the overproduction of written matter.

'You would like to see literary production come entirely to an end?' said Milvain.
  'I should like to see the business of literature abolished.'
  'There's a distinction, of course. But, on the whole, I should say that even the business serves a good purpose.'
  'What purpose?'
  'It helps to spread civilisation.'
  'Civilisation!' exclaimed John, scornfully. 'What do you mean by civilisation? Do you call it civilising men to make them weak, flabby creatures, with ruined eyes and dyspeptic stomachs? Who is it that reads most of the stuff that's poured out daily by the ton from the printing press?' (23–4)

Milvain goes on to entertain John Yule's position, claiming that if he were to adopt such views himself he "might make a good thing of writing against writing. It should be my literary specialty to rail against literature" (25).

Milvain says this mostly in jest; he is guiltier of journalistic excess than anyone in *New Grub Street*. But it would be dangerous to assume that this mistrust of written production, this neo-Swiftian revulsion at the proliferation of endless mediocre matter, is solely the province of John Yule. In the following chapter, his brother Alfred, who will later suffer so terribly in the realm of authorship, claims "the evil of the time is the multiplication of ephemerides. Hence a demand for essays, descriptive articles, fragments of criticism, out of all proportion to the supply of even tolerable work" (37). A short while later Alfred's daughter Marian – an aspiring writer herself – falls into a similar reverie in the gloomy reading room of the British Museum:

> She kept asking herself what was the use and purpose of such a life as she was condemned to lead. When already there was more good literature in the world than any mortal could cope with in his lifetime, here was she exhausting herself in the manufacture of printed stuff which no one even pretended to be more than a commodity for the day's market. What unspeakable folly! (106–7)

Clearly Alfred Yule's rant and Marian's disenchantment result from a specific culture of reviews and ephemera: it is this kind of writing, easily and endlessly reproduced, that provides such an expedient target for satire and scorn. It is striking, nevertheless, how often Gissing allows such rhetoric to slip into a more generalized exasperation about the creation of any new writing at all. Marian's later remark to her father – "I love books, but I could wish people were content for a while with those we already have" – is a complaint no longer confined so safely to any specific kind of writing; and Reardon's weary decree at the end of the first volume – "I must cease to write altogether" – is the uncomfortably total desolation of an author who, much like Gissing himself throughout much of his career, has watched personal failure in vocation engender a more comprehensive despair (314, 166).[19] The reading room of the British Museum, that normally sacrosanct Victorian space where Gissing himself spent so many hours, is rendered in tones and colors barely distinguishable from those of the Grub Street alleys and modest drawing rooms where the aspiring chattering classes mostly dwell. For Marian the reading room is not only gloomy; it threatens to become "a trackless desert of print" (107). Milvain likes to call it the "valley of the shadow of books."

And just as the different zones of the novel seem to blur into one another, each serving so dubious a role in this culture of words, so the various characters all risk falling into the sight of the satirist's scope. The novel clearly satirizes the ingratiating Milvain more than the vulnerable Biffen or the weak Reardon, but all three are writers, and therefore all are guilty denizens of Grub Street. We begin to wonder if perhaps the only viable lesson to be gained from all this is Reardon's idea that he should cease to write altogether. It is effectively the same conclusion reached by Nancy Lord, the heroine of Gissing's 1894 novel *In the Year of Jubilee*.

Nancy spends much of that book trying to become a novelist herself, but in the end she can only hide her manuscript in a drawer: "its author spoke of it no more."[20]

The struggle of Reardon and Biffen to get their fiction into print in *New Grub Street* makes Nancy's effort look minor by comparison. But in *New Grub Street* the real problem is that most of London suffers rather from a *surfeit* of writings, just as it teems with a surplus of writers. There is simply too much unmanageable waste. These countless books and journals are just so many objects that flood the market in their great bulk and number.[21] It is, of course, no accident that the Yule family money comes from paper manufacture and a paper-mill in Hertfordshire. In his early scene with the Yule brothers, Jasper impishly blames this industry, and John's role in it, for the glut of writing in London: "'I understand that you have devoted most of your life to the making of paper. If that article were not so cheap and so abundant, people wouldn't have so much temptation to scribble" (23). Readers of *New Grub Street* have neglected to point out the allusion to Pope here, but Jasper's remark is an echo of the final prefatory section of the *Dunciad Variorum*, "Martinus Scriblerus, of the Poem":

We shall next declare the occasion and the cause which moved our Poet to this particular work. He lived in those days, when (after providence had permitted the Invention of Printing as a scourge for the Sins of the learned) Paper also became so cheap, and printers so numerous, that a deluge of authors cover'd the land.[22]

This is a sort of reversal, *avant la lettre*, of the classic Ian Watt model of the rise of novel-reading: instead of concentrating on the demand-side of middle-class readership, it focuses on the supply-side of paper factories and their cheaper mode of operation.[23] Gissing satirizes this surfeit of paper more effectively than any English writer since Pope. He never forgets to remind us that books in *New Grub Street*, whatever their value, simply take up space. When Marian in one scene reaches for a book, literature is compared to "table garnishing"; when Reardon sinks into dire poverty, the first thing he must sell off is his book collection, especially the more expensive volumes. Our narrator explains that in general "books are cheap, you know. At need, one can buy a Homer for fourpence, a Sophocles for sixpence" (91; 140–1). Though Reardon earns little money from it, this is where the liquidation must inevitably begin, for written matter is the one unchanging mass in the world of this novel, the one palpable reality.

In his insistence on this theme, Gissing indeed owes much to Pope and Swift, who had mastered and codified this kind of satire on writing in the eighteenth century. (With respect to Augustan culture more generally, *New Grub Street* makes clear that its greatest debt is to Dr. Johnson and Boswell, to whom the novel frequently alludes; Milvain's remark about "Sam Johnson's Grub Street" is only the first of many references.)[24] The novel's panorama of the world of literature often resembles a darkly Augustan vision of writing gone wild. A visit to the cheap reading-rooms where Sykes, one minor character in *New Grub Street*, pays a penny to have a desk where he can write his autobiographical opus "Through the Wilds of Literary London," yields a glimpse of a phantasmagoria – "ink blotches, satirical designs, and much scribbling in pen and pencil" (377) – that would not be out of place among familiar images from *The Dunciad* ("showr's of Sermons, Characters, Essays,/ In circling fleeces whiten all the ways") or the *Epistle to Dr. Arbuthnot* ("It is not Poetry, but Prose run mad").[25] Swift himself inhabited this sort of deranged prose in *A Tale of a Tub*, where the countless prefaces, digressions, glosses, and blank spaces – not to mention all the pseudo-spatial allusions to corners and surfaces and affixed codicils – all play on the preposterous materiality of a culture where there is too much published matter, a mad cosmos that Swift's hack calls "this vast World of Writings."[26] (Byron's "English Bards and Scottish Reviewers" sounds the same exasperated note: "Another epic! Who inflicts again/ More books of blank upon the sons of men?")[27] *New Grub Street* falls squarely in this main tradition of satire. This tradition is fueled by the same antipathy to publishing and journalism that Walter Benjamin emphasized in Karl Kraus, sworn nemesis of journalistic mediocrity and idiocy, who spends his life in a "landscape of hell … a landscape in which every day fifty thousand tree trunks are felled for sixty newspapers."[28] Like all these satirists, Gissing in *New Grub Street* is fundamentally and, of course, paradoxically at odds with the very fact and existence of publishing. The novel seethes at "the flood of literature that pours forth week after week" (456). We cannot help wondering if a satirical masterwork like *Candide* is right to declare of publishing and the selling of books that there is "no occupation in the world that should disgust us more."[29]

Gissing clearly knows these classic satirical antecedents, but his position on the proliferation of writing, much like the title of his novel, both acknowledges the Augustan precedent and registers a very contemporary reality. *New Grub Street* must contend with a flood of thick novels just as it has to confront the superfluity of journalistic ephemera, since it emerged from a late Victorian culture in which the three-decker novel, though on its way to extinction – the system collapsed in 1894, three years after the publication of *New Grub Street* – still exerted considerable force. Even Milvain, midway through the novel, holds forth on "that well-worn topic, the evils of the three-volume system," which he calls "a triple-headed monster, sucking the blood of English novelists" (203).

In an important sense *New Grub Street*'s attitude toward a culture of writers and writing is fuller and more comprehensive than the posture of its Augustan precursors, despite its great debt to that tradition. Gissing's book cannot only ridicule the follies of this culture; as a realist novel it must also describe its inner workings. In this respect we should keep in mind a prominent aspect of the nineteenth-century realist novel – its own tendency to criticize the business of literature – when reading *New Grub Street*. Gissing's portrait of writers who find themselves in quickly shifting circumstances of success and failure can remind us of the Thackeray of *Pendennis* or the Flaubert of *L'Éducation sentimentale* as easily as it can recall Swift or Pope. In particular *New Grub Street*'s scenes of journalistic attack, the lunges and ripostes of criticism, seem to take their inspiration from Balzac's *Illusions perdues*. In the second chapter of Gissing's novel, Jasper Milvain draws Alfred Yule's attention to an issue of *The Study*: "'Did you notice that it contains a very favourable review of a novel which was tremendously abused in the same columns three weeks ago?'" (21) This is notably prescient of the seemingly contradictory judgments of *New Grub Street* itself, which were to appear in the *Author* and the *Saturday Review* after the novel's publication, but it also calls to mind Lucien de Rubempré's lessons in the necessary hypocrisies of reviewing.[30] In Balzac's novel Lucien cannot at first understand how a critic might eviscerate a writer one day and glorify him the next. His own experiences in this sort of journalistic pragmatism are, as much as anything else in Paris, what enable him to understand the ruthlessness of reality, to see "les choses comme elles sont" or "things as they are."[31]

In Gissing's version this kind of lesson is digested with a varying degree of ease depending on the character. Alfred Yule displays the invective – he writes a long, angry work called "English Prose in the Nineteenth Century," and in the literary sphere he believes that "in the very interest of the public it was good that certain men should suffer a snubbing" (97) – but he does not master the necessary parry, and he never really recovers from the *Current*'s disparagement of his writing. When his hopes of starting a new publication are dashed – he had planned to use his daughter's inheritance from an uncle, but that inheritance turns out to be paltry – his defeat is total, since he can never be in the position of controlling literary public opinion. The final chapters of *New Grub*

Street find Jasper Milvain, on the other hand, entirely proficient in the rules of the game. He tells his sister Dora that he has just written a favorable review of "Mr Bailey, Grocer" for the *West End*, but he then proceeds to craft a more guarded appraisal for the *Current*. "You wouldn't suspect they were written by the same man, eh?" Jasper asks Dora. "No," she replies, "You have changed the style very skilfully" (455). Milvain is atypical of Gissing's characters for possessing such dexterity. Most others care too deeply about the authenticity of their opinions, and they end up getting dragged through the mud of Grub Street. But Milvain is like the writer-critic Warrington in *Pendennis*, who acknowledges that "we are all hacks": entirely unsentimental, and therefore totally hard-nosed, about the professionalized and vulgar business of publishing.[32] In the final analysis Gissing, like Balzac and Thackeray before him, satirizes this entire plunge-and-riposte culture by exposing the lie behind most critical opinion. And yet, like Balzac, he situates this whole foolish process within the realist confines of an intricately sketched society, so that when an author is wounded by an attack upon his writing we witness the very real pain that he suffers. Once again we encounter a systemic satire oddly concurrent with the kind of sympathy that can only emerge from a realistic depiction of recognizable human situations. Late Victorian realism cannot merely engage in a satire on writing, as the Augustan model did. It must also dramatize it.

The difficulty in discussing the satire in Gissing emanates largely from this problem: we struggle to reconcile all the contempt and disdain with his own participation in this culture, and in the end we realize that his satire is consequently an ambivalent one. It can often be easy, when reading *New Grub Street*, to lose sight of its far-reaching condemnation of an immense society, since the specific dramas of the novel – the deteriorating marriage of Edwin and Amy Reardon, Alfred Yule's slow descent into blindness and financial collapse – can be so heartrending in the excruciating detail of Gissing's method. But, of course, it is also these very dramas that point the way to that large-scale condemnation. At a certain point in the Reardons' suffering, when it becomes clear that Edwin's literary struggles are causing the disintegration of their marriage and ultimately his death, we realize that any system that could create such unnecessary calamity is essentially ridiculous. The realism of detail thereby leads to a satire of scope.

There is a peculiar passage toward the end of the novel where Gissing steps back from the narrative to address this very question – and to address the reader – directly. He appears to acknowledge the ridiculousness behind his tormented writers' ordeals; and he seems to worry that we will over-estimate the satirical intent behind such characterizations:

The chances are that you have neither understanding nor sympathy for men such as Edwin Reardon and Harold Biffen. They merely provoke you. They seem to you inert, flabby, weakly envious, foolishly obstinate, impiously mutin-ous, and many other things. You are made angrily contemptuous by their failure to get on ... But try to imagine a personality wholly unfitted for the rough and tumble of the world's labour-market. From the familiar point of view these men were worthless; view them in possible relation to a humane order of society, and they are admirable citizens. Nothing is easier than to condemn a type of character which is unequal to the coarse demands of life as it suits the average man. (425–6)

This is a pivotal moment in Gissing's fiction. It is a sort of apologia, Gissing's equivalent to George Eliot's defense of her art in chapter 17 of *Adam Bede*. Gissing cannot tolerate a misreading of his novel in which the satire is overestimated because it is divorced from the particular contingencies of the story. He seems to rail against the system while exonerating the individual people caught up in it: this is a spirit native to much of his fiction of the 1880s, like *The Nether World*. Like George Eliot in *Adam Bede* and indeed across her fiction, Gissing exhorts us to look closely at the "coarse demands of life," for we cannot evaluate a culture's failings or folly without witnessing and recognizing how people must live within it. This is one of the central lessons of realism in the Victorian novel.

But it is less clear how great an immunity from the lashings of satire Gissing intends this lesson to provide his represented world. His letters of the late 1880s and early 1890s are striking for their insistence on the satirical intent behind his fiction. In 1885 he explained that he wanted *Demos* to be "rather a savage satire on working-class aims and capacities"; in 1889 he insisted that his title *The Emancipated* was chosen for its "satirical sense"; the next year he emphasized his "*satiric* intention throughout" that novel; in 1894 he defended another title, *In the Year of Jubilee*, by claiming "it is satirical, & in keeping with the tone of the book."[33] On March 7, 1891, he announced to his sister Ellen: "With 'New Grub Street' I am pretty well pleased; you will enjoy its satire and general bitterness."[34] And so although within the pages of *New Grub Street* he instructs his reader to suppress the impulse to condemn or scoff at such seemingly miserable specimens, Gissing made sure that his own correspondents did not overlook the satire that he so fervently hoped would define his fiction of these years. These two seemingly contradictory concerns, this dual pressure to underline both the realist pathos and the satirical core of his fiction, are perhaps the clearest reflection that Gissing's 1891 novel about writers was so oddly pulled in two apparently different directions. It proposed that the business of literature be abolished, but it insisted that those who toiled within that business be pitied.

THE SCORNER OF AVERAGE MANKIND

Within this business and cosmos of literature Gissing seems to diffuse himself – the image of himself as a writer – across several figures: Reardon most of all, but (as I have been suggesting) also Biffen and even Milvain too, not to mention, in small ways, even minor characters like Whelpdale.[35] Reardon surely comes closest as a parallel to Gissing the realist: he is not suspiciously doctrinaire about realism as Biffen is, and the little we know of Reardon's respected novels suggests a subtle and refined psychological realism with which Gissing would have identified. There is little of the satirist in Reardon, however, and the caustic figures that do exist in the novel (Alfred Yule, most prominently) bear little resemblance to the Gissing who insisted so adamantly on the satirical essence of his fiction.

We need to turn to a different novel to find a character who can be said to represent a real analogue to Gissing the satirist. *Born in Exile*, published only one year after *New Grub Street* in 1892, provides a model in its protagonist, Godwin Peak. In contrast to the many interconnected writers who split the attention of *New Grub Street*, Peak stays fixed at the center of *Born in Exile*; indeed Gissing's original title for the novel was *Godwin Peak*. And though it is obvious throughout *New Grub Street* that its creator sees aspects of himself in Reardon, Gissing never professed the same affinity for him that he did, in a May 1892 letter, for the hero of *Born in Exile*. Though taking pains to clarify that the tone of the novel was "by no means identical with that of Peak's personality," Gissing nonetheless made a plain confession: "Peak is myself – one phase of myself."[36]

Godwin Peak aspires to be a London journalist, but the nature of his aspiration cannot be said to resemble that of *New Grub Street*'s scribblers. Once in the capital he moves within a circle of freethinkers, and the main plot of *Born in Exile* involves the composition and anonymous publication of his blasphemous article, "The New Sophistry," which assails the hypocrisies of the Anglican Church. Peak's resentment of institutions, especially the Church, stems largely from an acute complex of class inferiority – his lower-middle-class humiliations dominate the novel – as well as his scientific leanings, which are incompatible with Christian orthodoxies. But the inspiration behind Peak's writings also issues from a kind of vague and innate sense of opposition, from his perpetual status as a contrarian in a universe of euphemism. At first he struggles to find the best way to articulate this native impulse. In one early scene, thinking about how he might slam a hateful book proposing to reconcile science and religion, he cannot sleep at night for the wrath boiling within him: "his brain throbbed with a congestion of thought; he struggled to make clear the lines on which his satire might direct itself."[37] With time, however, the writer with the cankered muse learns to express himself with greater fluency and precision. Later in the novel, as Peak begins to display "his powers of savage eloquence," Gissing makes it clear that to be eloquent is necessarily to be antagonistic (151). Peak agrees with a friend that "the task of the modern civiliser is to sweep away sham idealisms"; later, after the publication of the dangerous article, Gissing writes of Peak that "no intellectual delight, though he was capable of it in many forms, so stirred his spirit as that afforded him by a vigorous modern writer joyously assailing the old moralities" (164, 283). In *Born in Exile* the development of the intellect, the coming-into-being of the writer, is the same story as the evolution of the satirist. Peak's essay, later called "a tremendous bit of satire" (281), is a salvo aimed specifically at the Church but intended more generally for a culture which he resists with hostility.

The parallel between Gissing and Peak is, however, far more complex than merely one of shared satirical purpose, or independence from the degradations of social pressures. The main theme and crisis of *Born in Exile* is Peak's quandary in reconciling his satirical freethinking with his quest to ingratiate himself into a higher stratum of English society, as represented by the Warricombe family. He pretends to hold devout Anglican views, and he even studies to become a clergyman, in order to impress Mr. Warricombe and especially his pious daughter Sidwell, with whom Peak falls in love. Suddenly the fiery atheist has assumed the guise of a parson, and we are left on a kind of uncertain terrain perhaps comparable to that of *New Grub Street*: like Jasper Milvain, only with more tentativeness, shame, and bald hypocrisy, Peak turns to compromise and soul-selling as a pragmatic way of escaping what would otherwise be a life of poverty and failure. Unlike Milvain, Peak fails: he is found out. But like Reardon and indeed his creator Gissing, Peak is perpetually "in exile": stranded between authenticity and the kind of labor and humiliation that people without money must subject themselves to, and which necessarily contaminate any preexisting authenticity. This is one of the recurring problems that Gissing struggled with throughout his career, as recorded nearly everywhere in his correspondence – and, of course, it is one of the central themes of *New Grub Street* as well.

And so the parallel between Peak and Gissing comes down to two main things: satire and shame. Given *Born in Exile*'s great attention to Peak's religious hypocrisy, and the disgrace resulting from it, it is easy to come away from the novel thinking mostly about his shame. But we should not lose sight of the real and even proud identification that Gissing clearly felt with his angry and censorious protagonist. Peak's confession to Sidwell after his exposure as the author of "The New Sophistry" – "my strongest emotions seem to be absorbed in revolt; for once that I feel tenderly, I have a hundred fierce, resentful, tempestuous moods" (332) – is a genuine expression of an authentic sensibility, rendered with little irony on Gissing's part; and it demonstrates that such a stance is a question of temperament rather than of conscious politics or religious affectation, and so is essentially unchangeable. Peak remains an exile from society; his sad death at the end of the novel places him in the tradition of Edwin Reardon rather than Jasper Milvain. He fails in his effort at self-transformation, and therefore he loses his grasp of the pragmatic realism so necessary amidst the harshness of all Gissing's novels. But Godwin Peak's authentic character, his essential satirical and oppositional self, survives the middle section of the novel: after his exposure he is still a non-believer, an outsider, and (after a long period of deceit) a truth-teller who finds himself all alone. When the disguise is swept away, this is all that is left. Gissing can claim that Peak is "one phase of myself" because of this elemental congruence of the true self and the satirical self: satire and realism are two ways to describe the work of a writer who conceives of himself as a truth-teller. In this respect Gissing's hero bears a resemblance to certain Ibsen figures from the same period, the finest example being Dr. Stockmann in *An Enemy of the People*, for whom telling the truth necessarily means departing from the majority opinion.

To describe Peak in such terms, however, is not to confuse this brand of desired authenticity with virtuousness or compassion. A major current running through *Born in Exile* is Peak's wide-ranging misanthropy, his oft-expressed revulsion for the masses. He is prone to outbursts of invective directed against the populace, particularly the urban poor: "I hate low, uneducated people! I hate them worse than the filthiest vermin!"; they are to him "the squalling mass, the obscene herd of idiot mockers" (29, 95). For such opinions the narrator calls Godwin Peak "the born rebel, the scorner of average mankind" (139). Among the most remarkable scenes of *Born in Exile* are those where Peak finds himself in the midst of the crowd he hates so fiercely but which still, because of his own humble origins, lays some claim to him. In the novel's second part he chances upon a public ceremony in Hyde Park and pauses "at the edge of a gaping plebeian crowd" while a carriage of aristocrats passes by: "here he stood, one of the multitude, of the herd; shoulder to shoulder with boors and pick-pockets." Peak gazes longingly at the grandeur of the carriage and turns to scorn the masses around him: "he hated the malodorous rabble" (103).

Surely the most interesting thing about *Born in Exile* is the strange relationship between Peak and Gissing – it is a relationship of intermittent identification and distance, affinity and repudiation. The great challenge in reading the novel is determining where author stands in relation to hero, particularly regarding this unyielding contempt for the masses.[38] In John Carey's polemic, *The Intellectuals and the Masses*, Gissing is criticized for being the first to articulate the position that Carey believes will define English intellectuals in the modernist period: "Gissing seems, in fact, to have been the earliest English writer to formulate the intellectuals' case against mass culture, and he formulated it so thoroughly that nothing essential has been added to it since. The case has not been developed or advanced; it has simply been repeated."[39] For proof of such formulation Carey cites not only *Born in Exile* but also *New Grub Street, In the Year of Jubilee, The Whirlpool,* and indeed most books dating back to Gissing's first novel, *Workers in the Dawn.* With respect to *Born in Exile,* though Carey allows for some distance between Gissing and Peak, he emphasizes the self-portraiture behind the characterization: "much of what Godwin believes in, Gissing himself never renounced or outgrew. Godwin's fulminations ... are eminently Gissingite." Carey is willing, in part, to acquit Gissing of culpability in this modernist pattern of elitist contempt; the defense is that Gissing, like no other English novelist, knew poverty himself, and so can both disparage the masses and render their lives with true accuracy: "other writers imagine, but Gissing knows" (113–15). This aptitude for a certain realism, in Carey's view, saves the novelist from some of his own satirical invective. But it does not prevent Carey's genuine dismay with Gissing, or his profound censure of the author of *Born in Exile* for being so prescient of the elitism of Wells, Lawrence, and Wyndham Lewis, even if Gissing really did "know" the poor masses he was writing about. "Knowledge of this kind cannot be mitigated or assuaged," writes Carey. "It breeds, and bred in Gissing, both social guilt and its opposite – a black amalgam of disgust, despair, and loathing that vented itself in denunciations of the masses and their degradation" (116).

Fredric Jameson also regards Gissing's view of the general population with considerable skepticism; in *The Political Unconscious* he refers to the "people" rather than Carey's "masses," but the subject is essentially the same.[40] Jameson focuses on *The Nether World*'s difficult position with respect to philanthropy: Gissing seems to denounce both the reformers and the urban poor they seek to rescue. And just as the philanthropic tendency within the fiction is never successful, so is it doomed to failure as a narrative tactic for Gissing. It leaves the novelist, in Jameson's view, with little more than the disinterested realist representation of the "solidity of objects": "Gissing thus finds himself limited to something like an indicative mode" (196). Here Jameson stresses the alienated figure in Gissing's novels, whether the alienated intellectual in the later fiction or the character caught between social classes more common in the 1880s novels. Both are defined by their unease in being perpetually out of place, and by their railing against things without ever effectively changing them. Jameson rightly sees in these scenarios a pattern of *ressentiment*, made all the more interesting in Gissing's fiction because the author (in *Demos*, for example) seems also to resent his hero's *ressentiment* (202). This is a fine illustration of Gissingite ambivalence, in this case regarding the novelist's struggle with the problem of the masses: Gissing seems to be both against the masses and against those who are against them.

The comparison of the alienated intellectual within the fiction to the author behind the fiction is an inevitable one, and if we are to think of Gissing as innately a satirist, a novelist drawn intrinsically to satirizing (among other things) the entire business of literature, then the comparison becomes all the more necessary. The detested masses of people in the novels, after all, bear an unsettling resemblance to the glut of written matter that provides the basis for so much of the satire in *New Grub Street*. In that novel, Whelpdale, with Jasper Milvain's encouragement, hatches a plan to transform an existing paper into a periodical for the "quarter-educated" people spilling out everywhere: they can read, "but are incapable of sustained attention" (460). This is the narrator's view of such cynical ventures in culture and education for those quarter-educated: "To the relatively poor (who are so much worse off than the poor absolutely) education is in most cases a mocking cruelty" (40). In *The Reading Lesson*, Patrick Brantlinger addresses this grim logic proposed again and again in *New Grub Street*: "the overpopulation of writers is, of course, linked both to mass education and the overproduction of journals and books of all sorts."[41] But this is an overpopulation not just of writers but of people generally. There is a direct, causal relationship between humans and books: with increased literacy, more people means more writing. There is more *matter* all around, and so it very often becomes difficult to distinguish one kind from the other. This is what makes Carey's and Brantlinger's emphasis on mass literacy so important – it is, the first argues, one of the primary motivations behind the intellectuals' disdain for the masses.[42] Carey writes:

> D.H. Lawrence vigorously develops this theme. 'Let all schools be closed at once,' he exhorts, 'The great mass of humanity should never learn to read or write.' Illiteracy will save them from those 'tissues of leprosy', books and newspapers ... T.S. Eliot is less Utopian than Lawrence, but he regrets, in his essays, the spread of education ... there are, he believes, too many books published.[43]

In Gissing the Popeian deluge of too many books cannot be dissociated from the rather late Victorian problem of too many people. There may not be a Father Time figure in Gissing's fiction, someone who sacrifices himself sensationally in the name of fighting overpopulation, but the masses surface frequently enough as a problem or dilemma in the different novels as to leave a sort of permanent, residual anxiety. In *The Whirlpool* it is Harvey Rolfe, one of the main characters, who voices this concern, claiming that the death of babies is nothing to grieve about: "we don't want to choke the world with people."[44] Any large gathering of people, in *The Whirlpool* and elsewhere, Gissing renders with considerable disgust and scorn. The mass seems always to crush the individual. Nancy Lord, in an early chapter of *In the Year of Jubilee*, breaks away from her escorts at the Jubilee Day procession and into the "trampling populace," a crowd of Londoners little different from a herd of cattle: "the slowly advancing masses wheeled to left or right at word of command, carelessly obedient ... there was little noise; only a thud, thud of footfalls numberless, and the low, unvarying sound that suggested some huge beast purring to itself in stupid contentment" (58).

In *The Nether World*, teeming with its squalid masses of the urban poor, Gissing exposes the horrors of overpopulation with more rigor than anywhere else in his fiction. The narrator of that novel, in quasi- or proto-Hardyan fashion, asks whether Clara Hewett's mother should "be blamed for bringing children into the world, when those already born to her were half-clothed, half-fed"; he calls London slums the "dens of superfluous mankind"; and in one bravura passage he describes the view of the City from Clara's window, a view so nightmarish it seems barely plausible:

Down in Farringdon Street the carts, waggons, vans, cabs, omnibuses, crossed
and intermingled in a steaming splash-bath of mud; human beings, reduced to
their due paltriness, seemed to toil in exasperation along the strips of pavement,
bound on errands, which were a mockery, driven automaton-like by forces they
neither understood nor could resist.[45]

Such visions might be said to represent Gissing's long view of the masses
in *The Nether World*: distance permits a certain pseudo-allegorical, disen-
chanted condescension. But these passages coexist with the long, excruciating chapters that examine the sufferings of individual people in closer
and more idiosyncratic detail, in the specific dramas of their poverty.
In an important sense the latter yield necessarily to the former. Gissing
immerses us in the realism of quotidian misery, then peels back to voice
his exasperation, his disgust for such a repugnant reality. We are reminded
of Juvenal's third satire: "the hardest thing that there is to bear about
wretched poverty is the fact that it makes men ridiculous."[46]

This, of course, is the same narrative method – a verisimilitude of detail
developing into a satire of breadth – employed so effectively in *New Grub
Street*. Gissing's rhetoric of disdain for the masses, so common in his
fiction, is conspicuously similar to the kind of language in which he evokes
the deluge of writing in the 1891 novel. Alfred Yule's campaign in *New Grub
Street* against the "multiplication of ephemerides" begins, in this context, to
sound a little like an extermination fantasy. Later in *New Grub Street*
Jasper Milvain even claims that "the struggle for existence among books
is nowadays as severe as among men"; and in light of the blurring of these
two categories in Gissing's imagination, the comparison no longer seems
very far-fetched (456). In effect there appear to be two entities most
frequently reviled in Gissing's fiction – books and people, both of which
represent a crisis precisely because they are too many in number and too
few in quality. Since the latter are responsible for the former they can often
be attacked with a single lash. And so the scorning of "average mankind"
tends to remind us that one of mankind's productions especially deserves
that lash: the business of literature above all must be abolished.

I emphasized earlier the importance of *New Grub Street*'s position of
dual judgment: its insistence on satirizing the system of Grub Street while
taking pity on some of its individual denizens. This stance is equally
characteristic of Gissing's attitude toward the masses more generally.
Nowhere is this attitude expressed so concisely as in one essential scene
midway through *Born in Exile*, where Peak tries to explain his actions to
Sidwell Warricombe. Here Gissing seems to align himself with Peak more
closely than anywhere else in the novel:

I can't pretend to care for anything but individuals. The few whom I know and love are of more importance to me than all the blind multitude rushing to destruction. I hate the word *majority*; it is the few, the very few, that have always kept alive whatever of effectual good we see in the human race. There are individuals who outweigh, in every kind of value, generations of ordinary people. (222–3)

This speech seems emblematic of a certain late nineteenth-century attitude: Peak's hatred of "the word *majority*" sounds like a clear echo of Ibsen's enemy of the people.[47] But Peak's tirade is also notably consistent with a major tendency of satire, particularly in the English tradition. This is a fundamentally Swiftian tendency, best articulated in the famous 1725 letter to Pope to which I alluded in the first chapter:

But since you will now be so much better employd when you think of the World give it one lash the more at my Request. I have ever hated all Nations professions and Communityes and all my love is towards individuals for instance I hate the tribe of Lawyers, but I love Councellor such a one, Judge such a one for so with Physicians (I will not Speak of my own Trade) Soldiers, English, Scotch, French; and the rest but principally I hate and detest that animal called man, although I hartily love John, Peter, Thomas and so forth. This is the system upon which I have governed my self many years (but do not tell) and so I shall go on till I have done with them.[48]

Peak's apologia is, indeed, so similar a statement to Swift's that Gissing seems to be invoking Swift directly.[49] (In fact earlier in the same scene Peak makes the same point in language even closer to Swift's: "I know, of course, that the trader may have his quiet home, where art and science and humanity are the first considerations, but the *mass* of traders, corporate and victorious, crush all such things beneath their heels" (217).) Both Gissing and Swift claim that it is possible to scorn mankind while still managing to love some of its individual specimens. In truth only experiential context can exonerate specific people: Peak must know someone to love him, and Swift must be able to identify someone as John or Peter or Thomas in order to spare him that "one lash the more" destined for the rest of the world. Indeed it is precisely this knowledge – immediate, personal – that makes it possible for people to be individualized: otherwise they would be merely segments of a throng. Swift here seems remarkably prescient of a major current of Victorian realism, as formulated best by George Eliot ("we may satirise character and qualities in the abstract without injury to our moral nature, but persons hardly ever"), and later so complicated by George Gissing.[50] The long view of mankind encourages satire; immersion in the particular permits sympathy. A fusion

of the two modes is an inevitable, necessary attitude for a novelist defined
by such ambivalence about person and people: the individual human
who has a name, but also the throngs that surround that person, and
threaten her with their vulgarity, on all sides. The lesson of Gissing may
be that only the realism of idiosyncratic detail can save us from satire's
otherwise ravenous appetite.

GISSING, DICKENS, AND IDEALISTIC REALISM

It is not, in fact, very common to discuss Gissing in relation to the Augustan
satirists. Gissing's far more obvious and acknowledged precursor – even
in the context of satire – is Dickens.[51] The Dickensian example was
foremost in Gissing's own mind and self-conception, inspiring his only
full-length works of criticism: the 1898 *Charles Dickens: A Critical Study*
and the series of prefaces to Dickens novels, the surviving nine of which
were collected in the posthumous 1925 volume *The Immortal Dickens*.
Both books acknowledge Gissing's immense debt to the earlier novelist,
perhaps nowhere as plainly as in the introduction to *The Immortal
Dickens*: "this it was that stirred me, not to imitate Dickens as a
novelist, but to follow afar off his example as a worker. From this point
of view the debt I owe to him is incalculable."[52] The phrasing here is a
remarkably candid and accurate statement of influence. Gissing's own
London, for example, always knows the Dickensian precedent but never
merely imitates it, and when, for example, a "lurid fog" or a "thick black
fog" hovers over *New Grub Street*, we are aware of *Bleak House*'s
presence without ever being overwhelmed by it (III, 422).

Gissing's allusion to his own work says something equally important
about these two volumes of criticism: they are as much concerned with
Gissing as they are with Dickens. Indeed it often appears that Gissing's
motive in studying the earlier novelist is to formulate theories about his
own writing – and to address certain literary debates that defined late
Victorian literature rather than the earlier years of Dickens's career.
In particular Gissing seems committed to focusing on the question of
realism in the novel. He never sets forth very systematically the terms
of the debate, but the inquiry remains: he wants to determine whether
Dickens was, in fact, "a realist." Often the answer appears to be no, since
novels like *Dombey and Son* and *Bleak House* share little of the Zolaesque,
pseudo-documentary griminess so characteristic of fin-de-siècle fiction.
In the 1898 book Gissing says as much explicitly: "It will be seen, of
course, that, theoretically, he had very little in common with our school

of strict veracity, of realism – call it what you please; the school which, quite apart from extravagances, has directed fiction into a path it is likely to pursue for many a year to come."[53] In the *Immortal Dickens* chapter on *Nicholas Nickleby* Gissing writes similarly that "the theories of so-called 'realism' had, of course, never occurred to him; a novel, to his mind, was a very different thing from a severe chronicle of actual lives" (93).

If Dickens is to be held up to the standards or assumptions of a "school" or a set of "theories" that go by the name realism, Gissing's verdict is that he cannot belong to such a category. The lurking reason is that in these volumes Gissing wants the late Victorian idea of "realism" to signify little more than a belabored or portentous procedure, striving quixotically for amoral objectivity: perhaps something like Harold Biffen's "Mr Bailey, Grocer." In the first Dickens book Gissing writes with unabashed admiration of Dickens's contrary tendency to "modify circumstances": "Our 'realist' will hear of no such paltering with truth. Heedless of Pilate's question, he takes it for granted that the truth can be got at ... but Dickens went further; he had a moral purpose; the thing above all others scornfully forbidden in our schools of rigid art" (73). At one point in *The Immortal Dickens* Gissing pauses to note with disapproval that "since Dickens's time there has arisen a school of fiction which, with incredible labour, strives to set before us the reality of things, to impress by a scrupulous fidelity of presentment" (216). Such passages recur often enough in the two books that Gissing's swipes at the "realist" school begin to seem awkward and even gratuitous. At times he seems more interested in voicing his ambivalence about what in 1895 he had called "the place of realism in fiction" than in discussing Dickens's novels themselves. He, of course, admires Dickens's strong, unabashed moral fervor, but often he wants more than anything to ridicule the more contemporary fiction that hid its mediocrity under its own pretentious, rigid rules of objectivity.

Elsewhere in the two volumes, however, Gissing seems rather more willing to apply the ever-vexed term to Dickens's art. Writing in the 1898 volume about the plausibility of emotion and characterization in Dickens, Gissing argues that "had the word been in use he must necessarily have called himself a Realist"; several chapters later, in relation to Dickens's portraits of Pecksniff's daughters and female characters more generally: "Here the master would have nothing to learn from later art; he is the realist's exemplar" (75, 155). Dickens believed in the authenticity of his characters, and he rendered them with unparalleled skill and honesty; he believed, in Gissing's words, in the "absolute reality" of the world of his fiction (75). This alone is enough evidence, says Gissing, to allow us to call Dickens a realist. And yet sometimes Gissing goes still further, isolating individual scenes in Dickens's fiction for their specific, unqualified verisimilitude. In *Charles Dickens: A Critical Study* the nineteenth chapter of *Martin Chuzzlewit* provides one such example: "Mr Mould and his retainers, the whole funeral from household to grave, seems to me such realism as no other novelist ever came near unto; for it is mere straightforward describing and narrating, without a hint of effort" (189–90). The motivation behind such statements cannot be merely Gissing's wish to applaud Dickens's great talent. Clearly these two volumes, the 1898 study in particular, find Gissing working through the same uncertainty about realism that defined his 1895 essay on the subject and indeed his rendering of "realists" in *New Grub Street*. When he praises Dickens for achieving a realism that no other novelist ever attained, he is not only celebrating Dickens; he is effectively disparaging many of his own contemporaries. And he is also, it is clear, fortifying his own defense against charges of "mere realism": by rendering the term elastic enough to accommodate Dickens, Gissing is, in effect, turning a slur into a potential accolade.

All this may seem like the sustained expression of one writer's doubt about a thorny literary term. What is so significant about Gissing's fixation on Dickens's realism is how naturally it develops into a consideration of the workings of satire in the novel. Gissing rarely delves into the question of realist representation without reflecting upon the polemical quality of this representation, the way such a mode can be used for censorious and satirical ends. Toward the end of *Charles Dickens: A Critical Study* he compares Dickens to Balzac, noting that a major difference seems to separate the two, "a difference which seems to involve the use of that very idle word 'realism.'" Gissing explains:

Novels such as those of Balzac are said to be remorseless studies of actual life; whereas Dickens, it is plain, never pretends to give us life itself, but a selection, an adaptation. Balzac, calling his work 'the human comedy', is supposed to have smiled over this revelation of the littleness of man, his frequent sordidness, his not uncommon bestiality ... Dickens has just as much right to his optimism in the world of art, as Balzac to his bitter smile. Moreover, if it comes to invidious comparisons, one may safely take it for granted that 'realism' in its aggressive shapes is very far from being purely a matter of art. The writer who shows to us all the sores of humanity, and does so with a certain fury of determination, may think that he is doing it for art's sake; but in very truth he is enjoying an attack upon the order of the universe – always such a tempting form of sport. Well, Dickens was also combative, and enjoyed his palpable hits; only, his quarrel was

with certain people, and certain ways of thought, never with human nature or
the world at large. (216–17)

The distinction here between the Balzacian and the Dickensian could not
be more illuminating, either as a personal observation from George Gissing
or as a theory of novelistic satire more generally. Gissing has identified one
of the most important distinctions in satirical writing. In a sense it is quite
similar to Thomas Hardy's own 1899 division between Swiftian and Dickensian humor, even if Hardy, for his part, aligned himself with the Swiftian.
According to Gissing, Balzac's brand of aggressive realism seemed to make
all humanity its target; Dickens's satire, on the other hand, was more
selective. One is wide-ranging, prone to misanthropy; the other discrimin-
ates and redeems some of us even while convicting others. The "certain
people" that Dickens combated could be identified: they were provincial
schoolmasters, bureaucrats in Chancery and the Circumlocution Office,
unsavory French villains. Gissing clearly admires this method of keeping
the combat circumscribed and specific. Dickens is "wroth with institutions," Gissing writes a few pages later, "never bitter against fate, as is so
often the case in 'realistic' novels of our time" (221).

But this is an extremely peculiar stance for Gissing, of all writers, to
assume. All his references to "realist" writers speak disapprovingly of their
tendency to attack everything in the name of being exhaustive. Yet it
would be difficult to absolve Gissing himself of this very condemnation:
in *New Grub Street*, in *Born in Exile*, and indeed across his dark fiction of
the 1880s and 1890s, his own satirical tendencies take in far more than they
leave out, and, as a result, his novels lack most of the enduring benevo-
lence that exists at least somewhere in every Dickens novel. The preference of the individual to the masses, best articulated by Godwin Peak, is
palpable; but it never prohibits Gissing from indulging this more radical,
pervasive satire, just as it never stood in the way of Swift's. And so while
Gissing learned enormously from Dickens, he departed from him in this
crucial respect. Raymond Williams argues the same point:

Gissing looked back to Dickens and recognised that 'he taught the English
people a certain way of regarding the huge city', but in Gissing himself, and
perhaps in London by the 1880s, the paradoxical Dickensian movement of
indignation and recognition had separated out into a simpler structure: indignant
or repelled observation of men in general.[54]

It is their common terrain of London, especially the London slums, which
might first encourage us to assimilate Gissing to Dickens. But this major
difference in the representation of urban life – which is, for both novelists,

really the representation of *life* in general – thwarts any easy confeder-
ation. Williams notes that even when Gissing describes Dickens's London
he has a tendency to render the city "more single and more organised"
(224). In 1899 Arnold Bennett made a similar observation, writing that
Gissing "sees the world not bit by bit – a series of isolations – but broadly,
in vast wholes."[55] In the final analysis it may be difficult to understand
why Gissing would go so far to distinguish Dickens from the "realists,"
with an obvious and stated preference for the former, if virtually any
reader would place him – at least with respect to the scope of his satire – in
the second camp. Gissing seems as perplexed about the proper direction
of satire in the novel as he is unsure about the place of realism. In his two
books on Dickens, however, he does appear to discover that there exists
some profound connection between the two.

In *Charles Dickens: A Critical Study* Gissing adds this observation to his
comparison of Dickens and Balzac: "There are orders of imaginative
work. A novel is distinct from a romance; so is a fairy tale. But there
can be drawn only a misleading, futile distinction between novels realistic
and idealistic. It is merely a question of degree and of the author's
temperament" (217–18). Gissing's idea of this "futile distinction" must
be central to any study of the relation of realist narrative to satire.
"Realistic" implies a kind of fiction that is neutral, dispassionate; "idealistic" suggests rather a literature infused with moral purpose. Gissing's
claim that the two are, in fact, interpenetrating seems inevitably correct.
What is so noteworthy is his phrasing.

In 1889 he had been the subject of an article written by his German
friend and correspondent Eduard Bertz called "Ein Real-Idealist."[56]
Six years later, after the publication of *In the Year of Jubilee*, an anonymous reviewer in the *Spectator* claimed that Gissing must "be regarded not
as a realist, but as an idealist of the new school."[57] And after his death the
seemingly paradoxical idea of "idealistic realism" seemed to define the
many posthumous appraisals of Gissing, as critics tried to make sense of
the uncommon career that had just ended. In 1904 the *Atlantic Monthly*
published an unsigned homage to Gissing entitled "An Idealistic Realist,"
which opened by complaining that "in the vocabulary of criticism the
word 'realism' has been soiled with all ignoble use" but specified that
"Gissing was a realist controlled by an ideal."[58] Arthur Waugh, writing in
the *Fortnightly Review* that same month, began his evaluation by taking
note of "the inextinguishable conflict between realism and idealism" and
argued that Gissing had "the making of a realist" and "training in realistic
method": the author of *New Grub Street* wrote "not at all to illustrate a

theory, but simply to picture life." But that was not a sufficient account of Gissing, according to Waugh: "realist as he was in the practice of art, he was at heart an idealist of idealists," since he could not help seeing "in all the world around him, perpetual evidence of the foiled ambition of a striving and ever disappointed humanity."[59]

In Gissing's fiction, and in the criticism it has inspired, the ancient philosophical division between realism and idealism seems rather like a porous border, a blurred and outdated margin. This is one of the main lessons of his often convoluted 1882 essay "The Hope of Pessimism," where he wonders whether the limited philosophy typical of the "mass of mankind" may embody a sufficient ideal in itself:

Granting that we cannot rise to a perception of the absolute, that we are hopelessly imprisoned in our universe of phenomena, then let us not only accept these limitations, but make it a characteristic of moral excellence to resolutely shut the mind against yearnings for transcendental flights, and dedicate every thought to this so solid-seeming earth on which we tread, grapple with its material difficulties, study its conditions, enter into its transient joys and sorrows as though they were the be-all and end-all of human consciousness.[60]

Gissing's proposition is not without its irony, but his essay never comes out very explicitly against it. Indeed one of the great achievements of Gissing's fiction is that it consistently challenges us to determine whether "idealistic realism" is a contradiction in terms. No reader has disputed that Gissing relied on the narrative methods and attitudes so characteristic of late Victorian realism, but there has never been much consensus about the idealism, the moral rationale, behind them. In 1880, when Gissing was just embarking on his career, he described his ambition in a way that seems much at odds with the criticism he would write on Dickens nearly two decades later:

Certainly I have struck out a path for myself in fiction, for one cannot of course compare my methods & aims with those of Dickens. I mean to bring home to people the ghastly condition (material, mental & moral) of our poor classes, to show the hideous injustice of our whole system of society, to give light upon the plan of altering it, &, above all, to preach an enthusiasm for just & high *ideals* in this age of unmitigated egotism & 'shop.' I shall never write a book which does not keep all these ends in view.[61]

Gissing's decree of "showing" sounds a lot like Hardy's declaration when he first decided to write the novel that would become *Jude the Obscure*: "There is something [in this] the world ought to be shown, and I am the one to show it to them."[62] To "show" us hideous injustice is for Gissing, as for Hardy, an intensely moral act, even as it relies on the apparent detachment of realist narrative. In Gissing's words of 1880 there is even the suggestion of a possibility for a corrective to the misery of the poor (a plan of altering "our whole system of society"), though by the time of *New Grub Street*, a decade later, his satirical realism would no longer permit such glimmers of faith. Gissing forces us to ask whether a resolute truth-telling in fiction can be anything other than a vehicle for primarily idealistic and deeply moral ends. This was essentially Virginia Woolf's point when she began her 1923 essay on Gissing by calling him "an imperfect realist."[63]

But many readers of Gissing have seen the problem of idealistic realism differently. Holbrook Jackson, in his 1913 study of the 1890s, insisted rather that "the more typical realists of the Nineties, George Gissing and George Moore, seem to be devoid of deliberate social purpose."[64] Orwell, writing thirty-five years later, concurred with Jackson, for although he had great admiration for Gissing ("merely on the strength of *New Grub Street*, *Demos* and *The Odd Women* I am ready to maintain that England has produced very few better novelists"), he argued that the novelist had "no strong moral purpose. He had, of course, a deep loathing of the ugliness, emptiness and cruelty of the society he lived in, but he was concerned to describe it rather than to change it."[65]

Perhaps we can ultimately reconcile such evaluations with Gissing's own proclamation of his idealistic motives – perhaps his was an authentic idealism that never professed itself explicitly, a moral sense that seized upon recognized facts in order to rail against contemporary conditions without ever adhering to a specific program or politics. This was likely Orwell's point. Gissing's fiction despaired but refused to propose a false or facile remedy for the conditions that gave rise to such despair: Gissing would presumably have argued the same of the novels of Dickens.[66] In the end we can find satisfactory terms for Gissing's art only in the rhetoric of apparent paradox: in categories like "idealistic realism"; in the phrase of a review of *The Nether World*, which called the novel a "realistic jeremiad"; or in Gissing's own words in a 1900 letter to Edward Clodd, where he declared his allegiance with those who "know how to joke in earnest."[67] Such expressions may be the only way to describe fiction that constantly treads the murky border between realism and satire.

REALISM'S SUICIDE

In "The Limits of Realism in Fiction," written in 1890, Edmund Gosse claimed that the movement in question was coming to an end. "It is now declining ... my conviction is that the limits of realism have been reached;

that no great writer who has not already adapted the experimental system will do so; and that we ought now to be on the lookout to welcome (and, of course, to persecute) a school of novelists with a totally new aim." These limits, Gosse noted, "seem to have been readily discovered by the realists themselves."[68] I argued earlier that this diagnosis was remarkably prescient of Thomas Hardy and *Jude the Obscure*; it is equally true of George Gissing and *New Grub Street*. Gissing might, in fact, be said to go further than Hardy: he effectively dramatizes the difficult life and sad death of realism itself.

Here we return to Harold Biffen, the aspiring realist whose effort to write and publish his novel "Mr Bailey, Grocer" occupies so much of Gissing's interest in the novel. Toward the end of *New Grub Street* Biffen finally reaches completion of the manuscript, though in Edwin Reardon's judgment this is a dubious achievement: "to the public it would be worse than repulsive – tedious, utterly uninteresting. No matter; it drew to its end" (426). After struggling with the final half page of the book, Biffen at last writes "with magnificent flourish 'The End'" (427) and, unable to sleep, leaves his cold flat (he has neither coal nor wood) to take a walk. When he returns he finds his house on fire: a drunken fellow lodger has kicked over a lamp and set the whole building ablaze. Biffen panics: "Desperate with the dread of losing his manuscript, his toil, his one hope, the realist scarcely stayed to listen to a warning that the fumes were impassable; with head bent he rushed up to the next landing" (429–30).

The rest of the chapter traces Biffen's improbable rescue of the only copy of "Mr Bailey, Grocer." He races upstairs and through the smoke to reach the manuscript, then breaks down a door, climbs atop the roof, wraps the pages in his coat and throws the bundle to the street below, leaps onto an adjacent roof to escape the approaching flames, and with the help of a neighbor's ladder manages to descend to the street. At first it seems that the coat has been lost, but eventually Biffen is able to find it and the manuscript bundled within. The whole episode is so gripping in its high-wire detail that we are likely to forget momentarily how ridiculous it is: Biffen nearly dies for the sake of his tedious realist opus. Even the realist himself understands the absurdity of the situation. Meeting with Reardon two days later, and contemplating the frantic rescue of "Mr Bailey, Grocer," Biffen imagines what the newspapers might have written had he died in the attempt: "The *Daily Telegraph* would have made a leader out of me. 'This poor man was so strangely deluded as to the value of a novel in manuscript which it appears he had just completed, that he positively sacrificed his life in the endeavour to rescue it from the flames'" (437).

Over the next few chapters Reardon dies in poverty and obscurity, and Biffen is plunged into despair: he has lost his only friend, and he realizes more than ever how hopelessly in love he is with Reardon's widow, Amy. "Mr Bailey, Grocer," turned down by two publishers, is finally accepted at one house, but the reviews are "either angry or coldly contemptuous." One weekly derides the novel in a short, scathing review: "Here is another of those intolerable productions for which we are indebted to the spirit of grovelling realism" (485). Biffen sinks deeper into solitude, poverty, and misery: though in love with Amy, he is not so deluded as to think that she would ever want him. Soon he runs out of money and any will to live; he comes to know "the actual desire of death, the simple longing for extinction" (491). His embrace of the prospect of dying brings him a certain serenity at last. One afternoon, returning home from the British Museum reading room, Biffen buys several bottles of pills, writes a letter to his brother, goes to the heath at Putney Hill, and – once the sun has set completely – prepares to die. It is one of the most extraordinary moments in Gissing's fiction.

The moon was now hidden from him, but by looking upward he could see its light upon a long, faint cloud, and the blue of the placid sky. His mood was one of ineffable peace. Only thoughts of beautiful things came into his mind; he had reverted to an earlier period of life, when as yet no mission of literary realism had been imposed upon him, and when his passions were still soothed by natural hope. (493)

If Harold Biffen, in his combination of suspect theorizing and palpable suffering, can be said to embody his creator's ambivalent attitude toward realism, then his suicide marks Gissing's own uncertain conclusions about the fate of realism in fiction. It is a particularly wicked touch to align Biffen's transcendent quietude in the moments before death with that "earlier period of life," before he had fallen victim to his doomed mission of literary realism. The whole scene seems allegorical, but the allegory is more complex than it might at first seem. Of course it is effectively realism and its strictures that have killed Biffen, since his devotion to "Mr Bailey, Grocer" has proved his undoing; if he had been a savvier kind of writer, in the mold of Jasper Milvain, he might have survived the trials of New Grub Street. And yet with Biffen's suicide, realism in a sense also kills itself, since with Reardon dead as well, and with only Jasper Milvain, among the novel's major writer-figures, still standing, Biffen – realism's only surviving avatar – takes the cursed movement with him to the grave. Or perhaps there is one final interpretation. This pivotal scene in Gissing's fiction marks the moment when the Real kills the Realist, when the pressures of the real world – competition, isolation, poverty – overwhelm the writer who pretends to capture them in his fiction. Gissing's realism effectively gives the lie to Biffen's realism. And *New Grub Street*, the novel that dramatizes and satirizes the realist movement like no other work of fiction, vanishes into an infinite regress.

Biffen's suicide may propose a cruel ending to the era of realism, but it does not actually mark the end of *New Grub Street*. Gissing has other cruelties remaining, mostly involving the indefatigable and immovable Jasper Milvain. The novel, in fact, begins with him as well: the opening scene is set over breakfast at the Milvain house. Jasper hears the parish church clock strike eight, cracks an egg, and remarks "with cheerfulness": "There's a man being hanged in London at this moment." (He then adds presciently, as if forecasting the entire novel in miniature: "There's a certain satisfaction in reflecting that it is not oneself.") This dark initiation is entirely typical of Gissing's openings: *Born in Exile* and *The Odd Women* begin in much the same spirit. In *New Grub Street* Milvain's inaugural announcement sets the tone for his crafty disposition and indeed for the harsh mood of the novel in general. By the end of the narrative, with Reardon and Biffen both dead, Milvain marries Reardon's widow Amy, whom Reardon lost (except for a brief reconciliation before his death) and Biffen could never hope to win. Milvain meets with further journalistic success – he at last becomes editor of *The Current* – and effectively fortifies his status as the exemplary figure of survival amidst the otherwise universal debris of Grub Street failure. The final lines of the novel find Jasper and Amy agreeing that the world is a glorious place for rich people, as she sings and plays the piano while he reclines "in dreamy bliss."

This very dark send-off is wholly consistent with the novel it concludes, but it can still leave us perplexed about *New Grub Street*'s final word. In one sense the novel ends much like that consummate masterpiece of satirical realism, *Madame Bovary*. Milvain, that is to say, bears a certain unmistakable resemblance to Homais, the figure so consistently satirized and despised for his petty self-promotion, for his philistinism, and for his utter indifference to anything more transcendent than bourgeois society's image of him. Both Homais and Milvain survive to the final page and beyond, after everyone else has been crushed; Milvain's crowning position of power as editor of *The Current* is his equivalent to Homais's *croix d'honneur*.

Yet in Gissing's version Jasper Milvain is not quite the fool: he is the scorner of fools, and the manipulator of fools. Late in the novel he tells his sister with some authority that "fools will be fools to the world's end. Answer a fool according to his folly; supply a simpleton with the reading he craves, if it will put money in your pocket" (460). This is not the kind of statement with which Flaubert would entrust Homais. Milvain's aphorism is in alarming harmony with the lessons of Gissing's novel, and our inevitable uneasiness derives as much from our knowledge that Milvain is right as it does from the obvious and unwavering fact that he should be loathed. In his peculiar way Milvain (unlike Homais) is not guilty of hypocrisy, that favorite target of satire: he is something quite terrifying, but he knows exactly what he is doing and confesses it freely. Gissing both satirizes Milvain and assigns him the truth, just as he simultaneously inhabits and mocks Biffen and, indeed, the entire project of literary realism. Milvain's philosophy is a form of realism too, even if he wisely steers clear of the school of fiction that calls itself by that name. His survival beyond the final page of *New Grub Street* marks Gissing's own realization of a nauseating dual proposition. Realism may be a folly that we should be prepared to mock, but folly is a reality that we may be sadly forced to endure.

CHAPTER 4

The English critics
and the Norwegian satirist

THE MOST FAMOUS MAN IN THE ENGLISH LITERARY WORLD

Realism, for English critics of the last two decades of the nineteenth century, was the essential subject in dispute: they wanted to define what it was, and they wanted to determine what it was good for. Did the new literature come closer than earlier forms to representing everyday life credibly? Did "realism" signify a kind of representation that did not flinch before the squalid or the sordid? Were these books actually operating on the premise of authorial neutrality and objectivity (and was this even something writers should aspire to)? Or was it all a sham, a subterfuge to conceal a prurient imagination craving to drag a polite readership through the mud?

These questions revolved mostly around fiction and native English novelists: Hardy and Gissing are the two finest examples. But a comprehensive study of English criticism from the later years of the nineteenth century, when the realism disputes raged most violently, makes clear that the central case was neither a novelist nor an English writer. It was Henrik Ibsen, whose plays, along with their English reception, shaped the literary culture of fin-de-siècle England as decisively as the work of any other writer. The critics debating realism sparred over Ibsen's theater more contentiously than over the novels of Hardy or Gissing, of Balzac or Flaubert or even the notorious Zola. And despite the difference in genre and nationality, Ibsen's dramas embodied the same governing idea about realist representation that I have traced in his English novelist contemporaries. For Ibsen, as for Hardy and Gissing, realism in its most audacious forms became indistinguishable from an austere and antagonistic mode of satire. Ibsen's reception in England has always been a source of curiosity for scholars of late Victorian culture; it is well known that the productions of Ibsen on the London stage in the early 1890s laid bare the pruderies and philistinism of much of the British public. Most of these scholars have commented in one way or another upon the vexed English reaction to what was understood to be the "realism" (in staging, in language, in subject) of the plays. But to discuss Ibsen's realism without confronting the satirical or polemical quality of that realism – as many scholars have tended to do – is to miss the point entirely. Because Ibsen was at the forefront of literary culture in England, because he was always the critics' favorite bugbear and enemy, the reception of his theater provides the most illuminating and comprehensive case study of the critical reaction to satirical realism in late Victorian England. Any inquiry into the disputes over realism in literature – and any formulation of a theory of satirical realism – must pass through Ibsen.

The first year of Ibsen's notoriety in England was 1889: in the *Fortnightly Review* that July, William Archer declared him "the most famous man in the English literary world." The controversy over Ibsen's plays was just starting to take hold of the English public. *A Doll's House*, with Janet Atchurch in the role of Nora Helmer, had recently finished its three-week run at the Novelty Theatre, and a group of angry London reviewers, led by Clement Scott, had been loudly condemning the drama as both indecent and inscrutable. Archer, who had translated the play, and who had already become one of the principal interpreters of Ibsen in England, set out to identify the main objections of the anti-Ibsenites, whose jeremiads had transformed an obscure Norwegian into a literary celebrity. "It is said, in the first place," Archer explained, "that he is not an artist but a preacher; secondly, that his doctrine is neither new nor true; thirdly, that in order to enforce it, he oversteps the limits of artistic propriety."[1]

A Doll's House was London's first real exposure to Ibsen, the first production of his plays on the English stage.[2] But Archer had already been studying the Norwegian dramatist for many years: he was well acquainted with the arc of Ibsen's career from the earliest verse plays through *A Doll's House* and indeed beyond – by 1889 Ibsen had already written five subsequent dramas. It was this familiarity that enabled Archer, in his *Fortnightly* article, to classify *A Doll's House* as part of a newer phase in the playwright's career: as one of Ibsen's "realistic plays" (31). Archer's phrase could not have been more pertinent to the ongoing controversy. It was the very formulation of Edmund Gosse, one of Ibsen's other chief interpreters of the period, who wrote in the *Fortnightly* only six months earlier of Ibsen's "severely realistic conception of what dramatic form should be"; his plays were "a series of sternly realistic dramas."[3]

Archer and Gosse were both emphasizing something essential about Ibsen's theater and the simultaneously perplexed and outraged response that it had already generated in England. Archer noted that *A Doll's House*'s detractors believed that Ibsen was guided by a "doctrine," an irritating tendency to preach and moralize – but he specified that this hectoring tone was thrown into stark relief by the disarmingly contemporary and realist staging of the play. Gosse had also known Ibsen's drama for many years: he had been the first Englishman ever to publish an essay on Ibsen, in 1872. He would describe the situation in 1889 in similar terms. In his own article, Gosse wrote that Ibsen's "realistic" dramas were, in fact, a form of "diagnosis," that they were dedicated to identifying "the disease of which this poor weary world of ours ... is expiring" (110). Archer and Gosse had both studied Ibsen's verse satires from decades earlier, plays like *Love's Comedy* and *Peer Gynt*; but both critics recognized that this newer phase of the dramatist's career, introduced to English audiences through the Novelty Theatre's staging of *A Doll's House*, signaled a new way of transmitting the seemingly didactic or diagnostic energies of satire. Ibsen's satirical intensity had now taken the form of a more direct and realist idiom.

It is no accident that Archer and Gosse – English critics – zeroed in on the realism of Ibsen's dramas. Of all the nations where Ibsen had a profound influence, nowhere did the evaluation of his drama turn so persistently and so essentially on the question of realism as it did in England – not in Germany, France, or the Scandinavian countries. Pascale Casanova, in *The World Republic of Letters*, takes the reception of Ibsen in England and France as a "superb example of the different ways in which an author's work may be annexed by two literary capitals having discrepant interests in embracing it." Ibsen's plays were "seen as models of realism" in London, models of symbolism in Paris. Casanova argues that in both capitals "directors and critics took advantage of Ibsen's relative weakness as a foreigner": because Ibsen wrote in a "minor" language and literature, he exerted little authorial power in the foreign theater and marketplace. In England, then, he was easy fodder for appropriation by the natives in their own cultural disputes or political programs. Casanova's prime example is the (non-English) George Bernard Shaw, whose subversive political views necessitated an embrace of realist and naturalist literature and therefore a "social" interpretation of Ibsen. (In France, meanwhile, the avant-garde was instead committed to a platform of symbolism – realism being a long-expired movement – and therefore to an appropriation of the Norwegian dramatist as a fellow traveler of Maurice Maeterlinck and the pro-symbolist theater director Aurélien Lugné-Poë.)[4]

Casanova is absolutely right about this divergence. From 1889 to the turn of the century, England was fixated on the realist quality of Ibsen in a way that the French would have found antiquated. But it is possible that the reasons for this appropriation were not merely political or self-seeking. English critics and audiences could have been particularly attuned to the realism of Ibsen's dramas precisely because they recognized in them a sphere and an experience unnervingly close to their own. It is a commonplace in the history of German criticism to treat Shakespeare as if he were a natively German writer; it would be tempting to do something similar with Ibsen and England, and to consider his theater as the near-native expression of a late nineteenth-century English culture. Ibsen himself – along with many of his Victorian interpreters – seemed receptive to a certain conflation of Norwegian and English literature and culture. In an 1872 letter to Gosse he wrote that "the English people are very closely related to us Scandinavians" and confessed that "having my works presented to the English reading public" was the matter of "chief importance to me"; he lamented (as he also did to Archer in 1895) that his English was so poor.[5] Ibsen never visited England, but his letters to Gosse and Archer testify to the genuine and longstanding kinship that he felt with the English.[6]

Many observers in England also recognized this kinship. In 1884 Edward Aveling argued in the socialist monthly he edited, *To-day*, that Ibsen's plays seemed to speak directly to the social problems that defined his contemporary Victorian society.[7] Henry James, reviewing *Hedda Gabler* in 1891, remarked that Ibsen's function "was to tell us about his own people; yet what has primarily happened is that he has brought about an exhibition of ours."[8] The proximity of Ibsen's Norway to late Victorian England was a favorite theme of George Bernard Shaw in particular. In the opening chapter of *The Quintessence of Ibsenism*, first written for the Fabian Society in 1890 and then published in 1891, Shaw asked:

How then is it that Ibsen, a Norwegian playwright of European celebrity, attracted one section of the English people so strongly that they hailed him as the greatest living dramatic poet and moral teacher, whilst another section was so revolted by his works that they described him in terms which they themselves admitted to be, by the necessities of the case, all but obscene?[9]

The answer, as Shaw had discovered, was precisely this unsettling resemblance of the world of Ibsen's plays to contemporary England. In an 1895 essay, later collected in *Our Theatres in the Nineties*, Shaw declared that "*The League of Youth, An Enemy of the People*, and *Rosmersholm* are as true to English as they can possibly be to Norwegian society." The following year, writing about *Little Eyolf*, Shaw returned to the same theme, responding to Clement Scott's allegation that Ibsen was "suburban": "But if you ask me where you can find the Helmer household, the Allmers household, the Solness household, the Rosmer household, and all the other Ibsen households, I reply, 'Jump out of a train anywhere between Wimbledon and Haslemere; walk into the first villa you come to; and there you are.'" This "suburban life," retorted Shaw, "is the life depicted by Ibsen."[10] Well into the following century, many years after Shaw had definitively left dramatic criticism for playwriting, he was still arguing for this universality of Ibsen's drama – but, in particular, for its bearing upon England. In the preface to the 1919 *Heartbreak House*, while discussing the international relevance of Chekhov's theater, Shaw compared the Russian playwright to Ibsen, writing that Chekhov transcended Russia "just as Ibsen's intensely Norwegian plays exactly fitted every middle and professional class suburb in Europe."[11] From "Europe" Shaw made it clear that he was not excluding his adopted England.

Shaw was not only interested in Ibsen; he was interested in Ibsen as seen through the prism of England. So too were all the critics who responded with such energy to the Norwegian dramatist, whether they extolled him or loathed him. For many, like Ibsen's main late Victorian translator William Archer, the writer's strange digestion into English culture – sometimes happy, sometimes uneasy – was nearly as worthy of analysis as the dramas themselves. In his 1901 essay "The Real Ibsen," Archer wrote: "if his fame endures for another fifty years, someone will doubtless write a 'History of Ibsen Criticism in the Nineteenth Century' to the no small entertainment of our grandsons."[12] Archer meant this in jest: the vehement and often ludicrous opposition of so many anti-Ibsenites would stand as proof of a philistine Victorian culture. The Ibsen controversy was often the reflection of English pruderies; much else of the anti-Ibsenites' resistance can be described as the usual, skeptical bafflement of those who bear witness to a radically new and disorienting form of art.

But a history of Ibsen criticism in the nineteenth century can be much more than an occasion to laugh at the late Victorians for their priggishness or ignorance. The critics who confronted Ibsen were not merely fools like Clement Scott; they were also William Archer, Edmund Gosse, Henry James, Bernard Shaw, and James Joyce. For these figures, "realism" was not a meager slur for Ibsen's plays. It was a recognition of the dramas' particular and peculiar mimetic – and polemical – force. A history of Ibsen criticism can therefore be an investigation into a culture wrestling with specific problems of genre, trying to define what to expect from certain modes of representation. Clearly there are differences between realism in fiction and realism in drama. Methods of theatrical performance have no true parallel in novels or our reading of them; the language of realist fiction is not always analogous to the dialogic essence of drama. Nor were the writers' own views of something called realism, and of their participation in it, identical: Ibsen's self-image as a realist differs from (for example) Gissing's. These differences will not be ignored here. But the similarities between Ibsen's realism and the novelistic realism I have been examining are too remarkable to disregard merely out of deference to such variances. Both kinds of realism were forms of revolt against received ideas of progress, and – despite Shaw's insistence on the social prophet Ibsen – in both cases this revolt was therefore a non-corrective one. Both realisms understood satire as the outermost limit of realist representation. Indeed the audacious and spectacular finales of nearly all Ibsen's plays – from Nora's door slam in *A Doll's House* to Hedvig's suicide and Relling's concluding spit of disgust in *The Wild Duck*, from Hedda Gabler's similar suicide by gunshot, with the ensuing inanity of Tesman's and Brack's stunned responses, to the avalanche that buries Rubek and Irene in *When We Dead Awaken* – are similar to Father Time's own Swiftian finale: all these scenes expose the violent shock or outrageousness of image and idea that lies at the boundary of representational possibility. (Ibsen literalized the notion of limit and boundary: he actually concluded his dramas at this moment of violence, such that the curtain drops at the very point of extremity.) And both novelistic realism and dramatic realism met with a nearly identical critical bafflement and condemnation. This last is one of my primary concerns in this chapter. I am interested in the way that critics and observers perceived Ibsen's realism as a kind of censure, and in the fact that the English critics always relied on two words – *realism* and *satire* – in their effort to make sense of Ibsen's theater. The murkiness surrounding the interpretation of Ibsen remains a central fact of fin-de-siècle English culture, if only because the dramatist occupied such a supreme position in that culture. A history of Ibsen criticism is in essence a history of criticism in the late Victorian era.

ENTER THE NORWEGIAN SATIRIST

In England, Ibsen was called a satirist long before he was ever named a realist. In January 1873, only months after writing his first, brief pieces about Ibsen for the *Spectator*, Edmund Gosse contributed a much longer essay to the *Fortnightly Review*, for the purpose of introducing the playwright in detail to English readers. Gosse's title was "Ibsen, the Norwegian Satirist." His earlier pieces for the *Spectator* had, in fact, already given great prominence to the satirical temper of Ibsen's dramas. A July 1872 review of *Peer Gynt*, for example, praised the "draperies of allegorical satire" of a play that brilliantly "satirises, as in a nutshell, everything vapid, or maudlin, or febrile" in Norwegian society. Ibsen, as Gosse described him to *Spectator* readers, was "a man who pours out the vials of scorn upon vice."[13]

The following year, with "Ibsen, the Norwegian Satirist," Gosse would bring to the fore the theme announced by his title. The article opens with Gosse's evocation of "a vast and sinister genius" living in exile in Dresden, "Promethean, a dramatic satirist." Gosse explains:

Modern life is a thing too complex and too delicate to bear such satire as thrilled through the fierce old world ... Modern satire laughs while it attacks, and takes care that the spear-shaft shall be covered in roses ... As the ages bring in their advancements in civilization and refinement, the rough old satire becomes increasingly impossible, till a namby-pamby generation threatens to loathe it altogether as having "no pity in it." The writings of Ibsen form the last and most polished phase of this slow development and exhibit a picture of life so perfect in its smiling sarcasm and deliberate anatomy, that one accepts it at once as the distinct portraiture of one of the foremost spirits of an age. Ibsen has many golden arrows in his quiver, and he stands, cold and serene, between the dawn and the darkness, shooting them one by one into the valley below, each truly aimed at some folly, some affectation, in the every-day life we lead.[14]

At first glance Gosse's Ibsen of 1873 may seem unfamiliar to twenty-first-century readers – and indeed may not have been entirely recognizable to most Victorians in the audience of *A Doll's House*, only sixteen years after this essay was published in the *Fortnightly Review*. The Ibsen of the later, better-known prose dramas can hardly be deemed such a smiling or serene figure. But Gosse's early vision of Ibsen was the Ibsen of three verse plays in particular: *Love's Comedy*, *Brand*, and *Peer Gynt*, what Gosse's article called the "three great satires" (77), "a great satiric trilogy" (88). In "Ibsen, the Norwegian Satirist" Gosse compares these three dramas to God's fury in the book of Ezekiel and the violent invective in the satires of Juvenal; his point is that in such a context the Norwegian satirist looks rather temperate. Gosse attributes the "cold and serene" Ibsen's aloofness mostly to the precise formalism of the poetry: all three plays are applauded for the beauty of Ibsen's poetic line, the "perfection of faultless verse" (84). It is this very formalism, Gosse implies, that allows Ibsen's satire to elude the roughness and ferocity of Old Testament thunderings or Juvenalian diatribes.

And yet Gosse's ostensible point here – that satire in the late nineteenth century necessarily laughs while it attacks – is not particularly representative of his larger perspective on Ibsen, even within this same early article. Much of his 1873 portrait of the Norwegian satirist depicts a sober and unremittingly stern writer, lashing mankind for its grave and intrinsic folly. Gosse's most illuminating phrase in the excerpt above is his last: Ibsen shoots his arrows at the follies and affectations of the "every-day life we lead." This is a remarkably perceptive, even prescient, observation. None of the three "great satires" can be easily classified as realist portrayals of the everyday, certainly not in the way that *Ghosts* or *A Doll's House* or *Hedda Gabler* would so often be described sixteen years later. All deeply allegorical, these three plays inhabit other modes: *Peer Gynt* is a kind of picaresque mock-epic, *Brand* is driven by an uncompromising, fanatical, neo-Biblical severity, *Love's Comedy* Gosse himself called epigrammatic and a "lyrical saturnalia" (84). But as early as 1873 Gosse could insist that Ibsen's theater was fundamentally concerned with everyday experience.

Ibsen's plays presented ever-expanding and indeed universal targets for their invective – broad vices like foolishness, hypocrisy, spinelessness – and therefore seemed directed at a world unsettlingly recognizable. In *Brand*, for instance, "all society is reviled for its universal worldliness, laziness, and lukewarmness" (85); *Peer Gynt* is a "lampoon on which silly people hail each new boaster as the Man of the Future, and worship the idol themselves have built up" (86). These are verse dramas, each a "clear-cut jewel of satire" (86), but for Gosse they are nonetheless concerned with contemporary life and its common follies. A sober view of present experience and a furious critique of that experience could not be separated from one another. Ibsen's satiric impulse is, according to Gosse, so innate, so native to his genius – "he was born to be a satirist" (77) – that his dramas, in representing the most elemental experiences, had to pass though this prism of ridicule.

With "Ibsen, the Norwegian Satirist," Gosse proved himself a critic of remarkable insight, much as he would two decades later with "The Limits of Realism in Fiction." Both essays are especially fluent in evaluating the combative, aggressive literary modes so characteristic of late nineteenth-century literature. Ibsen himself would recognize Gosse's critical acumen; he was particularly grateful to Gosse for such a favorable introduction to English readers. In February 1873, just after he was sent the *Fortnightly* article, the playwright wrote to his enthusiast: "I value your criticism more than that of any of my other friends – and this because of the real, intimate, poetic understanding revealed in everything that you have been good enough to write about me. How can I thank you enough for your last exhaustive article!"[15] In *Brand* and *Peer Gynt*, after all, Ibsen had written dramas embodying Gosse's central theory, that he was a born satirist. When Brand, in the first scene of the 1865 play, says that "I felt, dimly, the difference/ Between what is and what should be; between/ Having to endure, and finding one's burden/ Unendurable," he is speaking the thinly veiled apologia of a playwright whose art constantly deplores the pervasive failings of the world around him.[16] The enemy in these verse satires tends to be something larger, more essential, than any particular segment of society, even if Ibsen does make sure to mock schoolmasters, public officials, and certain nationalities, especially the Norwegians. As Brand announces in the first act, "It is/ Our time, our generation, that is sick/ And must be cured"; he claims later that he is the "chastiser of the age" (28, 51). In the 1867 *Peer Gynt* – less relentlessly solemn than *Brand*, more faithful to the comic tradition of satirical theater – the satire nevertheless has a tendency to expand to similar universal proportions. In act 4 Peer tells a young girl: "Men, my child, are a most untrustworthy race"; in his peregrinations in the final act, asking a stranger whether "mankind" has taken a turn for the better, he receives this reply: "Quite the contrary. They've deteriorated disgracefully./ Most of them are only fit for the casting-ladle."[17]

Such pronouncements, entirely characteristic of Ibsen's 1860s verse plays, clearly left an impression on the young Gosse. And though the name Ibsen did not reverberate with much intensity within English criticism until 1889, it is significant that in the previous decade Gosse had introduced him to England in this way. Gosse would frequently refer, in later writings, to his earlier Ibsen articles, with their tremendous emphasis on the satirical aspect of the dramatist's work. In the introduction to his 1907 book, *Ibsen*, Gosse paid tribute to Archer's faithful efforts on behalf of Ibsen, as both translator and defender, but also noted that "thirty-six years ago some of Ibsen's early metrical writings fell into the hands of the writer of this little volume, and that I had the privilege, in consequence, of being the first person to introduce Ibsen's name to the British public."[18] This, in turn, is an echo of his 1889 *Fortnightly* article "Ibsen's Social Dramas" – the article in which he talks of the diagnostic quality of Ibsen's "sternly realistic dramas" – which opens with Gosse's remark that in the 1870s "the name of Ibsen was absolutely unrecognised in this country; it is a pleasure to me to know that it was I who first introduced it to English readers" (107).[19] English readers and audiences after 1889 were thereby referred to a figure from the 1870s who was, before anything else, a satirist.

Gosse remained the most consistently articulate English interpreter of Ibsen, even after the playwright's death in 1906; and he stayed faithful to his essential ideas concerning Ibsen's art. In his 1907 volume, Gosse titled the chapter covering the years 1857–1867 "The Satires." It was during these years, Gosse writes of Ibsen, "that the harshest elements in his nature were awakened, and that he became one who loved to lash the follies of his age" (85). The English critic then makes an interesting claim about English literature: this golden moment of Norwegian satire seems to have coincided with an English neglect of that same mode. Gosse writes:

With regard to the adoption of that form of poetic art, a great difference existed between Norwegian and English taste, and this must be borne in mind. Almost exactly at the date when Ibsen was inditing the sharp couplets of his *Love's Comedy*, Tennyson, in *Sea Dreams*, was giving voice to the English abandonment of satire – which had been rampant in the generation of Byron – in the famous words: "I loathe it: he had never kindly heart,/ Nor ever cared to better his own kind,/ Who first wrote satire, with no pity in it." What England repudiated, Norway comprehended, and in certain hands enjoyed. (86)

Gosse here seems rather prone to generalization: by "English" he seems to mean Tennyson. Still, this is a generally accurate judgment of English satire in the 1850s and 1860s – if, that is, Gosse means only lyric satire, as his phrasing implies. He does not seem to have in mind Dickens, for example, who was forging such elaborate novelistic satire during these years; and his dates precede those of the fin-de-siècle period, when the satirical realism of *Jude the Obscure* and *New Grub Street* would prove to be such a dominant mode. For all the similarities between Ibsen's Norway and late Victorian England, as Shaw and others remarked in their reactions to the later prose plays, Gosse does make a case for the gap between the two literary cultures a few decades earlier, at mid-century. Aside from certain aspects of Browning, there was no major verse satire in English literature during the years of *Brand* and *Peer Gynt*. Surely this is a primary reason for Gosse's longstanding emphasis on the satire in Ibsen: the Norwegian's corrosive wit and invective had taken the young English enthusiast by surprise.

Gosse's chapter on the 1857–1867 "satire" period is one of the finest English evaluations of these years of Ibsen's career. But it is just as illuminating for its turn-of-the-century perspective on the workings of satire generally as for its description of one Norwegian playwright's practice of that mode. Gosse seems to recognize this period as a transitional phase in satirical writing, with Ibsen as its exemplar, its most prominent practitioner. Satire, that is to say, was evolving toward a realist idiom. As in his earlier "Norwegian Satirist" essay, Gosse makes subtle reference to the proto-realist impulse native to Ibsen's early verse satire. "He was always an observer," Gosse writes, "always a clinical analyst at the bedside of society, never a prophet, never a propagandist" (94). This is an important description of a notably detached form of satire, a diagnostic rather than corrective mode: a satirical writing that, while couched in impeccable verse, is an analysis rather than a forced prescription. The medical analogy is familiar: Gosse had used a similar metaphor in his 1889 "Ibsen's Social Dramas" when he wrote of Ibsen's diagnosis of the "disease of which this poor weary world of ours ... is expiring" (110).

Gosse's rhetoric is instructive, even beyond its specific reference to Ibsen. Here is a description of satirical realism in its broadest sense; it calls to mind, in particular, the purest avatar of that mode, Flaubert. This is not merely because the metaphor evokes the intersection of medicine and satire in the Flaubertian imagination – the foolish doctor Charles Bovary, for instance – but rather because it recalls the strikingly similar critical reaction to Flaubert's fiction. The best example is Sainte-Beuve's 1857 review of *Madame Bovary*, in which he wrote with exuberance: "Son and brother of distinguished doctors, M. Gustave Flaubert wields the pen as others wield the scalpel. Anatomists and physiologists, I find you everywhere!" The icon of Flaubert the anatomist was immortalized in J. Lemot's famous caricature of the author brandishing his scalpel, having just ripped out the heart of Emma Bovary.[20]

To compare the writer to the clinical analyst at the bedside of society, or to the coroner wielding his instrument, is to make a specific observation about a form of realist literature that – like satire – is committed to identifying the problems and maladies inherent in contemporary experience. But neither Flaubert nor Ibsen, in these analogies, is construed as prescribing any kind of remedy.[21] They are solely diagnosticians, scientists whose task is some kind of detached vivisection or autopsy. A satirist who proposes some corrective to folly – or even a writer like Zola, whose entire *Roman expérimental* hinges on the analogy of the crusading novelist to the experimental physiologist – might be a good doctor, seeking to restore society back to health. Satirical realists like Flaubert or Ibsen, on the other hand, restrict themselves to standing by the bedside, chronicling everything, and then – when their inspection is complete – walking away in dismay and in scorn. This repudiation of a corrective purpose is the central fact of satirical realism in the nineteenth century, realism's great inheritance from the tragic pessimism of Juvenal and Swift. And so if earlier forms of Victorian realism can be connected to the advances and discoveries of nineteenth-century science – in the criticism of Gillian Beer and George Levine, for example – then satirical realism, by century's end, can be aligned only with an austere kind of scientific inquiry, one which offers no consolations of enlightenment or amelioration.[22]

In the 1907 study, Gosse writes of *Brand*: "Here Ibsen comes not to heal but to slay; he exposes the corpse of an exhausted age, and will bury it quickly" (107); later, comparing Ibsen to Tolstoy, he observes: "Tolstoi analyses a morbid condition, but always with the purpose, if he can, of curing it; Ibsen gives it even closer clinical attention, but he leaves to others the care of removing a disease which his business is solely to diagnose" (135). The Ibsen of the mid-1860s had not yet left verse for prose, nor had he come to set his scene so obstinately in the drawing rooms of middle-class life. But the stern realism of the major prose plays, those dramas that would so enthrall and perplex English critics and audiences, was already embedded in his verse satires. In this respect the distance from *Peer Gynt* to *Ghosts* was notably short.

IBSEN AND THE ILLUSION OF REALITY

Ibsen's first play after *Peer Gynt* was *The League of Youth*, completed in 1869. This was his first prose drama; after *Peer Gynt* he would never write another play in verse. It would not be grandiloquent to say that Ibsen's shift from verse to prose was one of the most significant events in the career of any major European writer. This shift brought the playwright inexorably into the realist idiom that would define his place in late nineteenth-century and then modernist literature – into the theater that would have such a profound influence on Shaw, Joyce, and many others. The turn to prose continues to be a central theme in Ibsen studies: Toril Moi, in her recent *Henrik Ibsen and the Birth of Modernism*, cites it as one of the keys to the playwright's radical modernism.[23]

Ibsen himself recognized, in the very first days of this new prose phase, the momentousness of his transition. In an 1868 letter to the Copenhagen publisher Frederick Hegel he noted the plain difference between the previous year's *Peer Gynt* and his work-in-progress, *The League of Youth*: the new play, Ibsen clarified, "will be in prose . . . it deals with forces and frictions in modern life." Six months later, writing to the Danish critic Georg Brandes, Ibsen explained in similar terms the aims of his new drama: "I have stayed on the level of ordinary, everyday life ... I am very anxious to hear what you have to say about my new work. It is written in prose, which gives it a strong realistic coloring."[24]

In 1873, four years after the completion of *The League of Youth*, Ibsen finally finished his historical prose play *Emperor and Galilean*. This was the same year that Edmund Gosse's "Ibsen, the Norwegian Satirist" would give the dramatist his first prominent introduction to English readers. It was this article that began the extensive correspondence between the two – a correspondence that would therefore flourish just as Ibsen's career as a prose writer was starting to take shape. At first Gosse expressed some hesitation about the dramatist's abandonment of verse, and in January 1874 Ibsen responded by explaining the method behind *Emperor and Galilean*:

> You say that the drama ought to have been written in verse and that it would have gained by this. Here I must differ from you. As you must have observed, the play is conceived in the most realistic style. The illusion I wished to produce was that of reality. I wished to produce the impression on the reader that what he was reading was something that had actually happened. If I had employed verse, I would have counteracted my own intention and defeated my purpose. The many ordinary, insignificant characters whom I have intentionally introduced into the play would have become indistinct and indistinguishable from one another if I had allowed all of them to speak in the same meter. We are no longer living in the days of Shakespeare ... My new drama is no tragedy in the ancient sense. What I sought to depict were human beings, and therefore I would not let them talk the 'language of the Gods.' (144–5)

Gosse cites this letter in his 1907 volume, noting that such a revolt against verse drama was characteristic of the late nineteenth century: Alphonse Daudet, in 1877, had come to a similar conclusion. But Gosse argues that "no poet, however, sacrificed so much, or held so rigidly to his intention of reproducing the exact language of real life, as did Ibsen" (149). This sacrifice was the sacrifice of lyrical cadence and fantasy; and as Gosse saw it, it was a sacrifice made most precipitously in these first prose plays. The decade from 1869 to 1879 might be considered the transitional phase in Ibsen's career, from the earlier verse plays to the unbroken sequence of prose masterpieces, beginning with the 1879 *Doll's House*. The plays of these years – *The League of Youth*, *Emperor and Galilean*, and *The Pillars of Society* (this last generally considered Ibsen's first work of social realism) – are the work of a playwright adapting his theater to a new mode and rhetoric, though retaining much of the combative energy from the verse satires of the previous decade.[25] As critics like Gosse observed, the satirical expression was therefore noticeably sparer. "The subject of *The Pillars of Society*," Gosse remarks in *Ibsen*, "was the hollowness and rottenness of those supports, and the severe and unornamented prose which Ibsen now adopted was very favourable to its discussion" (150). Another way of saying this is that whereas *Peer Gynt* had been funny, *The Pillars of Society* – despite its own reliance on caricature – seemed a predictor of the unnervingly stern later dramas.[26] Gosse was tracing the transformation of satire from its earlier, exuberant manifestations into the severity of a more realist form.

The period of Ibsen's major realist drama is framed by the years 1879 and 1890 – by *A Doll's House* and *Hedda Gabler* – and, in particular, includes, beside those two plays, *Ghosts, An Enemy of the People, The Wild Duck,* and *Rosmersholm.* (Ibsen also wrote *The Lady from the Sea* during these years.)[27] In England these six plays were first staged between 1889 and 1893, the main years of the Ibsen controversy; all six were commonly debated in relation to the question of "realism." Of these, *A Doll's House* and *Ghosts* incited the most argument and antagonism. This was largely because the specific topics these two plays presented at least on the surface – feminist revolt, the scandal of hereditary disease – promised their own inevitable controversy. With *A Doll's House* the general impression of the English was that they were under some kind of assault, waged with the aggression of an unsettling realism: Joyce would later call this the "uncompromising rigor" of the plays of the early eighties.[28] In the *Theatre* of July 1, 1889, the indefatigable Clement Scott attacked the play for embodying "such unpleasing realism."[29] A similarly hostile article ("The Foolishness of the Ibsenites") in the unrelated, American-published *Theatre Magazine* six months later claimed that *A Doll's House* was simply Ibsen's attempt to unnerve people, *pour épater le bourgeois.* Ibsen was "mainly desirous of doing something irregular and improper," the article claimed. It rejected the play's claim to "realism" altogether, noting with incredulity that *A Doll's House* was "heralded as a play that went straight to human nature and treated it with the honesty of the new realism," when, in fact, it "presented us with a weak monstrosity that does not belong to normal life."[30] Blustery critics like these were not alone, though, in objecting to the play's method of channeling antipathy through the plain language of everyday life – whether or not such a method was deemed realistic. In his *Autobiography* W.B. Yeats would recall his own experience in the 1889 audience of *A Doll's House*: "I hated the play ... I resented being invited to admire dialogue so close to modern educated speech that music and style were impossible."[31]

The "realism" of Ibsen's prose plays was, in a sense, largely a question of factors such as this – his innovative reliance on spare and straightforward language. Dramatic dialogue of this kind could provoke the censure of Yeats; but it could also stir the enthusiasm of Gosse (who wrote so favorably of Ibsen's "exact language of real life") or George Moore, who similarly praised *Ghosts*'s rejection of hexameters for "the simple language of a plain Norwegian household."[32] Ibsen's realism could, just as well, be a matter of staging – the everyday interiors in the London productions that inspired Henry James's admiring encapsulation of the

ugly interior on which his curtain inexorably rises ... the hideous carpet and wall-paper and curtains ... the conspicuous stove, the lonely centre-table, the 'lamps with green shades', as in the sumptuous first act of *The Wild Duck*, the pervasive air of small interests and standards, the sign of limited local life. It represents the very clothes, the inferior fashions, of the figures that move before us.[33]

Stagings like this were not, of course, unique to England; an account of the very first performance of *A Doll's House* (in Copenhagen in 1879) expressed awe at this aspect of the play's originality: "it is beyond memory since a play so simple in its action and so everyday in its dress made such an impression of artistic mastery."[34]

Such reactions to Ibsen remind us, of course, that realism on the stage arises from a very different set of circumstances from those inherent in realist fiction. I am emphasizing, in this chapter, the critical response to the staging of Ibsen's plays, not the reading of them; and the debate about Ibsen's realism was a debate mostly about the way these plays appeared on the London stage. Yeats and Gosse and Moore were hearing Ibsen's dialogue in the theater; James was seeing those carpets and lamps while sitting in an audience. The longstanding tradition of criticism on dramatic realism has always focused on questions of mise-en-scène no less than on textual matters. With Ibsen in particular, the stage notes for the prose plays are innovative in the precision of their directives: the "tiled stove decorated with fresh birch-branches and wild flowers" in *Rosmersholm*, for example, or the "lamps with green shades" that James admired in *The Wild Duck*. (Even if such directives originate in the text of the plays, it was, of course, the late Victorian stage that put this kind of realism of appearances into practice – that codified it.) Indeed, just as it is a commonplace that *Brand* and *Peer Gynt* are essentially impossible to produce on stage – too vast, and requiring too many sets – there has long been a consensus that the realist prose plays, in particular, *require* performance. One of the earliest Ibsen partisans to make this claim was Joyce, in his review of *When We Dead Awaken*: "if any plays demand a stage they are the plays of Ibsen ... they were not written to cumber the shelves of a library" (62).[35]

Theorists of dramatic realism in general have traditionally zeroed in on these same elements of production, even when they are discussing realism in broader social terms. Stephen Lacey, to take one example, acknowledges Raymond Williams's tripartite definition of realism in drama as it emerged in the nineteenth century – for Williams, the essential characteristics were the secular, the contemporary, and the socially extended (or the extension of representation to a greater range of society, notably with regard to class) – while also examining the "theatrical articulation" (or performance) of realist drama. New Wave British drama, to take the case of Lacey's focus, relies on totems of everyday bourgeois or working-class experience in order to construct a "plausible social reality" which would inevitably become the subject of critique in most British theater of the 1950s and 1960s.[36] This is not merely a naturalism relying on a pseudo-scientific scrupulousness of mimesis, the kind of "naturalism" to which Brecht always objected.[37] Brecht had advocated a realism that did more than simply make "reality recognizable in the theatre": "one has to be able to see through it too."[38]

The parallels to Ibsen are clear – as are the parallels to realist fiction, in the way I have been discussing it. My interest here does not lie in dramaturgy or the history of realism on the stage as such, but rather in the significant parallels between modes of realism in drama and in fiction. Just as historians and theorists of drama have tended to compare these kinds of elements of production and mise-en-scène to the machinery of realist fiction – "stage scenery might be nothing but canvas and paint, but it was the theatre's equivalent of the element of description in the novel," according to J.L. Styan – so I am emphasizing here Ibsen's portrayal of the everyday for essentially polemical and satirical ends.[39] In Ibsen's major prose plays, techniques like those that absorbed his contemporaries – common speech, simple dress, the banal objects of bourgeois life; what Virginia Woolf would later call Ibsen's "paraphernalia of reality"[40] – were not in any sense ends in themselves. They were not realistic devices merely to be admired as totems of a recognizable contemporary existence, merely for the sake of an aesthetically detached or muted realism. It is true that Ibsen may have first set forth from this goal of detachment. His letters from 1882 and 1883, in particular – the years he was composing *Ghosts* and *An Enemy of the People* – testify to his great aspiration to a certain pared-down verisimilitude. "My intention was to produce the impression in the mind of the reader that he was experiencing something real," he wrote in 1882, the same year that he expressed his wish that his spectators should think they were "actually experiencing a piece of real life." In 1883 he explained to one actress that his art was "writing the straightforward, plain language spoken in real life" and told a prominent Swedish director that the effect of *An Enemy of the People* "depends a great deal on making the spectator feel as if he were actually sitting, listening and looking at events happening in real life."[41]

And yet these very same letters make clear that the illusion of reality exists for a furious, often polemical purpose. In that 1882 letter, Ibsen denies that *Ghosts* preaches "nihilism" – a common charge against the play – and claims instead that "it preaches nothing at all. It merely points out that there is a ferment of nihilism under the surface" (201). This is a similar phrase to that of Hardy, who remarked that the novel that would become *Jude the Obscure* exposed something that "the world ought to be shown," or to the declaration of Gissing, who wanted his fiction to "show the hideous injustice of our whole system of society."[42] Ibsen's effort to "point out" such nihilism carries the same moral imperative as Hardy's or Gissing's task of "showing": it is a forceful moralism that relies on realist devices. That same month (January 1882), just as he was declaring his ambitions toward the representation of "real life," Ibsen announced the fiercely independent and antagonistic attitude that he wanted to maintain, by means of such realist drama, toward the society he was excoriating: "I stand like a solitary sharpshooter at the outpost, acting entirely on my own" (202).[43] In this light, Gosse's phrase of a decade earlier, in "Ibsen, the Norwegian Satirist" – that Ibsen shoots golden arrows "one by one into the valley below, each truly aimed at some folly, some affectation, in the every-day life we lead" – sounds remarkably prescient (75). By the 1880s Ibsen had grown even more naturally into this role as a sort of marksman realist.

Ibsen's notes for his work-in-progress *Ghosts* serve as a kind of manifesto in this respect. First he expresses his wish that the play be "a realistic picture of life," then he alleges that "the trouble is that mankind as a whole is a failure."[44] Indeed in *Ghosts* Ibsen provides an instructive analogy for his own method, in the form of Mrs. Alving's remark to Pastor Manders that when she began, years earlier, to examine the seams of his devoutness and learning, "I only wanted to pick at a single knot; but when I had worked it loose, the whole fabric fell apart" (63). To look closely, says Ibsen, is to see through received ideas and to discover the facts that lead to despair; and to arrive at this despair compels the observer to lash out at the innate human folly that generates such a reality. The basic structure of the prose dramas invariably follows this pattern. Social order is upset by a character's detection, and then exposure, of the hypocrisy, sham, or stupid artifice weakly supporting present conditions: this is the experience and the lesson of Nora Helmer in *A Doll's House*, Oswald Alving in *Ghosts*, Dr. Stockmann in *An Enemy of the People*, John Rosmer and Rebecca West in *Rosmersholm*, and the disillusioned heroine of *Hedda Gabler*. In this sense the arc of discovery in each of these plays is a version of Ibsen's own. The endpoint of this arc is the recognition of intrinsic human error and fraudulence, and the arc itself therefore equals a kind of satire; but the conditions along it are always plausible and austere. It is, in other words, satire attained by realist means.

The most discerning interpreters of Ibsen in the late nineteenth century were quite conscious of this fundamental connection in his imagination, between what could be called verisimilitude or evidence and this native, despairing impulse toward satire. The French critic Auguste Ehrhard made this quite plain in his 1892 book about Ibsen: "because he is a realist, Ibsen is a pessimist." When Ehrhard describes this "experience"-based pessimism, he could be just as easily writing about Flaubertian satire:

The experience of life confirms his distressing opinion that the ailments of the soul are incurable, and that vice, folly, and lies will continue to triumph in this world ... The horror of the world as it exists is expressed with even greater passion, and despite this ardor, Ibsen sees people and things with the most lucid vision.

Or Ehrhard's phrasing could sound like a description of the fiction of Gissing, positioned uneasily between realism and idealism: "Idealist in argument, Ibsen is an admirable realist through the way in which he presents it."[45] The realist manner of presentation was both a technique and a philosophy: an aesthetic technique that sought to produce a certain verisimilitude, to be sure, but also a philosophy in the sense that such combative satire would seem imperative only if the follies it attacked were inherent in actual contemporary experience, and therefore if censure resulted from – and formed an essential part of – knowledge. Hjalmar Hjorth Boyesen, an American writer and scholar born in Norway, who wrote an 1894 book on Ibsen, agreed that in *A Doll's House* such censure depended fundamentally on the realist method. "The satire is the more scathing," Boyesen wrote in relation to the play's spare dialogue, "and the gradual unravelling of the tragic elements that lurk in a perfectly normal relation is the more terrifying because of this scrupulous avoidance of high-colouring or overstatement."[46]

Critics in Scandinavia had thought about this question in a similar way. Georg Brandes – whose major study of Ibsen and Björnson was translated into English in 1899, thereby joining the critical conversation of Gosse, Archer, and Shaw – had written of the moral character of Ibsen's pessimism, which was "akin to contempt and indignation"; but he immediately clarified that this "gloomy way of looking at things," this "peculiar bias that forces him to depict life in just this manner," was due to an empirical, crystalline realism: "in the last analysis, however, there is no other answer than that he represents life as it presents itself to him."[47] The conclusion is familiar: Ibsen was drawn instinctively to satire because he was faithful to what he observed in the world.

What was under observation was often something that much of Ibsen's readership and audience identified as ugliness. Repulsive themes like disease in *Ghosts* or suicide in *Rosmersholm* and *Hedda Gabler* were the primary cause for the nauseated response of so much of the London press. Many of these reactions were collected with amusement by William Archer in his April 1891 *Pall Mall Gazette* article "'Ghosts' and Gibberings": "an open drain: a loathsome sore unbandaged; a dirty act done publicly; a lazar-house with all its doors and windows open ... candid foulness ... absolutely loathsome and fetid ... gross, almost putrid indecorum ... literary carrion ... as foul and filthy a concoction as has ever been allowed to disgrace the boards of an English theatre," and so on.[48]

But the pursuit of ugliness could, for other observers, be construed as a quasi-heroic act instead. George Eliot's ars poetica in chapter 17 of *Adam Bede* – in which her homage to the "homely existence" captured in Dutch genre painting triggers her reflection that "I am not at all sure that the majority of the human race have not been ugly" – provides an instructive lesson here, even if she is largely advocating a sympathetic rather than censorious judgment (166–7). An intrepid realism unearths the ugly; a committed satire rails against it. Boyesen concluded his 1894 volume on Ibsen by declaring: "he has the courage to look the ugliest truths in the face without flinching, and to record what he sees and feels with a relentless disregard of revered conventionalities" (316–17). Henry James, in his essay on *Hedda Gabler*, offered a similar formulation:

In his satiric studies of contemporary life, the impression that is strongest with us is that the picture is infinitely *noted*, that all the patience of the constructive pessimist is in his love of the detail of character and of conduct, in his way of accumulating the touches that illustrate them. His recurrent ugliness of surface, as it were, is a sort of proof of his fidelity to the real.[49]

This is perhaps the finest précis of Ibsen's strain of realism. The satire of the plays depends on the author's scrutiny, his acute eye for detail; the inevitable ugliness that results from this scrutiny is only the purest evidence of a steadfast realism, Ibsen's "fidelity to the real." James's formulation could apply to a great portion of the brash literature of the era: this is an apt description of the entire panorama of late nineteenth-century satirical realism. And it is a reminder of the strong resemblance of Ibsen's dramatic mode of satirical realism to its novelistic guises in the fiction of Hardy or Gissing.

James, in this 1891 essay, takes *Hedda Gabler* as his point of departure, but from there he proceeds to offer his most extensive reflections on Ibsen's art generally. He returns several times to the question of satire, nowhere more penetratingly than in one passage:

Some of his portraits are strongly satirical, like that, to give only two instances, of Tesman, in *Hedda Gabler* (a play indeed suffused with irrepressible irony), or that of Hjalmar Ekdal, in *The Wild Duck*. But it is the ridicule without the smile, the dance without the music, a sort of sarcasm that is nearer to tears than to laughter. There is nothing very droll in the world, I think, to Dr. Ibsen; and nothing is more interesting than to see how he makes up his world without a joke. (236)

James's basic point marks an inevitable discovery in any study of satirical realism in the nineteenth century, though it is especially pertinent to Ibsen's prose dramas: these plays are rarely very funny. *Ghosts* and *Rosmersholm* and *Hedda Gabler* refuse the comic frenzy and picaresque humor that define much of *Peer Gynt*, or even the somewhat more temperate wit of *Love's Comedy*.[50] In a play like *Little Eyolf* the drama reaches such unbearably bleak, heartrending extremes that it can be easy to forget that the same dramatist had ever inhabited such a comic mode.

This same question has surfaced before: can it still be called satire if it seems so devoid of humor? *Jude the Obscure*, deeply indebted to Hardy's readings in the satiric tradition, is nevertheless so relentlessly desolate that it can appear to bypass or else transcend that tradition within its own pages. The question is ultimately impossible to answer with any certitude: it necessarily depends on our understanding of satire's proximity to comedy, as I discussed in the first chapter. James, reviewing *John Gabriel Borkman* six years later in 1897, noted that Ibsen's attitude was "a result of so dry a view of life, so indifferent a vision of the comedy of things. His idea of the thing represented is never the comic idea."[51] Oswald Crawfurd, writing in the *Fortnightly Review* in 1890, had similarly warned: "If we look into the Ibsen drama to see how far it contains the elements of genuine comedy, we shall be grievously disappointed."[52] This was a common late Victorian reaction to Ibsen's theater, especially among his detractors: the plays were too severe in their lashings, too unremitting in their ridicule, to provide any moments of humor. Along the spectrum of plays on the London stage in the final years of the nineteenth century, Ibsen's stern dramas were situated on the opposite end from the drawing-room comedies of Wilde or (though the structure of Ibsen's plays is always meticulous, and though it is true that in his early plays, especially, Ibsen still bore the marks of Scribe) the theatrical artifice of the *pièce bien faite*.[53]

On the evidence of *Jude the Obscure*, of *New Grub Street*, of *Ghosts* and *An Enemy of the People* and *Hedda Gabler*, satirical realism in the late nineteenth century cannot be said to be a mode of humor or wit. It is a mode of aggression. First it identifies specific targets in the world, then it expands its sights to include such a vast field of contemporary experience that it develops into an absolute satire. To be absolute means to condemn universally, to subject mankind itself to a broad attack. The late Victorian critics' usual method of identifying this mode was to call it "pessimism": this label was attached routinely to Hardy, Gissing, and Ibsen. Such pessimism does not provoke laughter in any conventional sense; it takes in too much of the pain of common experience, and spares too little, to allow for such comfort. Its methods of representation can be too lifelike to provide the distance that readers or audiences might require to laugh. And so, though satirical realism emerged from the ancient tradition of satire, it largely abolished its primary motor, which was humor. In this respect a darkly satiric Ibsen drama like *Hedda Gabler*, populated by fools but fundamentally and ruthlessly austere, is similar to Gissing's Grub Street, with its satiric ancestry but contemporary Victorian bleakness. William Archer, in his essay on *Hedda Gabler*, claimed that the play was so "detached," so "objective," that "one cannot even call it a satire, unless one is prepared to apply that term to the record of a 'case' in a work on criminology."[54] Archer had been a faithful observer of Ibsen from decades earlier, when the playwright had infused *Peer Gynt* with such comedy (even if it was a dark comedy indeed).

But Archer could now trace the strange arc that Ibsen's satire had followed, until it reached a hyperrealist extreme where the term "satire" might no longer even apply.

Readers and audiences rarely find it funny to be lectured at, and one of the primary charges leveled against Ibsen was that he was a preacher. (This was Archer's main observation in the *Fortnightly* essay where he called the Norwegian "the most famous man in the English literary world.") Ibsen's most consistent late Victorian detractor, Clement Scott, wrote that the London audience of *A Doll's House* was enthralled by the experience, but that he could not accept the work as true theater: "the sermon proceeded – it is not a play."[55] In 1891 the generally sympathetic Oswald Crawfurd similarly called *An Enemy of the People* "a sound bit of ethical teaching, a sermon shamming as a play"; Ibsen's main purpose was not to entertain or amuse his audience, but "to teach you."[56] What was perceived as Ibsen's preachiness hit its shrillest note with this play: *An Enemy of the People* is a barely veiled allegory of the author's own struggle with the small-mindedness and philistinism of the masses, and it attacks these masses with the greatest severity. It is Ibsen's purest satire among the prose dramas, the play whose purpose is most explicitly to attack and to scorn. Dr. Stockmann's crusade becomes unconditional in the way Ibsen's satire becomes absolute. "This whole community's got to be cleansed and decontaminated," he cries in the third act; later he despairs – in the abiding language of the satirist – that "the fools are in a terrifying, overwhelming majority all over the world!"[57] A filthy water supply is hardly a matter for comedy. In England the allegation that the Norwegian playwright was really a preacher, humorless and sanctimonious, was raised most frequently in relation to this play, first performed in London in 1893. In Ibsen's theater the satirist figure, the agent of derision and despair in the face of reality, took, in its purest incarnation, the form of ascetic men like Brand and Stockmann: scourges who refused to compromise with any kind of mediocrity. This kind of satire was not an opportunity for laughter; it was an occasion for punishment.

THE AMORAL, THE MORAL, AND THE IMMORAL IBSEN

The kind of late nineteenth-century literature that I call satirical realism emits such strong vapors of aggression that it can cloud our perception of the very genres that constitute it. Ibsen's English contemporaries knew that he was fueled by a fierce satirical impulse – and yet they were also aware that the censorious fury of his prose plays impeded the kind of laughter we typically expect from satirical art. His satire thereby became a matter of great dispute. The same can be said of Ibsen's realism: it was a subject that sparked fierce disagreement among his readers and critics.

The quarrel over the claim of "realism" has also been characteristic of the history I am tracing – of the late Victorian response to works of satirical realism, that strange hybrid mode. With *Jude the Obscure* much of the critical resistance hinged upon the implausibility and even absurdity of Father Time, who seemed to channel so much of the Swiftian darkness of Hardy's novel. Mrs. Oliphant found the boy and the infanticide to be not realism but "pure farce"; Havelock Ellis could not square the killing of the children, an episode he deemed "comparatively unreal," with the otherwise considerable realism of Hardy's method. Faced with *New Grub Street*, the late Victorians similarly struggled to reconcile Gissing's sober realism – and especially his direct and explicit engagement, within the novel, with that literary movement – with the sense that his gloom was a source of excess and an obstacle to credibility. In publications like the *Saturday Review* and the *Author*, critics might praise the persuasiveness or plausibility of Gissing's vision one week but contest them the next; a single journal could serve as the terrain upon which the conflict over realism in the novel would be fought.

In this respect the theater of Henrik Ibsen posed a dilemma very similar to that of Gissing's fiction. Again a debate arose concerning the "idealist" ambitions of realist literature: Ibsen, like Gissing, would force people to ask whether an "idealistic realist" was, in fact, a contradiction in terms. Oswald Crawfurd, in the same article where he called *An Enemy of the People* a "sermon shamming as a play," took on this subject directly:

In the recent controversy on Ibsen's dramatic and literary position he has been claimed by his friends as a realist ... he is a realist indeed in manner, in style, in dialogue: his characters talk with almost the pointlessness of real life, and have everything of real life but its redundancy; but this does not constitute a realist in any true sense, and the enumeration I have given of his characters and their motives will suffice to show that no purer idealist, no truer romanticist ever wrote for the stage.

Crawfurd goes on to ask whether this idealism, this effort to "better the world by his presentment of the doings of its inhabitants on his stage," is successful; he declines to provide an answer.[58] But the problem is nevertheless articulated in familiar terms. Ibsen's theater was polemical in a way that seemed at odds with its realist devices; literature this furious could not be said to be impartial, and "realism" was commonly thought to maintain a premise at least of neutrality. The vociferous opposition of so many anti-Ibsenites like Clement Scott took this stance as its point of departure: when Scott wrote of *A Doll's House* that "it is not a play," his point was that Ibsen was too sanctimonious, too obvious in the preaching of his lessons, to be judged on any kind of aesthetic or dramatic basis.

But the logic of such opposition can be taken further: in their most extreme forms, and even irrespective of their moral aims, devices that seem to belong to realism might lead to a kind of anti-realism instead. This was the apparently paradoxical thinking that disputed the horrendous scene of Father Time's killing of himself and his two half-siblings, and it is the same kind of logic – or illogic – that would generate such argument over Ibsen's spectacularly violent finales in particular. A "realistic" work would seem to be one that recoils before no scene, no matter how disturbing; but if that work pursues this ambition too far it will lead to a terrain of shock and excess that becomes ultimately implausible. For this reason, as I have said before, satirical realism treads always the boundaries of representation. And in this sense "realism" – grittiness, even sordidness, as it was often understood in late Victorian criticism – can come at the expense of "realism," if that term is to signify verisimilitude or credibility instead. The theater of Ibsen posed this very problem. In England the most influential writer on the topic was, in fact, not an Englishman but Max Nordau, whose *Degeneration* provoked such a strong reaction from the time of its translation into English in 1895. Nordau's volume was divided into five books, one of which was called "Realism" and another of which, "Ego-Mania," contained a chapter on "Ibsenism." But for Nordau realism and Ibsenism were two versions of the same thing: they were both a sham, and they were both to be abhorred as worthless forms of a degenerate fin-de-siècle culture.

Nordau was among the many late nineteenth-century writers who relentlessly disputed the very existence of something called realism. In *Degeneration* he insisted that "the word 'realism' itself has no aesthetic significance ... Applied to art and literature, it possesses no conception whatever." His opposition was so intense that it became something of an *idée fixe* in *Degeneration*: "The notion of so-called 'realism,'" he repeats, "cannot withstand either psychological or aesthetic criticism ... From whatever side we approach this pretended realism, we never succeed in seeing in it a concept, but only an empty word."[59] In one of the two "Realism" chapters the main object of Nordau's debunking is Zola, whose claims to science and experiment the author considers mere posturing.

The only thing Zola invented, according to Nordau, was the word "naturalism" – "substituted by him for 'realism'" – and such naturalism is really nothing more than the "premeditated worship of pessimism and obscenity" (491, 497). In this way realism (or Zolaesque naturalism) falls squarely in Nordau's catalog of moral and aesthetic disintegration in the arts.

But of all *Degeneration*'s villains – not only Zola, but also Wagner, Tolstoy, Nietzsche, the Parnassiens, and the Decadents – no single writer receives the intensity or degree of invective that Nordau directs at Ibsen. His section on Ibsen is twice as long as that on anyone else, and its favorable judgments are few. This chapter could just as easily have been called "Realism," or simply appended to the chapter with that title. Nordau's line of attack against the dramatist takes one main form: disputing the realism that Ibsen's admirers so often attributed to his work. Nordau begins by attacking the playwright's reliance on Aristotelian unities of time and space: Ibsen's "technique of fireworks," his explosive catastrophes, could never be expected to occur so epigrammatically. Any spectator interested in truth will instead "bring away from Ibsen's dramas an impression of improbability, and of toilsome and subtle lucubrations" (339–40). Ibsen has "become the model of 'realism'" to his admirers, whereas, in fact, "no writer has heaped up in his works so many startling improbabilities as Ibsen" (344). Nordau lists such improbable scenarios in *Ghosts, A Doll's House, The Pillars of Society, An Enemy of the People, Hedda Gabler, The Lady from the Sea, Rosmersholm,* and *The Wild Duck* in order to prove his point. Never can he bring himself to call Ibsen a realist without surrounding that term in thick and sarcastic scare quotes.

Some of the scenes that Nordau singles out he merely finds improbable: Helmer's silly banter to Nora in *A Doll's House*, the insurance advice that Pastor Manders gives to Mrs. Alving in *Ghosts*. Nordau, a trained physician, also contests Ibsen's claims to science and heredity, especially in *Ghosts* and *Rosmersholm*: "the poet has naturally no need to understand anything of pathology. But when he pretends to describe real life, he ought to be honest" (354). And yet in its assault on Ibsen's realism, *Degeneration*'s main target is what it insists is the plays' dubious heavy-handedness. Despite all the individual improbabilities of plot and character, it is ultimately the moralizing scourge of Ibsen's theater that interferes with the illusion of reality and vexes Nordau. He explains:

What he wishes is to denounce society, the state, religion, law, and morals in anarchistic phrases. Instead, however, of publishing them like Nietzsche, in brochures, he sticks them into his pieces at haphazard, where they appear as unexpectedly as the couplets sung in the naïve farces of our fathers ... Ibsen always begins by finding some thesis – *i.e.*, some anarchist phrase. Then he tries to find out beings and events which embody and prove his thesis, for which task, however, his poetical power and, above all, his knowledge of life and men, are insufficient. For he goes through the world without seeing it, and his glance is always turned inward on himself. (385–6)

Nordau resumes this line of argument a few pages later:

The pretended 'realist' knows nothing of real life. He does not comprehend it; he does not even see it, and cannot, therefore, renew from it his store of impressions, ideas, and judgments. The well-known method of manufacturing cannon is to take a tube and pour molten metal round it. Ibsen proceeds in a similar way ... He has a thesis – more accurately, some anarchistic folly; this is the tube. It is now only a question of enveloping this tube with the metal of life's realities. But that lies beyond Ibsen's power ... Where Ibsen makes strenuous efforts to produce a picture of actual contemporaneous events, he astounds us with the niggardliness in incidents and human beings evinced by the range of his experience. (404)

At first glance Nordau's view of Ibsen does not seem very different from the opinion of English anti-Ibsenites like Clement Scott, even if at times Nordau concedes that Ibsen has some innate literary skill. Nordau and Scott both reject a central assumption of the playwright's advocates: that the power of his dramas begins, at least, from a certain scrupulous realism.

But there is an interesting difference between Scott's version of anti-Ibsenism and Nordau's. For Scott, Ibsen was guiltiest of wallowing in the sordid: the dramatist seemed to rejoice in the stage representation of suicide, disease, pollution, and depraved sexuality. Nordau, on the other hand – and despite the relentlessly hectoring message of his own anti-degeneracy harangue – objected primarily to Ibsen's sermonizing, his insistence on bullying lesson at the expense of representational art. In Scott's view Ibsen was a grimy provocateur; in Nordau's he was a blatant preacher who merely wrapped his moralism in a tube of incidental detail. Both Scott and Nordau were disputing the realism of Ibsen's plays, but they saw the problem from opposite angles. If realism was conventionally assumed by the late Victorians to strive toward a certain amorality, it is clear that Scott found Ibsen too immoral, whereas Nordau found him too stridently moral. Nordau's accusation of didacticism connected directly to the strong late Victorian opinion that Ibsen was some kind of satirist, for if realism pretended to operate from a stance of neutrality, satire was understood as a moralism, a negative kind of morality. The fact that in the

1890s Ibsen, much like Hardy with *Jude the Obscure*, was effectively called amoral, moral, and immoral is a plain indication of the profound critical confusion regarding the combative literature of the era. It is also a testament to the endless complexity of Ibsen's dramatic art.

Degeneration enjoyed a substantial notoriety in late Victorian culture after its translation into English in 1895. Among the most prominent English-language responses was George Bernard Shaw's rebuttal, published later that year as "A Degenerate's View of Nordau" in *Liberty*, an American magazine with anarchist sympathies; it was eventually reprinted, in 1908, as "The Sanity of Art: An Exposure of the Current Nonsense about Artists being Degenerate." Shaw's aim was to contest Nordau's disapproving judgments of artists and writers, primarily Ibsen and Wagner; to expose *Degeneration* as merely an alarmist collection of "bogey-criticisms," "two hundred and sixty thousand mortal words, saying the same thing over and over again"; and to lay out, in very abridged form, the Shavian theory of art as inherently utilitarian and committed.[60] But in "The Sanity of Art" Shaw does not, in fact, delve very deeply into Nordau's specific claims about the writers in question. Regarding Ibsen, Shaw had already examined the plays in much greater detail, in the 1891 *Quintessence of Ibsenism.*

A much more detailed and absorbing English-language rebuttal to *Degeneration* was the longer volume *Regeneration: A Reply to Max Nordau.* Published anonymously in England and America in 1896, and now usually ascribed to Egmont Hake, *Regeneration* was a large-scale effort to debunk Nordau's argument about the prevalent degeneracy in fin-de-siècle European culture. The book challenges Nordau's rants against Wagner, Tolstoy, Zola, and several others; but, true to Nordau's own emphasis, *Regeneration* devotes its primary attention to Ibsen. The very title of the chapter on Ibsen and Nordau – "The Real Ibsen" – is a sly indication of the two-part task it seeks to accomplish. It will reclaim the playwright from the falsifying clutches of Nordau; and it will do so by tackling the very subject that had so consumed Nordau himself, the question of Ibsen's realism. The problem is stated clearly: "The puzzle is why Nordau is so anxious to show that Ibsen is not a realist, and how his not being a realist can possibly be construed into an argument in favour of his insanity."[61]

Regeneration sets out to reclaim the mantle of realism for Ibsen by disputing the main complaint in *Degeneration*: that the dramatist is guided by a self-involved moralism, and that this impedes any sense of lifelike plausibility.

Henrik Ibsen aims not at being a prophet, a teacher, or a regenerator of mankind either by literary or scientific methods. No one can detect in his works special ethics, or particular religious or social views. It is characteristic of his pieces – and according to many of his opponents a great fault in them – that he points no moral ... he aims at producing stern reality. (140–1)

Nordau's mistake, says *Regeneration*, is that he "impeaches Ibsen's reputation for realism, but takes this term in its most literal sense" (154). Ibsen's realism does not ultimately depend on specific advice about insurance in *Ghosts* or precise turns of phrase in *The Pillars of Society*. Ibsen can be called a realist because his characters are "individually true to nature ... strongly coloured types": in this respect the argument is just like Gissing's in defense of the realism of Dickens, who believed in the "absolute reality" of his characters. Nordau is too anxious that Ibsen preaches through his characters; he devotes too much time seeking a message that he will then want to refute precisely because it *is* a message. "Few people in the world really know what Ibsen's final object and real aims are," *Regeneration* counters, "but his immediate object, it will be granted, is to show his contemporaries what they really are, and so sternly and so cogently does he pursue this object that, while other dramatists show their spectators the defects of others, Ibsen lays bare their own" (162).

This volume never met with the kind of attention in England that Nordau's book attracted, and it has since been mostly forgotten among the minor critical works of the 1890s. But in a sense *Regeneration* understood the workings of Ibsen's theater in a way *Degeneration* never did, for it saw, fundamentally, that the realist vision of the plays was entirely coexistent with – indeed inseparable from – their censorious energy. To show one's contemporaries "what they really are" *was* to lay bare their defects: these two aspirations could not be dissociated from one another. This was satire as a diagnostic rather than a curative practice. Nordau's error was to assume, because the plays seemed like a furious protest, that there must be a series of easy lessons embedded in them. But, in truth, Ibsen's stern method allowed his condemnation to be wider, more elusive; his spectators, in the words of *Regeneration*, were faced finally with their own defects. It is, of course, the perspective of *Regeneration*, with its elastic understanding of what "realism" could mean in Ibsen, which has endured for Ibsen scholars, while Nordau's *Degeneration* remains one of the most ridiculous documents of fin-de-siècle cultural criticism. Toril Moi's central argument in her recent study of Ibsen – that Ibsen's modernism springs not from a rejection of "naïve" realism but from a break with nineteenth-century idealism – is an elegant formulation of this perspective.[62]

As Shaw too emphasized, Ibsen in his dramas consistently satirized the idealists – figures like Gregers Werle in *The Wild Duck* – who did what Nordau accused Ibsen himself of doing: "finding beings which embody a thesis." It was these satirized idealists, not their creator, who were the true engineers of what Nordau called the "tube." Ibsen, as *Regeneration* made clear, pointed no moral.

IBSEN, SHAW, REALISM, SATIRE

George Bernard Shaw, in "The Sanity of Art," may have been less thorough than the author of *Regeneration* in rebutting Max Nordau, but his role in the interpretation and propagation of Ibsen in England cannot be overstated. It was Shaw, of course, who made famous the term "Ibsenism." *The Quintessence of Ibsenism* – first written as an address to the Fabian Society in 1890, then published the following year – implied through its title that the Norwegian's writings, already notorious for a couple of years, constituted some kind of unified body of thought. Such an implication would not have been disputed by Edmund Gosse or William Archer; but neither critic had, at this early point, written such an extensive study of Ibsen, or suggested that there might exist an apparent philosophy that could bear his name.

From the time of the *Quintessence*'s publication through the last century of retrospective criticism, it has been generally agreed that for Shaw "Ibsenism" meant something close to "Shavianism": that his slim volume was rather more interested in promoting his own literary-political agenda than in offering a rigorous interpretation of Ibsen's plays.[63] It is true that the book often reads like the manifesto of a young artist, and that it is a foundational document in the development of Shaw's thinking from his earlier novels to his eventual dramas. But the *Quintessence* also bears certain traces of the larger fights about Ibsen that were being waged throughout English criticism. Shaw's study provides some of the earliest vestiges of Ibsen's place in his own thinking – a significance that would have such a profound influence on his own theater – and yet it also includes a direct engagement with the idea of "realism," even if by this term Shaw could mean something quite different from Clement Scott or Max Nordau or even William Archer. I am not interested here in a full-scale interpretation of Shavian drama, or of the Fabian contours of Shaw's thought. My interest lies instead in the ways his notion of Ibsenism would inform Shaw's own writing in the 1890s, especially in his familiar dual impulse toward satire and a form of essentially realist representation.

Among late Victorian observers of Ibsen, "realism" was a term that could range widely in implication: in Edmund Gosse's usage an expression of great praise, in Clement Scott's a sardonic euphemism for obscenity. For Shaw the realist is nothing less than a hero. In *The Quintessence of Ibsenism* "realism" is not primarily a literary device, or a sign of dedication to the representation of gritty or scandalous subjects. Shaw juxtaposes realism and idealism in a familiar manner, but he adds another term to the equation: philistinism. In Shaw's paradigmatic society of a thousand people, as outlined in the *Quintessence*, there are "700 Philistines and 299 idealists, leaving one man unclassified."[64] This last man is the figure Shaw calls "the realist," the only one bold enough to strip away the mask of mere abstractions worn by the idealists. The Philistines see no problem with their contemporary experience – in Shaw's main example, with the rigid British family arrangement – and the 299 idealists recognize it as a failure but lack the courage to "face the fact that they are irremediable failures, since they cannot prevent the 700 satisfied ones from coercing them into conformity with the marriage law" (29–30). The realist is the only one who will translate thought into action, conviction into policy. Shaw defends his choice to call this person the "realist" (rather than the "idealist") because Ibsen himself seems to rail against feeble idealists like Gregers in *The Wild Duck*. And so "the realist at last loses patience with ideals altogether, and sees in them only something to blind us, something to numb us, something to murder self in us ... the realist declares that when a man abnegates the will to live and be free ... then he is morally dead and rotten" (34).

This idea of the moral underpinnings of realism – a moralism that depends on a commitment in the realm of politics – can seem at odds with the more prevalent sense of the term in the late nineteenth century. Literary realism, at least on the surface, usually implied disinterestedness, detached observation, representation rather than action. Shaw himself declared that he did not want to associate realism with "Zola and Maupassant" (33). Indeed, the following year Shaw expressed a distaste for this sense of the term, as it was exemplified by French writers:

Again, in dealing with the drama, I find that the forces which tend to make the theatre a more satisfactory resort for me are rallied for the moment, not round the so-called French realists, whom I should call simply anti-obscurantists, but around the Scandinavian realists; and accordingly I mount their platform, exhort England to carry their cause on to a glorious victory, and endeavor to surround their opponents with a subtle atmosphere of absurdity.[65]

Shaw viewed Zola and the unnamed French dramatists as compilers of facts, enslaved to the literalizing tendencies of pseudo-science; Ibsen, however – the only "Scandinavian realist" to whom Shaw devotes any attention – was fueled by a purpose, a rage that sought social or political change. These assumptions about both Ibsen and Zola are not immune to objection or even refutation, of course. Ibsen never wrote a *J'accuse*. But for Shaw, Ibsen was the exemplary realist because of his central aim: to cut through a thicket of lies and commonplaces in order to expose a searing truth. Such is the rhetoric of the opening pages of the *Quintessence*. Shaw's paradigmatic realist is the figure who shuns the mask of idealism, who can see things clearly enough to know that seeing is not sufficient in itself.

But for Shaw, even despite his dismissal of Zolaesque naturalism, a realism of purpose is not entirely dissociable from a realism of technique and method. The majority of the *Quintessence* consists of his idiosyncratic play-by-play analysis, from *Brand* through *Hedda Gabler*. After discussing the early dramas, Shaw prepares his reader for the transition to *The League of Youth* and especially *The Pillars of Society* by describing Ibsen's position in the 1870s:

Having at last completed his intellectual analysis of idealism, he could now construct methodical illustrations of its social working ... he could see plainly the effect of idealism as a social force on people quite unlike himself: that is to say, on everyday people in everyday life: on shipbuilders, bank managers, parsons, and doctors, as well as on saints, romantic adventurers, and emperors. With his eyes thus opened, instances of the mischief of idealism crowded upon him so rapidly that he began deliberately to inculcate their lesson by writing realistic prose plays of modern life, abandoning all production of art for art's sake. (65)

Shaw's phrasing is reminiscent of Edmund Gosse's descriptions of Ibsen: Gosse similarly emphasized Ibsen's "stern realism" and his representation of "modern life." Although Shaw quarreled with the sense of realism that English literature seemed to have imported largely from French naturalism – a technical orthodoxy, with its pretenses of scientific proced- ure – he nevertheless understood that Ibsen's realism was, at least in part, a matter of method. The purpose that defined Ibsen's theater, as Shaw so stubbornly insisted, depended on the familiar realist underpinnings: the representation of "everyday people in everyday life," the abandonment of verse for prose. It is only through methods like these that Ibsen arrives at that Shavian objective, "the unflinching recognition of facts" (68–9).

Shaw would maintain that such realism was always in the service of something else; in this respect, though they would have never reached consensus about the value of the dramas, Shaw and Max Nordau would have agreed about the didactic essence of Ibsen. G.K. Chesterton later wrote that Shaw "informed everybody that Ibsen was not artistic, but moral; that his dramas were didactic, that all great art was didactic."[66] Chesterton did not mean this as a censure, but in general the criticism on Shaw has found this emphasis on didacticism in Ibsen to be a major error.[67] Keith May, in *Ibsen and Shaw*, encapsulates this view:

Shaw could not perceive that so great a dramatist, so momentous a European event as Ibsen might not be conducting a humanist crusade. Since Shaw wished to improve people he assumed that the satirically observant Ibsen had the same paramount desire. It is true that Ibsen sometimes entertained hopes of improvement (in his private utterances rather than his plays), but such hopes never amounted to a faith, while to Shaw, on the other hand, they unified as well as expressed his personality.[68]

May's reference to the satirical quality of Ibsen is crucial in this context. In the *Quintessence* Shaw rarely uses the term "satirist," but much of his description of Ibsen the realist presupposes an essentially satirical position. Shaw's realist is the figure who sees mere ideas as folly and wants to combat them. Again, the rhetoric of the *Quintessence* is instructive: the realist tears off masks, opposes the conspirators of silence, rails against conventions. In his dramas – *Mrs Warren's Profession* and *Major Barbara*, to take only two examples – Shaw would eventually equate clarity and truth with a fundamentally contrarian attitude toward despised conventions. This equation was born of his understanding of Ibsen. Shaw perceived "realism" and a satirical predisposition as being vitally intertwined in Ibsen's plays; the realist figure *is* the satirist figure, for he understands vague ideals as foolishness and writes for the stage as an act of exposure. It is folly that underlies experience. In order to see things clearly enough to transform them, the writer must confront this basic and fundamental truth of the satiric tradition. In this respect there is no Shavian drama without the precedent of Ibsen, even a misread Ibsen.

In Shaw's drama criticism of the 1890s, collected in *Our Theatres in the Nineties*, the name Henrik Ibsen surfaces in virtually every article, even when the play under review has nothing to do with the Norwegian playwright. The figure that Shaw evokes is consistent with the persona described in the *Quintessence*: a harsh and fearless realist who recoils from nothing. The experience of seeing an Ibsen play is, accordingly, never an occasion for ordinary pleasure. In November 1896 he compares seeing *Little Eyolf* to "a visit to the dentist"; the following month he writes that attending an Ibsen play is like enduring a flogging.[69] During these later years of the decade, just as his own career as a playwright was taking shape, Shaw was still describing Ibsen as an unmasker, whose revelations were the source of genuine discomfort for the spectator. In a review of *John Gabriel Borkman* in January 1897 Shaw wrote that "Ibsen, always terrible in his character of the Plain Dealer, is plainer than ever"; according to Shaw it was this quality, that of the "genuine realist," that continued to baffle English audiences even after the main years of the Ibsen controversies had passed.[70]

Shaw's years as an Ibsenite critic preceded, and then paved the way for, his own eventual emergence as a playwright. But, of course, he had already had a different career before the *Quintessence* launched him into dramatic criticism. Between 1879 and 1883 Shaw had written five novels; it wasn't until the mid-1880s, when these novels were being belatedly published, that he really shifted his attention to journalism. In the books that Shaw would later call "the novels of my nonage" the élan and wit of the dramas are already in full evidence. The protagonist of his 1883 novel, *An Unsocial Socialist*, railing against English small-mindedness and materialism, could be a figure in the later plays:

Modern English polite society, my native sphere, seems to me as corrupt as consciousness of culture and absence of honesty can make it. A canting, lie-loving, fact-hating, scribbling, chattering, wealth-hunting, pleasure-hunting, celebrity-hunting mob, that, having lost the fear of hell, and not replaced it by the love of justice, cares for nothing but the lion's share of the wealth wrung by threat of starvation from the hands of the classes that create it.[71]

Shaw's role as socialist combatant is already firmly in place. Indeed one of these early novels, *Cashel Byron's Profession*, is the tale of a prizefighter, and Shaw never declines an opportunity to suggest that the pugilist might be a potential model for the emergent writer.

And yet to trace Shaw's career in the late nineteenth century is to become conscious of a genuine shift in literary attitude from the novels to the plays. His cavalier satire, his derisive contrarianism, is as evident in *Cashel Byron's Profession* and *An Unsocial Socialist* as it would be in *Major Barbara* and *Arms and the Man*, but the novels are defined by a certain veneer of fantasy that Shaw would modulate in many of his dramas. This is not to say that Shavian theater rejected improbabilities, caprice, or whimsy. But the arc from the novels to the dramas passes through his writings on Ibsen, and it is clear that Shaw was influenced by a realism in Ibsen that involved representation in addition to social philosophy.[72]

In the 1901 preface to the early-1880s *Cashel Byron's Profession*, Shaw looks back with perpetual ironic amusement at his novel-writing days, when "I confess I felt like the peasant in the drawing room" (in the novel itself Lydia Carew, the woman with whom Cashel falls in love, suggests that the boxing ring may be "a better school of character than the drawing room"). In the preface Shaw takes comfort in the fact that "at last I grew out of novel-writing, and set to work to find out what the world was really like." Shaw essentially views the novels of his nonage as failures. "And so between the old stool of my literary conscientiousness and the new stool of a view of life that did not reach publishing-point in England until about ten years later, when Ibsen drove it in, my novels fell to the ground."[73]

Many writers discovered in this same period that it was the novel – *not* the drama – that proved to be their natural mode of literary expression. Henry James returned to fiction after the disaster of *Guy Domville*; Thomas Hardy justified his preference of novels to drama in the 1892 essay "Why I Don't Write Plays," which he contributed to the *Pall Mall Gazette*; George Gissing even expressed his wish that Ibsen had written fiction instead of theater.[74] But Shaw, during these same years, came to the opposite conclusion. As his preface to *Cashel Byron's Profession* suggests, and as so much of his Ibsen criticism seems to confirm, it was ultimately the encounter with Ibsen that set Shaw definitively in the direction of drama. In the preface to *Plays Unpleasant*, three plays written mainly in the 1890s, Shaw explains that an eye doctor in these years informed him that his vision was perfect, or "normal" as compared to most people's "abnormal" bad vision; Shaw then concludes that his "want of success in fiction" was due to the fact that "my mind's eye, like my body's, was 'normal': it saw things differently from other people's eyes, and saw them better."[75]

Many writers would equate such clarity with a specifically novelistic sensibility, but for Shaw this superior vision was at odds with the ornamental curlicues and popular pressures that he believed were inherent in most fiction. Only theater, Shaw believed, could guard him from such bagatelles. In this preface, too, Shaw instinctively connects this revelation to the arrival in his consciousness and in England of Ibsen. The years 1889–1893 were an era of the new, and Ibsen "was the hero of the new departure" (xii). It was precisely the advent of Ibsenism that turned Shaw to the crusade that he had described in the *Quintessence* as the "unflinching recognition of facts"; in the preface to *Plays Unpleasant* he defends the title "Unpleasant" in similar terms: "The reason is pretty obvious: their dramatic power is used to force the spectator to face unpleasant facts" (xxiv–xxv). The aggression in these plays shares the wide-ranging satirical realism that Shaw had learned from Ibsen, so that when he warns his readers that "my attacks are directed against themselves, not against my stage figures," we are immediately reminded of Ibsen's own equation of the theatrical illusion of reality with the recognition that, in his phrase, mankind as a whole was a failure (xxvi). True to the example of Ibsen, Shaw's exposure of unpleasant facts is a simultaneous embrace of realist representation and censorious ends. Though he would hardly abandon fantasy or whimsy in his later dramas, Shaw implies in these writings that it was the theater, not the novel, that allowed him to shape his native satirical impulse to a greater realist idiom. And so Shaw could choose to set the partisan lashes of his satire (what in the preface to *Mrs Warren's Profession* he calls "moral propaganda") in the recognizable spheres of middle-class northeast London in *Candida* or the Salvation Army in *Major Barbara*. Such locales are evidence enough of the strong influence of the Ibsen years.

And yet despite Shaw's great debt to Ibsen, and Shaw's frank acknowledgment that Ibsen pushed him toward confronting the realism of "unpleasant facts," there is a critical difference between the Norwegian's satirical realism and Shavian theater. That difference has everything to do with the larger constellation of satirical realism I have been identifying, and with that literature's lineage not in the comedy of Molière but in the dark satire of Juvenal and Swift. Bernard Shaw, that is to say, is a comic playwright before anything else: he might have pioneered what was essentially an intellectual comedy of manners, but it was still comedy.[76] The feuds (between women; between men; between men and women; between parents and children) that took place in Shaw's drawing rooms were, in that respect, very little like those in Ibsen's. And though some plays end in somewhat ambiguous sadness – *Mrs Warren's Profession*, for example – the more familiar concluding note is that of the fulfillment of the brilliant farce of ideas, as in *Major Barbara*. This elemental difference between the tragic mode of satirical realism and the comic mode of Shavian theater points to another very similar one: Shaw's comedy is a comedy of correction. Shaw's didactic and programmatic satire connects him to that long tradition of satires of correction, from Aristophanes through Molière to (in a more political sense of correction) Orwell. But, as I have insisted throughout this book, satirical realism – Ibsen's no less than Hardy's or Gissing's – is decidedly non-corrective. It is a satire that has relinquished the qualities most often attributed to satire:

humor, but also betterment – whether that notion of betterment takes political form or not. Ibsen would never call his work "moral propaganda," and apart from the most obtuse late Victorian anti-Ibsenites, very few readers or spectators would give it that name either.

In this respect it is revealing that when Shaw actually folds Ibsen explicitly into his own theater, the effect is a transmogrification of the latently tragic into the decidedly farcical. Shaw makes Ibsen nearly a character in *The Philanderer*, one of his three "plays unpleasant." In the preface, Shaw makes the familiar remark that in the 1890s "not only dramatic literature, but life itself was staggering from the impact of Ibsen's plays, which reached us in 1889."[77] Indeed the 1893 *Philanderer*, though at first a perfectly realistic-seeming play set in the drawing room of a London flat, soon begins to stagger under its own weight of Ibsenism. In the second act the scene shifts to the library of the newly founded Ibsen Club, where a bust of Ibsen looks down upon the room, and therefore upon the play. The debate in this act turns on some of the hot-button issues of the day – vivisection, the "New Woman," even the "New Humour" – all under the watchful eye of Ibsen. Shaw's stage directions are described in relation to the bust, so that a character "bolts into the recess on Ibsen's left" or "retires to the recess on Ibsen's right." The act itself, meanwhile, becomes largely a familiar exhibition of Shavian doctrine, with the playwright's mouthpiece at one point declaring: "I loathe all the snares of idealism" (121).

Shaw, so influenced by Ibsen's satire, had bizarrely forged a sort of satire *on* Ibsenism itself. In fact *The Philanderer* was not the only such satire in the late Victorian period. J.M. Barrie wrote a burlesque one-act parody of *Hedda Gabler*, produced at Toole's Theatre in May 1891. In 1893 a volume called *Mr. Punch's Pocket Ibsen*, written by F. Anstey, promised "a collection of the master's best-known dramas condensed, revised, and slightly rearranged for the benefit of the earnest student."[78] The book included satires of *Rosmersholm*, *A Doll's House*, *Hedda Gabler*, *The Wild Duck*, and *The Master Builder*. The characters in these spoofs all refer incessantly to Ibsen himself, and to the controversies that they had originally generated in his plays. Rebecca West: "Am I not an emancipated enigma?" Nora Helmer: "I see my position with the eyes of Ibsen." Haakon Werle: "I have a son who loathes me, and who is either an Ibsenian satire on the Master's own ideals, or else an utterly impossible prig" (24, 85, 147). The volume's most revealing moments of self-consciousness lampoon the idea of realism in particular. Brack in *Hedda Gabler* tells George Tesman: "you forget we are all realistic and unconventional persons here"; Hedda says she has found herself in a "realistic social drama"; Brack agrees that "we're realistic types of human nature, and all that – but a trifle squalid, perhaps." Gregers, in the lampoon of *The Wild Duck*, seeing that Hedvig is about to shoot herself rather than the duck, announces: "It will be a most realistic and impressive finale!" (101, 126, 132, 167).

Of course, in bringing Ibsen so outrageously to the center of the action, *Mr Punch's Pocket Ibsen* and *The Philanderer* both turn him into a subject for pure burlesque.[79] The allusions that both make to realism are entirely submerged in the farce of the whole endeavor; Ibsen is transformed, even in Shaw's admiring hands, into a touchstone for social issues and notoriety. But these two satires from 1893 encapsulate perfectly the perplexity that defined the most famous man in the English literary world – and that ended up surging through English criticism in the 1890s. The staging of *The Philanderer*, though outlandish, is nevertheless an affirmation of Ibsen's centrality in late Victorian culture. It is not a patient or nuanced evaluation of the plays in the tradition of Edmund Gosse or William Archer, nor is it a sustained polemic in the form of Shaw's own *Quintessence*. But the bust of Ibsen, keeping vigil over Englishmen arguing among themselves, still seems faithful to its era. If we are to find fault with it as a metaphor for Ibsen's authority in late Victorian England, we can do so for only one reason: it is simply far too obvious.

CHAPTER 5

Truth and caricature in
The Secret Agent

Joseph Conrad completed *The Secret Agent* in 1906, but it was not until the following year that he first turned to crafting the title page and dedication to H.G. Wells. In June 1907 he wrote to his agent, J.B. Pinker: "I am thinking of dedicating the vol to Wells. I hinted something of that to him already. The full title I wish to run like this: "THE/ SECRET AGENT/ A Simple Tale." By the following month, when Conrad wrote directly to Wells to announce the dedication formally, the novel's subtitle had expanded: "To/ H.G. Wells/ The Chronicler of Mr Lewisham's Love/ The Biographer of Kipps and/ The Historian of the Ages to Come/ This Simple tale of the XIX Century/ is affectionately inscribed."[1]

Why did Conrad's "Simple Tale" become a "Simple tale of the Nineteenth Century"? The modest caption was suspicious enough on its own; now it was paired, almost paradoxically, with a rather grandiose declaration that Conrad's new novel had something consequential to say about the century just concluded. The most obvious explanation for Conrad's phrase is the book's chronology: based on the notorious Greenwich Park bomb outrage of 1894, *The Secret Agent* takes place in that same era, in 1887. It is a book that pivots on the fin de siècle: written just after the century's turn, set just before it. And yet it is clear that Conrad did not merely revise his subtitle to acknowledge a real-life analogue that he was usually eager to disavow anyway. Conrad wanted his simple tale to be an ironic elegy to something more than merely a nineteenth-century subject and setting. It was to be a different kind of book from his previous efforts; it was to be darkly ironic and murky in tone – closer in genre, perhaps, to late Victorian novels like *New Grub Street* than to *Lord Jim* or *Nostromo*. *The Secret Agent* is a pure byproduct of the final years of the nineteenth century – the Edwardian apotheosis of the satirical realism that characterized the late Victorian era – and therefore the inescapable final document in this study of satire in an age of realism.

To locate *The Secret Agent* at the crossroads of satire and realism is to understand fundamentally that the book occupies an uncommon position in Conrad's fiction. Such an understanding is entirely consistent with the author's: Conrad himself was the first to acknowledge that the novel was exceptional within his body of work. In May 1907 – a month before he crafted his first dedication to Wells, while he was still awaiting the proofs of the novel – he wrote to Pinker:

Do not doubt for a moment that I will do all I can to get the S.A. ready for the printer soon. If there is a hurry I will leave off Chance completely for a fortnight or so. I suppose it will be just as well. My only anxiety was to get Chance forward – you understand. The S.A. however has its importance as a distinctly new departure in my work. And I am anxious to put as much 'quality' as I can in that book which will be criticised with some severity no doubt – or *scrutinised* rather, I should say. Preconceived notions of Conrad as sea writer will stand in the way of its acceptance. You can see this Yourself. (434)

Five months later, writing to R.B. Cunninghame Graham just after the publication of the novel, Conrad expressed things in similar terms:

I am glad you liked the *S Agent.* Vous comprenez bien that the story was written completely without malice. It had some importance for me as a new departure in *genre* and as a sustained effort in ironical treatment of a melodramatic subject – which was my technical intention. (491)

Twice Conrad uses that same formulation: *The Secret Agent* is a "new departure" in his work. The phrase, at first glance, may seem ironic – just as his claim that the book is "without malice" seems disingenuous. The 1907 novel, after all, is exceptional in part because it is *not* a departure: for the first time Conrad's narrative does not depart for the foreign terrain of the Congo, or Patusan, or Costaguana; instead it stays close to home, in the obscure streets and murky offices of London. In an earlier letter, written in French to the editor and translator H.D. Davray the previous November, Conrad makes this difference quite explicit:

Je viens de finir un roman (?) où il n'y a pas une goutte d'eau – excepté de la pluie, ce qui est bien naturel puisque tout se passe à Londres. Il y a là dedans une demi-douzaine d'anarchistes, deux femmes et un idiot. Du reste ils sont tous des imbéciles ... (372)[2]

There is not a drop of water in Conrad's new novel, of course, because he has left behind African rivers, the Java Sea, and the harbor of Sulaco;

in the phrase of his letter to Pinker, he is no longer Conrad the "sea writer." The novelist would say essentially the same thing in his 1920 Author's Note to *The Secret Agent*, where he distinguishes the London of the novel from the setting of his previous fiction, "that remote novel, *Nostromo*, with its far-off Latin-American atmosphere."[3]

But in this letter to Davray there is something more peculiar, more perplexing, than the emphasis on the novel's urban locale. For some reason Conrad places a mysterious parenthetical question mark after "roman." He cannot seem to bring himself to call *The Secret Agent* simply a "novel"; instead he feels compelled to call it a "novel (?)." In light of his repeated emphasis on the exceptional status of this book, it is tempting to ask why *The Secret Agent* cannot just be a novel, a novel in the sense that *Lord Jim* and *Nostromo* had been novels. The reason cannot simply be that in its subtitle Conrad called it a "tale." Conrad always stresses that two things are vitally different about *The Secret Agent*: it is set in London, and it is dominated by a pronounced irony. In the October 1907 letter to R.B. Cunninghame Graham, Conrad had called this "new departure" a "departure in *genre*," explaining that it was a "sustained effort in ironic treatment." Elsewhere in his correspondence Conrad writes of his commitment to the "ironic treatment of the whole matter"; and in the Author's Note he declares his "earnest belief that ironic treatment alone would enable me to say all I felt I would have to say in scorn as well as in pity."[4]

The great interest of Conrad's 1907 masterpiece lies in the simultaneity of these two qualities in his writing: his turn toward a far less remote setting and atmosphere, and his immersion in an irony more ruthless and more total than in any of his previous fictions. *The Secret Agent* is at once Conrad's most "realist" novel – if we are to understand the term in its late Victorian sense, as an unyielding immersion in facts and characterizations that are not always pleasant – and his most satirical book, his most mocking and censorious effort. Some readers of Conrad have remarked upon the shades of satire in *The Secret Agent*, focusing mostly on the tendency of characterization to slide into caricature: these critics will be considered here. But no one has asked what connects these harsh ironies to the novel's concomitant anti-mythic mode of representation and non-exotic sphere, to its dark urban realism. For Conrad, as for Hardy with *Jude the Obscure* and Gissing with *New Grub Street*, satire and a peculiar hyperrealism emerged strongest within the same novel.

With Conrad in particular, the mode of satirical realism – this convergence of scrupulous description and unrelenting ridicule – threatened, in his own estimation, to banish his London novel from the category in which his previous books rested more comfortably. The novel's claim to being a novel, with the implications of sympathy and expansiveness that Conrad seems to have associated with that form, began to wane; *roman* had to be followed by a question mark. "As to novels I have written something which is certainly fiction of a sort," Conrad wrote to Sidney Colvin in 1906, "but whether it's a novel or not I'll leave it to the critics to say" (381). This is the essential question that *The Secret Agent* poses. If it is not a novel then it must be something else: perhaps something best called a satire. Or maybe Conrad's "roman (?)," his "fiction of a sort," belongs to the hybrid genre that defined the late Victorian era he was dramatizing. *The Secret Agent* is as pure an exemplar of satirical realism as English fiction has ever produced, a book in which seeing and scorning become two words for the same thing.

THE WHOLE TOWN OF MARVELS AND MUD

Like Flaubert and Hardy before him, Conrad could never bring himself to embrace the term "realism" or the school of fiction that bore its name. In the 1897 preface to *The Nigger of the 'Narcissus'* he speaks out against the "temporary formulas" of the writer's craft – "Realism, Romanticism, Naturalism" – as doctrines that ultimately betray the novelist in his quest for a less namable truth.[5] His 1905 essay "Books" finds him using a similar phrase:

Liberty of imagination should be the most precious possession of a novelist. To try voluntarily to discover the fettering dogmas of some romantic, realistic, or naturalistic creed in the free work of its own inspiration is a trick worthy of human perverseness, which, after inventing an absurdity, endeavours to find for it a pedigree of distinguished ancestors.[6]

In both cases "realism" may be no worse than any other school of fiction that pretends to operate according to a set of rules or principles – but then it is no better either. Still, on certain occasions Conrad objected to realism and naturalism with particular vehemence, largely because his emergence as a novelist coincided with the heyday of those movements in England. In 1899 he said naturalism was "very old-fashioned"; in 1906 he called it mere "Zola jargon"; in a 1902 letter to Arnold Bennett he protested against any such doctrinaire program: "you stop just short of being absolutely real because you are faithful to your dogmas of realism."[7]

Still, it would not be unwise to invoke "realism" – even with its specific literary-historical connotations – when examining *The Secret Agent*. Such a critical perspective does not have to depend on the fact that the novel is based on a real-life event from 1894; nor does it need to proceed, as Norman Sherry does in *Conrad's Western World*, by trying to locate the actual personage upon whom Conrad might have based each character in his story.[8] Conrad himself freely remarked that something was different about his book of 1907, and that this was related in part to scene and perspective. Some of his most discerning readers have described this shift by reference to realism: Albert Guerard, for instance, writes of the "major change from the impressionist to the realist method" that marked *The Secret Agent* and Conrad's subsequent novel, *Under Western Eyes*.[9] Ian Watt's pronouncement could serve as the final word on the subject: "In short, although *The Secret Agent* is neither a historical nor a Natural- istic novel, its distance from reality, though varying, is never very great."[10] Such critical judgments should not evoke much controversy. They under- stand that *The Secret Agent* invites our invocations of "realism" if only in comparison to Conrad's earlier fiction: whereas his previous narratives had been set far away, with exotic characters and mythic allusion, this book is crisper in the detail of modern urban experience, mostly ordinary in characterization, and set in a far more recognizable sphere.

Conrad had already visited this recognizable sphere of London at least once before. On the opening page of *Heart of Darkness* we find Marlow and the crew of the *Nellie* at rest on the Thames: they are in Gravesend, but in the distance can be glimpsed "the biggest, and the greatest, town on earth" under a thick, gloomy haze.[11] London was indeed the world's biggest city; and if Conrad intends some irony in calling it the greatest, it is not the kind of irony that defines *The Secret Agent*. But in the roughly eight years that passed between *Heart of Darkness* and that novel, as London grew from a novella's framing backdrop to a novel's total uni- verse, the Conradian city was transformed utterly. *The Secret Agent* thrusts us into the city's streets from its very first page, as Adolf Verloc leaves his shop one morning; after the first chapter pauses to set the domestic scene, we continue with Verloc past Hyde Park Corner and through Knights- bridge on his way to the embassy in Chesham Square. As Conrad follows Verloc – and later Ossipon, Chief Inspector Heat, Winnie, and the other Londoners – he pauses frequently to linger on the streetscapes, all of which seem to refer back to all the others. At the end of the fourth chapter, for example, after Ossipon's first meeting with the Professor, the narrator describes an ordinary corner outside the Silenus bar:

In front of the great door way a dismal row of newspaper sellers standing clear of the pavement dealt out their wares from the gutter. It was a raw, gloomy day of the early spring; and the grimy sky, the mud of the streets, the rags of the dirty men, harmonised excellently with the eruption of the damp, rubbishy sheets of paper soiled with printers' ink. The posters, maculated with filth, garnished like tapestry the sweep of the curbstone. (65)

A vision like this would not be out of place in *New Grub Street* – indeed it seems to embody the very title of Gissing's novel. Each thing here is defined by its grime. The vendors are filthy; the newspaper is soiled by the very ink it is supposed to parade; the posters make the very sidewalk dirty; even the sky is polluted. Conrad seems to want every part of his urban scene to blend into the dirt of every other one: in his phrase the sky, streets, and men "harmonised excellently" with the damp newspapers, and ultimately with the posters and the curb. This filthy scene is entirely typical of *The Secret Agent*. Much later in the novel, after Winnie murders her husband, she flees the Verloc house for the city outside: "the whole town of marvels and mud, with its maze of streets and its mass of lights, was sunk in a hopeless night" (203). And at the end of that chapter, after Ossipon abandons Winnie on the train, he returns home through "distant parts of the enormous town slumbering monstrously on a carpet of mud under a veil of raw mist ... through monotonous streets with unknown names where the dust of humanity settles inert and hopeless out of the stream of life" (224).

Two things stand out most of all: the mud, and the sheer immensity of the capital. In the Author's Note, Conrad describes the genesis of the novel with a similar phrase: "the vision of an enormous town presented itself, of a monstrous town more populous than some continents and in its man-made might as if indifferent to heaven's frowns and smiles, a cruel devourer of the world's light" (6).[12] But something else recurs again and again, beyond merely the size of the city: at every opportunity Conrad focuses on the leveling effect of the different places and qualities of London, to the point that they cease to be very discrete or individualized at all. His favorite leitmotif is the mud; but every time he evokes the wholeness, the mass of lights, the enormity of a city of monotonous streets, he is emphasizing the absolute uniformity of the urban sphere, the city as aggregate.

To take any segment of Conrad's London is to take the entire city: it seems always to be a cross-section. For this reason it is dangerous to assimilate Conrad too closely to Dickens, even if at first glance *The Secret Agent*'s capital of fog and dirt seems to invite comparison to *Bleak House* and *Our Mutual Friend.* In *Bleak House* Chancery is very different from the Dedlock estate, which in turn is entirely separate from Tom-all-Alone's; in *Our Mutual Friend* the Podsnap house is not the same thing as the Harmon house. The zones of Dickens's satire are usually sequestered, cordoned off from much of the rest of the novel, such that Chancery or the Circumlocution Office of *Little Dorrit* typically seem like self-contained worlds. In Conrad there is little hope for such consoling partition. (And in this respect Conrad is remarkably similar to Gissing, in whose fiction I have insisted on an identical departure from the Dickensian model of quarantined satirical representation.) Martin Price, in still the finest study of Conrad and satire, arrives at the same conclusion:

> In Dickens's novels we often move between satire and the novelistic. Some characters exist entirely within a satiric world ... Dickens's freedom in moving between modes has the confidence of an author who is not hobbled by doctrines of realism and who is constantly in touch with the supple conventions of popular art. Conrad learned much from Dickens's verbal wit, but his effects are less exuberant and far more studied.[13]

Indeed it makes sense that Dickensian narrative would move "between" worlds. In Dickens there are heroes and there are villains; some figures are virtually angelic and others are purely caricatures. Different kinds of characters need to inhabit different kinds of zones. Conrad, on the other hand, flattens the sphere of representation, insisting on the uniformity of that sphere, such that everyone in his London of folly and mud will be forced to occupy the same realm as everyone else.

Perhaps it is inevitable that readers would compare the London of *The Secret Agent* to the London of Dickens: Dickens's version dominates English fiction, and subsequent novelists are fated to imagine the city in his shadow. But ultimately it may not be Dickens who provides the best model for the urban vision of Conrad's novel. *The Secret Agent* seems to owe a much greater debt to a more essential mode of satire, a strain that does not keep the censure quarantined, as Dickens does, but instead tends to view the entire city – and the entire *idea* of the city – as suspect and contemptible. The source of this tradition lies in Horace's satire on city and country (book 2, satire 6) and especially in Juvenal's furious third satire. Juvenal begins by commending his friend's decision to leave Rome for Cumae: "myself, I'd prefer a barren island to down-town Rome:/ what squalor, what isolation would not be minor evils/ compared to an endless nightmare of fires and collapsing/ houses, the myriad perils encountered in this brutal/ city."[14] Juvenal rails against the poverty, danger, insomnia, crowds, and shoddy housing that define Rome, directing his fiercest animus at the city's Greek population. There is no sanctuary in Juvenal's Rome; the only option is to escape it altogether.

Samuel Johnson's "London," written in imitation of Juvenal's third satire, views the eighteenth-century English capital in much the same way. Like Juvenal, Johnson sees no advantage to urban life if the alternative is the countryside – even if later in his career he would voice revulsion for the whole genre of pastoral.[15] "Who would leave," he asks at the beginning of the poem, "unbribed, Hibernia's land,/ Or change the rocks of Scotland for the Strand?"[16] In a sense Dr. Johnson's unrelenting London satire may be the most reliable precursor for Conrad's version of 1907. For Johnson, as for Juvenal, urban reality was the essential food for satirical treatment: indeed it was "London" that inspired Boswell's observation that "great cities, in every age, and in every country, will furnish similiar topicks of satire."[17] Conrad's imagination is informed by the same innate equation, and at times his capital city bears a rather striking resemblance to Dr. Johnson's. When he writes near the beginning of *The Secret Agent*, for example, that Verloc "generally arrived in London (like the influenza) from the Continent" (11), he seems virtually to be echoing Johnson's own verses for a capital city absorbing its filth from abroad: "London! the needy villain's general home,/ The common shore of Paris and of Rome;/ With eager thirst, by folly or by fate,/ Sucks in the dregs of each corrupted state" (lines 93–6). This does not mean that Conrad's position in *The Secret Agent* was a plainly xenophobic one – he himself, of course, was from beyond the English shore – but rather that he, like Johnson, was nonetheless drawn to the idea of a London contaminated by influences from without.[18]

And yet we must also remember that Conrad, unlike Juvenal or Johnson, does not really give us any sense in *The Secret Agent* of how a world beyond London might be, or indeed whether such a world even exists. There is no Conradian equivalent to Juvenal's Cumae or Johnson's Scotland; there is no Arcadia elsewhere. As Conrad himself had made clear in that 1906 letter to H.D. Davray, "tout se passe à Londres": *everything* takes place there. The monotonous streets never seem to lead outward. Even when Winnie, near the end of the novel, takes the train out of London, we do not follow her – we only hear of her eventual suicide as she crosses the Channel. The overall effect is an acute sense of urban claustrophobia. And so, in a fundamental respect, Conrad's design is far harsher than any traditional satire that opposes the vice of the city to the virtue of the country. In *The Secret Agent*, Conrad seems to say, the English city, unusually gray and particularly sordid as it may be, could, in fact, be representative of a far more universal condition, one that ignores municipal or, indeed, any sort of geographical boundaries. The novel's satire seems defined by the scope of its urban realism: this realism dictates and shapes the satire, and so if the city is rendered as a totality, and if there is no Dickensian demarcation of bad from good, then this world of filth and folly may be, simply, all there is.

This kind of absolute perspective – a perspective that tells us: this is what the world looks like, this is how dark and polluted it is, and sadly there may not be any alternative – is the sort of perspective that informed *Jude the Obscure, New Grub Street,* and many of Ibsen's prose dramas. It is a literary attitude that seeks to ridicule the world, but only by operating on the premise that this is exactly how the world is. In *The Secret Agent* such satirical realism functions through a synthesis of two interpenetrating points of view: by moving through the city slowly, following individual characters and thereby amassing great detail; and by viewing London from a greater distance, enabling a supreme perspective that can recall Hardy's predilection for satire from above. Conrad seems drawn, in particular, to pseudo-panoramic representations of the urban crowd as a teeming mass of indistinguishable people, in the fashion of Gissing in books like *The Nether World.* Such visions of the crowd are especially characteristic of the scenes involving the Professor, who snakes his way interminably through the dirty streets. In the fifth chapter he gets swept up in the throng:

He was in a long, straight street, peopled by a mere fraction of an immense multitude; but all round him, on and on, even to the limits of the horizon hidden by the enormous pile of bricks, he felt the mass of mankind mighty in its numbers. They swarmed numerous like locusts, industrious like ants, thoughtless like a natural force, pushing on blind and orderly and absorbed, impervious to sentiment, to logic, to terror too perhaps. (67)

It is almost beside the point to ask whether a passage like this is in the free indirect style or not, whether its voice comes from this character or from a detached narrator, since the novel's own perspective never differs much at all. This is the same perspective that informs most of the book and indeed marks its finale, as the Professor passes again "like a pest in the street full of men" and Conrad's narrative camera seems to lift above the crowd, much as it might at the end of a film.

In Conrad's fiction this point of view is not unique to *The Secret Agent.* Early in *Heart of Darkness,* for instance, Marlow recalls a moment on the

Congo when he could see that "a lot of people, mostly black and naked, moved about like ants"; when Marlow is back in Brussels, his resentment of "the sight of people hurrying through the streets to filch a little money from each other, to devour their infamous cookery, to gulp their unwholesome beer, to dream their insignificant and silly dreams" is, in a sense, a similar condescension toward the masses despite the change of locale and population (17, 88). In the later novel *Under Western Eyes,* Conrad compares Razumov's "large, neutral pity" toward another character, Ziemianitch, to "such as one may feel for an unconscious multitude, a great people seen from above – like a community of crawling ants working out its destiny."[19]

The people "seen from above" is a fine symbol for Conrad's suspicion and satirical detachment, even if the passage suggests that such a point of view can be a kind of pity for the multitudes. In truth the most illuminating word in this analogy – a word both accurate and misleading – is "neutral." If Conrad often assumes this detached kind of perspective, this long view, it must be said that he shades it to be at once a neutral, disinterested omniscient perspective *and* a vision of such disdain that we can no longer really call it neutral. Rarely is it a perspective of pity. This is the narrative eye of Hardy observing Jude Fawley from a robin's perch in a tree, or of Gissing looking down from Clara Hewett's window upon the paltry human beings of Farringdon Street in *The Nether World.* It is the essential narrative perspective of satirical realism – the literalization of Flaubert's *blague supérieure* – since it seems to embody both the neutrality of omniscience and the derision of ridicule. Indeed the view from above can be understood as belonging equally to the traditions of satire and realism. Kate Flint, in *The Victorians and the Visual Imagination,* credits the new aerial views of London from balloons in the 1860s with providing a more literal, thorough, and totalizing perspective on the urban scene below; Linda Nochlin makes a similar point that in nineteenth-century realist art the "most typical and novel Realist city view is the *distant* view" influenced by "the view of the city from above" pioneered by Nadar in his 1856 balloon trips over Paris and rendered in caricature by Daumier; and Alexander Welsh, in *The City of Dickens,* connects this same balloon perspective to the images of the city in Dickens's contemporaneous satire. In *Realist Vision,* Peter Brooks identifies a proto-realism in the images of the devilish agent peeking below rooftops in *Le Diable boiteux.*[20] When observed from the sky the teeming city can be seen in its totality, and the observer can therefore claim to know it with something approaching omniscient supremacy. But people glimpsed from far above – from the observation deck of a skyscraper, for example – always risk looking ridiculous: small and therefore insignificant. (This is precisely what Orson Welles's Harry Lime tells Joseph Cotten's Holly Martins in the famous Ferris wheel scene in *The Third Man*.) The realism of the view from above is therefore paired inevitably with a certain satirical disdain. In *The Secret Agent*, and throughout much of his fiction, Conrad zooms out from the specific details of the drama to expose humans for the locusts and ants they threaten to become, if only as a consequence of their sheer number. Everything can be seen as at the beginning of *The Secret Agent*'s second chapter: under a "peculiar London sun" that encompasses the entire city with its bloodshot stare.[21]

MAN AND MANKIND

The problem facing Conrad in *The Secret Agent* was similar to Gissing's quandary in *New Grub Street* and *Born in Exile*: how to take in both person and people; how to reconcile an impulse to scorn the masses with the pressure to represent individual human beings with nuance and perhaps sympathy. Usually it seems that Conrad imports his generalized condescension to the local satire of his specific characters. A quick overview of the residents of Conrad's London exposes a city of torpor, grotesquerie, pallor, and alternating obesity and gauntness: Adolf Verloc is "very corpulent," "burly in a pig-fat style"; Michaelis is "round like a tub, with an enormous stomach and distended cheeks of a pale, semi-transparent complexion ... round like a distended balloon"; Karl Yundt has a "faint black grimace of a toothless mouth" and a "skinny groping hand deformed by gouty swellings"; the Professor is always emaciated and filthy, defined by the "lamentable inferiority of the whole physique"; and Sir Ethelred has puffy eyes that "stared with a haughty droop on each side of a hooked, aggressive nose, nobly salient in the vast pale circumference of the face" (20, 16, 37, 43, 38, 52, 105–6). Conrad typically emphasizes the unsightliness of his characters right when he introduces them – especially if they are fat. J. Hillis Miller writes: "With something of a shock the reader realizes how many of the characters in *The Secret Agent* are fat. Conrad seems to be insisting on their gross bodies, as if their fatness were connected with the central themes of the novel."[22]

Obesity does indeed seem essential to the novel: these fat men, much like the shriveled men, embody the sickly city they inhabit. But Conrad's propensity for this kind of caricature does not sit well with many of his readers. Irving Howe, in *Politics and the Novel*, finds that with the anarchists, in particular, "the burlesque is too vindictive, the malice too cruel," and with regard to the Professor that "it is difficult to regard this grimy lunatic as anything but a cartoon"; Norman Sherry similarly finds every anarchist to be "a grimy cartoon."[23] To a great extent it is this cartoonish tendency that can recall Dickens so strongly. And at times the proximity to Dickensian characterization seems astonishingly close: when Conrad writes of Winnie's mother that "the married couple took her over with the furniture," or later that Stevie "had been taken over with his mother, somewhat in the same way as the furniture of the Belgravian mansion had been taken over," we are reminded of *Our Mutual Friend*'s Twemlow, introduced as a dining table in the Veneering house.[24] Conrad, like Dickens, is drawn instinctively to the kinship of the inanimate and the animate. The player piano in the scenes at the Silenus bar is a magnificent example of this idea: a machine that functions perfunctorily and unconsciously, without human participation, it is unnervingly similar to the idea of man as automaton, exceedingly flabby but not necessarily deliberate or even organic.[25]

And yet like the comparison of Conrad's city to Dickens's city, the analogy between Dickensian and Conradian versions of characterization is as misleading as it is tempting. In the era of *The Secret Agent*, Conrad's perspective on character was quite similar to his view of London: he seemed unable to keep his revulsion limited to specific people, much as he was incapable of imagining certain zones of the city to be exempt from the lashings of his satire. His letters of the period are striking for the way individual characterization is transformed into the despondency of generalized misanthropy. In October 1906 he writes to Pinker: "I feel quite wretched and overdone not with work but with the anxiety this beast Verloc causes me"; the following month he tells John Galsworthy: "I've finished Verloc, and am very sick of it. There is a month's work in it yet and perhaps more. I am in a state of such depression as I have not known for years"; the next year, when the revisions are nearly finished, he writes again to Galsworthy: "Now and then I steal an hour or two to work at preparing the Secret Agent for book form. And all this is pretty ghastly. I seem to move, talk, write in a sort of quiet nightmare that goes on and on. I wouldn't wish my worst enemy this experience."[26] By "Verloc" Conrad means the novel generally, but in each case it is the characters of that novel that trigger such disgust and antipathy. He never forgets to remind his correspondents that the agony of writing emerges from the contempt in which he holds his imagined people. In the November 1906 letter to H.D. Davray to which I alluded earlier, he makes this most plain: *The Secret Agent* is populated by "a half-dozen anarchists, two women, and an idiot. In any case, they're all imbeciles."

Conrad suffered from depression several times in his life, but disconsolate letters like these suggest that the malaise of 1906–1907 was a nausea that emerged specifically from such a relentless immersion in satirical representation, from such an unremitting program of derision. Desolation like this does not evoke Dickens, even if Dickens could surely despair in his private writings. Here Conrad reveals his more significant debt to his real precursor, Flaubert. Conrad's torture in composing *The Secret Agent* is strikingly similar to Flaubert's affliction and near self-immolation as a writer, especially as recorded in his letters to Louise Colet during the creation of *Madame Bovary*. Flaubert tried repeatedly to express the disgust that his characters instilled in him, nowhere more bluntly than in one August 1853 letter:

Bovary, which has been an excellent exercise for me, may end up causing me a disastrous *reaction*, since I've developed (and this is weak and stupid on my part) an extreme disgust for such common characters. That's why I've had so much trouble writing this book. I need to make a great effort to imagine my characters and then make them speak, because they repel me so profoundly.[27]

This is remarkably prescient of Conrad, who filled his own novel with repugnant figures: "they're all imbeciles." The peopling of *The Secret Agent* was not a question of satirizing certain inhabitants and redeeming others; for Conrad it was nothing less than a crucible of characterization. As with Flaubert, the unwavering commitment to the naked representation of human situations and specimens created an antipathy so severe that it rendered his task almost unbearable. Caricature is one thing when contained within circumscribed sectors of a novel, but it turns from a technique into an attitude when it pervades an entire fictional world. In *The Secret Agent* it became a total way of seeing things.[28]

With Conrad we get the sense that this profound revulsion existed inevitably at the furthest reaches of the realist project, where the relentless depiction of ugly detail and unflattering character blurs indistinguishably into satire. This is Flaubert's legacy, bequeathed not only to Conrad but to any writer who similarly pursues what Edmund Gosse called "the limits of realism in fiction." In this respect Conrad's experience writing *The Secret Agent* recalls not only Flaubert but also Robert Louis Stevenson, who joined the fray of the late Victorian realism debates with his 1883 essay "A Note on Realism." Stevenson – like most of his contemporaries, skeptical of the term and the school – nevertheless acknowledged that "we of the last quarter of the nineteenth century, breathing as we do the intellectual atmosphere of our age, are more apt to err upon the side of realism than to sin in quest of the ideal."[29] Stevenson endured his own struggle with the bleaker mode of late Victorian realism in his novella *The Ebb-Tide*, the composition of which engendered Flaubertian agony much like Conrad's. At first, despite his reservations about "realism," he announced to Sidney Colvin in 1892 that "I am a realist and a prosaist, and a most fanatical lover of plain physical sensations plainly and expressly rendered."

Soon, however, Stevenson began to worry about the "queer realism," "naked writing" and "vilely realistic dialogue" of his fiction; "I have got too realistic," Stevenson concluded.[30] In 1893 he wrote to Henry James: "it seems as if literature were coming to a stand. I am sure it is with me; and I am sure everybody will say so when they have the privilege of reading *The Ebb-Tide*. My dear man, the grimness of that story is not to be depicted in words. There are only four characters, to be sure, but they are such a troop of swine!" (214). Stevenson's experience now sounds familiar enough that we can understand it to be representative of his era. His troop of swine became Conrad's horde of imbeciles: for certain late Victorian and Edwardian novelists, the pursuit of squalid detail quickly resulted in a general distaste for the characters who have to populate their stories.[31] This distaste, in turn, engendered a near impasse in the very writing of fiction.[32]

The realist project of examining small and unheroic detail offers itself as the consummate fictional mode for looking at individual people. Satire, with its directive to identify shared and common folly, seems more naturally suited to presenting a wider, more allegorized canvas of human existence. As I have emphasized in my interpretation of other writers – George Eliot and George Gissing especially – the hybrid genre satirical realism thus poses a fundamental question about the relation of individual persons to a larger category called mankind. In *The Secret Agent* Conrad often obscures the very distinction, such that individual human action cannot be very easily distilled from the novel's essentializing pronouncements on human nature. Conrad's method here is his steady dependence on the word "mankind," one of the definitional terms of *The Secret Agent*. In his Author's Note he writes that the story of the 1894 Greenwich Park outrage that gave rise to the novel exposed "a mankind always so tragically eager for self-destruction" (5). In the novel itself the word appears so systematically as to become the key motif in the highly regulated pattern of Conrad's narrative. Verloc possesses "the air common to men who live on the vices, the follies, or the baser fears of mankind"; the Professor feels "the mass of mankind mighty in its numbers"; the London rain exposes "the lofty pretensions of a mankind oppressed by the miserable indignities of the weather"; an Italian restaurant betrays "an atmosphere of fraudulent cookery mocking an abject mankind in the most pressing of its miserable necessities"; a cabman's paltry fare "symbolised the insignificant results which reward the ambitious courage and toil of a mankind whose day is short on this earth of evil"; in that same scene Stevie, "like the rest of mankind," mistakenly trusts the "organized powers of the earth"; and, on the final page, we are reunited with the Professor once again, as he averts his eyes from the "odious multitude of mankind."[33]

In fact, this is only a short list. The word surfaces so regularly in *The Secret Agent* that it begins to seem nearly as ridiculous as the mankind Conrad has set forth to mock. In many cases "mankind" is invoked in the most banal contexts: the rain, a restaurant, the cost of a cab ride. But sometimes Conrad appears to be entirely serious in making such declarations. His reference in the Author's Note to the self-destructiveness of mankind, or the Professor's announcement in the final chapter that "mankind ... does not know what it wants" (227), give us no reason to interpret them with much irony: they seem fully consistent with the vision of the novel. In the figure of the Professor, Conrad has hardly created a representative for himself, but when he writes that this mad terrorist has moments of "dreadful and sane mistrust of mankind" (67), we cannot help feeling that there is a bizarre underlying identification, a sneaking sympathy that cannot be repressed.

Indeed such axioms and judgments recall Conrad's description of the main character in his early story "An Outpost of Progress": "He had been all his life, till that moment, a believer in a lot of nonsense like the rest of mankind – who are fools."[34] Conrad, that is to say, usually invokes mankind in order to scorn it, and to transform his judgment of one character into a much grander and more withering condemnation. In this respect the final line of the Author's Note – "I have not intended to commit a gratuitous outrage on the feelings of mankind" – seems remarkably disingenuous, like much of the Note ("there was no perverse intention, no secret scorn for the natural sensibilities of mankind at the bottom of my impulses").[35] To scorn mankind, then to disavow such abuse: Conrad too often wants to have it both ways. But in the final equation his decrees against mankind are too rigorous, and too frequent, for his concomitant gestures in humanity's defense to be particularly capable of overriding them.

At first such grand assertions about mankind's ignorance and foolishness seem to indicate a strong confidence on Conrad's part: that he knows exactly what humans are and what humans are not. But in truth the author of *The Secret Agent* was radically uncertain about the definition and shape of mankind. Conrad's aphorisms should ultimately be seen as evidence of his effort to ascertain the essential properties of man – what ultimately constitutes man – as much as they may attest to his apparent conviction that all men are fools. This kind of hesitation peers out from behind motifs like furniture and the player piano, but in *The Secret Agent* Conrad's uncertainty about mankind is expressed most consistently through the juxtaposition of man and animal. I have already indicated the Conradian predilection for related metaphors: his comparisons of a human crowd to a colony of ants, for example. But in *The Secret Agent* the method goes beyond the metaphorical. Conrad seems intent on situating his men – usually fat, grotesque beasts in the first place – alongside creatures of an ostensibly subhuman intelligence: idiots, then ultimately animals themselves. As a result the line becomes blurred, and the precise relation and distance obscured, between man and beast.

The idiot in *The Secret Agent* is, of course, Stevie; and it is with Stevie that we walk the novel's line between varieties of beast. Conrad introduces him as "easily diverted from the straight path of duty by the attractions of stray cats and dogs, which he followed down narrow alleys into unsavoury courts" (13). A remark like this might pass unnoticed were it not for the novel's great set piece, the cab ride of Stevie, Winnie, and their mother in the eighth chapter. As they make their way through the city in their decrepit vehicle, Stevie's attention is focused entirely on the frail horse that is only barely able to pull them along:

Stevie was staring at the horse, whose hindquarters appeared unduly elevated by the effect of emaciation. The little stiff tail seemed to have been fitted in for a heartless joke; and at the other end the thin, flat neck, like a plank covered with old horse hide, drooped to the ground under the weight of an enormous bony head. The ears hung at different angles, negligently; and the macabre figure of that mute dweller on the earth steamed straight up from ribs and backbone in the muggy stillness of the air. (128)

The drama of the scene is essentially two-fold: the group's difficulty traveling in such a dilapidated cab, and Stevie's intense distress as he watches the suffering of the horse. The horse is not the only "mute dweller" here. Stevie too is an essentially non-verbal creature, though the cab ride does motivate him to speak most of the few words he is able to utter in the novel. When the driver whips the horse, and even after the cab ride is over, Stevie releases a series of pained grunts and cries: "Don't whip," "It hurts," "Bad! Bad!", "Poor! Poor!", "Poor brute," "Bad world for poor people," "Beastly!" (122–32).

Our first reaction may be to laugh at Stevie's howls – much as we want to laugh at the image of an idiot chasing cats and dogs down alleyways. There is an uneasy sort of humor here, in the nearness of humans and their folly to animals that share familiar characteristics – in the case of the horse, pain. This nearness carries a whiff of the ridiculous, much like the opening and closing chapters of Conrad's first novel *Almayer's Folly*, where a monkey will not stop peering and grinning at the cursed title character.[36] But Conrad's satire in these scenes is typically grave. Stevie occupies a surprisingly privileged place in *The Secret Agent*: amidst all these human fools, he alone seems to have some access to the world of animals, and thereby to the most visceral and basic forms of pain. His idiocy is in part a decoy. Stevie's brute grunts are the most unambiguous and authentic expressions of sympathy and compassion in this novel, and they yield one of Conrad's most significant observations: "The contemplation of the infirm and lonely steed overcame him. Jostled, but obstinate, he would remain there, trying to express the view newly opened to his sympathies of the human and equine misery in close association" (131).

In light of Conrad's incessant emphasis on "mankind" and its failings, we cannot ignore any remark that tests the boundaries of the human by revealing how closely they are shared by the animal. Indeed, earlier in the novel, Conrad – apparently invoking Aristotle's observation (in *On the Parts of Animals*) that man is the only animal that laughs – seems to reverse the Aristotelian theory when he writes that Chief Inspector Heat, "though what is called a man, was not a smiling animal"; in the 1920 Author's Note he modifies the statement only somewhat: "Man may smile and smile but he is not an investigating animal" (96, 4).[37] In both cases the lesson seems clear: man is finally not much different from beast. And aphorisms about the abjectness of mankind in particular lead directly, in the Conradian imagination, to suggestions that our wretchedness is unnervingly similar to animal (in chapter 8, equine) suffering. Indeed the unique brilliance of the cab scene is due largely to Conrad's blurring of normally fundamental categories: idiocy and intellect, human and animal. The result is that we cannot know exactly what to think. Stevie's realization that the infliction of pain is "Bad! Bad!" is about as close as any character in *The Secret Agent* comes to expressing some kind of truth about anything. "He felt with great completeness and some profundity," Conrad writes of the idiot boy, and it is unclear just how ironic he is; Stevie's morality, we are told, is "very complete" (131–2). Stevie's limited intelligence permits a certain clairvoyance about suffering that only feeling can generate. In this respect Conrad looks ahead to Orwell's Ministry of Love in *Nineteen Eighty-Four* or Elaine Scarry in *The Body in Pain*: pain may be the most basic or inexpressible fact of experience, a truth that overwhelms language.

The theme of the clairvoyant fool is hardly Conrad's invention: he follows plainly in the tradition of Shakespeare, Cervantes, and Dostoevsky. But the more interesting literary ancestry has to do with this particular emphasis on the proximity of human to animal, especially in terms of the suffering of animals. The smudged margin between man and beast is a topos in the satirical tradition, from Aristophanes to Swift's Houyhnhnms and Yahoos. And yet *The Secret Agent* is an essentially realist novel; it cannot stage human-animal drama in quite so fantastical a mode. Conrad, here as elsewhere, evokes Flaubert more than any other writer.[38] Within a genre owing equally to satiric impulse and realist discipline, he chips away at the definition of man by underlining man's closeness to beast.

In each of his novels Flaubert does the same thing: sometimes in a particular scene suggesting our likeness to animals, sometimes bringing the subject to the very fore of the narrative. The *comices agricoles* scene of *Madame Bovary* stages Rodolphe's seduction of Emma alongside the prizes for pigs and cattle outside; in *Salammbô* human battles are interspersed with vast panoramas of monkey carcasses and mutilated elephants; in *L'Éducation sentimentale* Madame Arnoux's dream about a barking dog turns out to arise from the real coughing of her son in the next room. In the later fiction, in particular, Flaubert seems specifically interested in human reaction to animal death and suffering. *Un coeur simple* recounts the tale of the simple woman Félicité's devotion to her parrot, which she stuffs when it dies.[39] *La Légende de Saint Julien l'Hospitalier* tells the story of Julien's conversion from killing all sorts of beasts – mice, birds, bears, boars – to feeling intense remorse for his sadism and finally renouncing it. And in *Bouvard et Pécuchet* the title characters begin by subjecting various animals to horrendous torture (magnetizing a dog, killing three steers when a phlebotomy experiment backfires) but, at the end of the book, become horrified by their barbarism and abandon their animal experiments.

Flaubert gives the impression of wanting to understand some essential quality of mankind by observing its behavior towards beasts. Usually these scenarios feel like satire: we are both mocked for behaving like animals and disparaged for treating them so terribly. In a sense our conduct is illustrative of our behavior towards each other, since cruelty and folly define our own relations. But there may be one hope for our salvation, based on a capacity for sympathy and a suspension of our native impulses: this may be the only way we can evade the censure directed at us. This is the lesson of Saint Julien, of Félicité, of Bouvard and Pécuchet. And it is the lesson of Conrad's Stevie, the one human in *The Secret Agent* who manages to notice that animals suffer, and whose protests against pain are the lone antidote to the homicide, suicide, and general beastliness that define the novel. Stevie's brief utterance "Beastly!" is indeed the most succinct expression of *The Secret Agent*'s fundamental attitude. We are to be scorned for behaving like animals; and it is our failure to live up to what should be demanded of mankind that calls into question the very value of that category.

THE INVINCIBLE NATURE OF HUMAN ERROR

If "mankind" is one of the fundamental terms of *The Secret Agent*, one of the novel's two lexical and thematic foci, the other is a word that surfaces almost as regularly: "folly." Sometimes in Conrad's fiction the two subjects are paired, as in the early remark that Verloc possesses "the air common to men who live on the vices, the follies, or the baser fears of mankind" or the aside in "An Outpost of Progress" about "the rest of mankind – who are fools." Foolishness in word or theme defines nearly every page of *The Secret Agent*. Newspapers, for instance – those "rubbishy sheets of paper soiled with printers' ink," and which, in the final chapter, are so inadequate in reporting Winnie's death – are "invariably written by fools for the reading of imbeciles"; from different vantage points Verloc is defined by his "inexplicable folly" and Mr. Vladimir by his "truculent folly"; for Chief Inspector Heat, the hunting of anarchists – the ostensible business of so much of the novel – is simply "all foolishness" (159, 63, 187, 78). These are all very different statements. But one reason that the various sectors of Conrad's London seem so united, and movement between them so fluid, is that the Verlocs, the anarchists, Mr. Vladimir from the Embassy, the people in the street, and sometimes the agents of law enforcement themselves are all subject to the verdict that what may define them is that they are fools.

"Folly" was a term of remarkable resonance for Conrad well before he wrote *The Secret Agent*. His first novel, after all, was called *Almayer's Folly*;

the word reverberates there much as it does in the later novel. The title refers directly to Almayer's half-finished house, but it embodies the entire sequence of delusions and failures that leads to his demise. It is not only the house that is foolish but also "the undying folly of his heart" and the general "earthly folly" from which only death can deliver him (162, 167).[40] And in the 1911 novel, *Under Western Eyes*, the word reappears with especial frequency, nowhere more tellingly than in one archetypal Conradian dictum. Early in the book Razumov contemplates his involvement in Haldin's death and realizes: "events started by human folly link themselves into a sequence which no sagacity can foresee and no courage can break through" (61). The line is instructive for two reasons. It calls attention, first of all, to the relation between folly and the Conradian idea of an event. Nearly every Conrad narrative is centered around or culminates in an act of error, a blunder in judgment: Jim's leap off the *Patna*, then his avoidable death at the hands of Doramin; Nostromo's similar mistake meeting his end with a bullet from Giorgio Viola's gun; and, most obvious of all, Stevie's fateful bomb-detonating stumble on his way to the Greenwich Observatory, the altogether ridiculous action that is described only indirectly but which nevertheless stands at the center of *The Secret Agent.*

And yet the remark in *Under Western Eyes* about "events started by human folly" is equally significant for another reason: the seemingly infinite scope that Conrad seems to imply by it. Human folly and error, much like "mankind," have a tendency to surface aphoristically in Conrad's fiction – rarely do they seem to refer to a single act only. In his essay "Books" Conrad offers a sort of ars poetica that expresses this tendency in ambiguous terms: "Of all the inanimate objects, of all men's creations, books are the nearest to us, for they contain our very thought, our ambitions, our indignations, our illusions, our fidelity to truth, and our persistent leaning towards error."[41] It is hard to tell if this defense of books is supposed to be uplifting or despondent. To situate "our persistent leaning towards error" alongside the novelist's vital tasks (the evocation of thought, the pursuit of truth) is to suggest that folly is as innate to mankind as consciousness – and therefore as compulsory a subject for the writer of fiction. It is a fundamental human characteristic. And it is altogether familiar to a reader of *The Secret Agent* or *Under Western Eyes*, where a conversation between Razumov and Sophia Antonovna gives rise to "the notion of the invincible nature of human error" (199–200). Here we should remember that in his *Secret Agent* dedication to H.G. Wells, Conrad reserved special praise for *Kipps*. Near the end of

Wells's 1905 novel the narrator steps back to observe of the title character and his wife: "The stupid little tragedies of these clipped and limited lives! . . . it is the ruling power of this land, Stupidity. My Kippses live in its shadow."[42]

And in evaluating the absoluteness, the supremacy of folly and error in *The Secret Agent*, we should keep in mind the Conrad narrative that most revealingly prefigures his simple tale of 1907. This is his first short story, "The Idiots," published in the *Savoy* in 1896 and included two years later in *Tales of Unrest*.[43] A man traveling in Brittany, who narrates the tale, comes across a woman who has given birth to four consecutive idiots: two twin boys, another boy, and a girl. Over time the narrator pieces together the family's back story, which in a phrase that foretells *The Secret Agent* he calls "a tale formidable and simple."[44] The wife is distraught by each birth, devastated that she and her husband can produce only idiot children. When he tries to have sex with her again, she cannot imagine engendering a fifth idiot, so she stabs him in the throat and kills him. She is haunted by the murder and eventually commits suicide by throwing herself off a cliff into the sea.

Conrad critics have generally overlooked this remarkable early story, mentioning it mostly in passing for its stylistic debt to Maupassant. But it is tempting to see in it the very germ of *The Secret Agent*. Its plot is notably prescient of the plot of the 1907 novel: a mother (or mother-like sister) of idiots kills her husband, then herself. Its underlying mythic theme is even more telling. "The Idiots" reads like a parable: idiocy is widespread, self-perpetuating, and ultimately inevitable – it is impossible to defeat it. To have more children is to produce more idiots. The ensuing horror of reproduction recalls Father Time's in *Jude the Obscure*, not to mention Gulliver's disgust and contempt upon returning to England after his experience among the Houyhnhnms, when the sight of his children reminds him that "by copulating with one of the *Yahoo*-Species, I had become a Parent of more; it struck me with the utmost Shame, Confusion and Horror."[45] (In this respect Swift and Hardy and Conrad all look ahead to the concluding decree of Larkin's "This Be The Verse": "Get out as early as you can,/ And don't have any kids yourself.")[46] The suggestion in Conrad's story that idiocy is the natural human condition, the normal order, calls to mind the line from *Under Western Eyes* about "the invincible nature of human error": in light of "The Idiots," that word *nature* becomes even more terrifying. This aphorism can, in effect, be rearranged: Conrad seems also to believe in the invincible error of human nature. Folly and essence are interchangeable. It is worth noting that the following story in *Tales of Unrest* is "An Outpost of Progress" with its denunciation of "the rest of mankind – who are fools."

In *The Secret Agent* there are several points where Conrad hints that the characters themselves may be aware of a universal, inescapable folly – usually in the form of some vast practical joke. In the early conversation with Mr. Vladimir, when the First Secretary at the shady embassy gives the directive to throw a bomb at astronomy, we read of Verloc that "suddenly it dawned upon him that all this was an elaborate joke"; later on, after the bombing, the Assistant Commissioner calls the whole affair "a ferocious joke"; near the end of the book, as Ossipon is finally able to piece together what has happened between Stevie, Verloc, and Winnie – the main story, that is, of the novel – Conrad writes that "the fooling of everybody all round appeared more complete than ever – colossal" (31, 166, 217). The Assistant Commissioner, assessing the case, may as well speak for Conrad himself: "There is a peculiar stupidity and feebleness in the conduct of this affair" (109). These are strange moments, since they raise an essential question concerning the knowability of Conrad's version of the Flaubertian *blague supérieure*. They make us wonder whether these satirized humans realize that they are targets of a grand satire. Usually in Conrad's fiction we get the opposite impression – that people are being lashed but lack any agency to understand or at least react in any effective way. The antagonistic forces are simply too elusive and overwhelming. In *Lord Jim*, for instance, Marlow says of Jim's tribulation that "there was the jeering intention of a spiteful and vile vengeance; there was an element of burlesque in his ordeal"; three pages later he refers to "the infernal powers who had selected him for the victim of their practical joke."[47]

We can almost imagine such intermittent allusions to a satirical deity in *The Secret Agent*, except that in the gritty urban sphere of the novel even ironical references to infernal powers might seem somewhat out of place. Still, it is possible to say that such references in *Lord Jim* and other earlier novels of Conrad the "sea writer" have, in fact, been subsumed into the amplified realism of *The Secret Agent*, and that the "element of burlesque," or the agent of the "practical joke" exists quite simply at the level of narration. There is no Marlow to mediate in the third-person narration of *The Secret Agent*. The persona who mocks Verloc, Michaelis, and the others is not a malicious divinity; it is none other than the storyteller himself. Conrad's narrator is detached enough in his irony that the satire of the novel – its mode of attack – is indistinguishable from the demonstrative realism of this narrator's very procedure.

One extraordinary moment in the novel exemplifies this idea perfectly. It comes near the beginning of the cab ride scene, as Winnie, Stevie, and their mother wait in front of their home for their ride:

Winnie, with her hat on, silent behind her mother's back, went on arranging the collar of the old woman's cloak. She got her handbag, an umbrella, with an impassive face. The time had come for the expenditure of the sum of three and sixpence on what might well be supposed the last cab-drive of Mrs Verloc's mother's life. They went out at the shop door.

The conveyance awaiting them would have illustrated the proverb that 'truth can be more cruel than caricature', if such a proverb existed. Crawling behind an infirm horse, a metropolitan hackney drew up on wobbly wheels and with a maimed driver on the box. (120–1)

This, of course, is the infirm horse that will so captivate and sadden Stevie. The cabdriver himself – described as having an "enormous and unwashed countenance . . . a bloated and sodden face" – takes his place alongside Conrad's many grotesques. But what is most peculiar about this passage is its reference to "the proverb that 'truth can be more cruel than caricature,' if such a proverb existed." Critics of *The Secret Agent* have consistently ignored this line, even though it seems to express the precise conundrum that the novel presents. Perhaps it is easily overlooked because it is concealed in what might at first seem to be an inconsequential scene, or maybe the phrase itself is simply too awkward: Conrad cites a proverb that he then tells us does not even exist.

This gnomic phrase is nevertheless the novel's central pronouncement. Caricatures are cruel: we need only the bumbling Verloc, the obese Michaelis, the bloated cabdriver, to understand this. But "truth" is something more slippery. A reader of *The Secret Agent* could, in fact, be forgiven for assuming that truth *is* caricature, since revolting, grotesque beings populate every corner of the novel; their cartoonish follies seem to be the one unchanging reality. By definition, though, caricatures depend on exaggeration. One could say that there is an inherent paradox in the idea of caricatures: they exist by dint of non-factual embellishment, yet it is embellishment that provides their claim to veracity. Conrad seems to be saying that truth is caricature without any need for exaggeration. Michaelis's distended balloon of a body, like the lamentable inferiority of the Professor's whole physique, is simply true and factual. It is proof of a satire that does not need to abandon realism.

Conrad was far too skeptical of the term "realism" ever to maintain that "truth" in fiction was simply a matter of documentary evidence: J. Hillis Miller overstates things a bit when he claims that "Conrad's truth is the exact opposite of precise images and events," but he is right that it was a far vaguer and more transcendent question than, for example, the scientific pretensions of Zolaesque detail.[48] Still, we cannot forget that Conrad invokes the proverb to make way for the arrival of a very specific image: the infirm horse and its maimed driver, who has a hook in place of a left hand. It is a moment as saturated in the detail of the hideous everyday as any other in the novel. And so – with this offhand and all but throwaway line, but which is nevertheless the most explicit reference in all his fiction to caricature – Conrad articulates what should be taken as *The Secret Agent*'s ars poetica. It is nothing less than an affirmation of the hybrid strangeness of his "roman (?)," this centaur with the head of a realist novel and the body of a wild satire. There is no need, says Conrad, for cruelty to depend on hyperbole. Realism is necessarily satire, and in its purest form satire is inherently a kind of realism. The cool detachment of novelistic omniscience does not require any assistance from fantasy or the unreal in its task of exposing the fools, the ogres, and the idiots.

THE OTHER SIDE OF IRONY

The past century of criticism has generally agreed that the tone, perspective, and structure of *The Secret Agent* are all governed by a comprehensive and unifying irony. Conrad's ironic mode has invariably struck readers as *consistent*: it seems to touch every page of the novel; and our resulting impression is of Conrad's total mastery of his material, his even hand in meting out steady doses of sarcasm, what Ian Watt calls a "control that approaches serenity."[49]

There is less consensus, however, about the implications or ends of such a uniformly austere irony. F.R. Leavis praises the subtlety of tone and perspective that he believes forms this irony; he means to pay the book a compliment when he writes that its "kind of irony involves a limiting detachment (we don't look for the secrets of Conrad's soul in *The Secret Agent*)."[50] But some readers profess rather more caution and hesitation, even while acknowledging the formal virtuosity of Conrad's method. Frederick Karl's comment that "the novel's irony appeared to give the novelist a devastating authority, even an arrogance" expresses the reservation of many Conradians that *The Secret Agent*'s disdain is too off-putting, too great a departure from the generous expansiveness of *Lord Jim* and *Nostromo*; R.A. Gekoski concludes that most of the novel's characters are "finally unworthy even of the sustained scorn to which they are subjected" and that Conrad's stylistic virtuosity comes "at the cost of complexity of thought and emotion."[51]

Perhaps no one has questioned the place of irony in *The Secret Agent* as thoroughly as Irving Howe. In *Politics and the Novel* Howe's resistance to Conrad's detachment at first seems to be a specific disapproval of the writer's refusal to articulate a clear politics. Soon, however, Howe's critique grows into a larger indictment of Conrad's elusive misanthropy.

> *The Secret Agent* is the work of a man who looks upon the political spectacle – as, a little too often, the whole of life – from a great and chilling distance, and who needs to keep that distance in order to survive. Conrad's growing alienation from the modes and assumptions of modern society, which has nothing in common with literary fashion but is an utterly serious response, seems to me profoundly impressive; too often, however, the impressiveness has more to do with sociological and ethical statement than literary value. Conrad's critical distance, the sense he communicates of writing as a man who has *cut himself off*, may win our sympathy, but it has unhappy consequences for the novel ... What one misses in *The Secret Agent* is some dramatic principle of contradiction, some form of resistance; in a word, a moral positive to serve literary ends. Conrad's ironic tone suffuses every sentence, nagging at our attention to the point where one yearns for the relief of direct statement almost as if it were an ethical good. (95–6)

Howe's misgivings, that is, have to do with the very pervasiveness and uniformity that I have argued define Conrad's brand of satirical realism: the homogeneity of his London, the essentializing aphorisms about "mankind," the disgust with his characters who are all imbeciles anyway. Howe cannot abide a satire that refuses to qualify or distinguish, especially in political terms; in his view Conrad's "irony has turned in upon itself, becoming facile through its pervasiveness and lack of grading" (96).

The ironic thing about all this emphasis on Conrad's irony is that in *The Secret Agent* – unquestionably a book that relies on its steadfast, arch detachment from its characters – often it seems that Conrad is not being very ironic at all. The question of Conrad's irony, that is, becomes a problem of distinguishing what we mean by that endlessly thorny term. It is possible to be sardonic without being ironic; a novelist can keep a tremendous distance from his characters and yet at times also say exactly what he means. When Conrad scorns "mankind" so plainly and repeatedly, or when he lodges specific insults at his individual characters, we can say that he is being ironic (he is being detached, sarcastic) or that he is being wholly non-ironic, since he hardly seems to intend the inverse of his damning and absolute pronouncements. If *The Secret Agent* is indeed a work of irony, it may be said to oscillate between Wayne Booth's "stable" and "unstable" ironies. In his often impassive narration of events, the narrator describes what is happening as if he were not too invested in it, and therefore invites us to reject the surface meaning of the narration; and yet elsewhere the novel pursues a campaign of such disdain that it leaves mostly ruins, a thorough negativity, and we are thereby denied the relative comfort of simply electing the contrary meaning of what is being offered. Booth's observation that "irony is used in some satire, not in all; some irony is satiric, much is not" can also be read in reverse: some satire is ironic, but some is definitively not. The levels of irony in Conrad's satire may be numerous, but that does not, in fact, mean that they are uniform.[52]

Conrad himself would not have disputed the critical emphasis on *The Secret Agent*'s irony. In his letters from the era that I quoted earlier, Conrad makes clear that the "new departure of genre" was a matter of intensifying irony: he underlines his "sustained effort in ironical treatment of a melodramatic subject." The juxtaposition of these two terms – irony and melodrama – exposes the complexity inherent in balancing extreme detachment with the dramatization of human scenarios, especially those involving the Verlocs: the difficulty of joining cruel satire with a story that could potentially foster sympathy. In this respect Conrad's ironical treatment seems obviously connected to his bouts of nausea while composing the novel. But there may be an interesting paradox inherent in this very connection. The narration of *The Secret Agent* is typically detached and cold; yet the novelist who creates this narration does not seem to benefit from this detachment, since the experience of writing becomes the source of such profound despair. In a letter to Pinker in October 1906 Conrad writes that "the ironic treatment of the whole matter is not so easy as it looks . . . I tell you it's no joke – not to me at any rate."[53] Irony fails as a defense against painful investment; indeed, if irony is to mean the cruelty of aloofness, it may be said to be one of the primary sources of pain.

This kind of irony thereby ends up posing a difficult problem in relation to the question of humor, so commonly associated with ironic narrative. In theory, the ironic detachment that infuses so much of *The Secret Agent* should generate a good portion of comedy, as indeed it often does. But Conrad seems to be speaking mostly in earnest when he says that the novel is no joke: not in his agonized writing of it, surely, and nor perhaps in the solemnity of its grand satire directed at the total folly of the city below. Much like Hardy – who wrote to John Addington Symonds that "all comedy, is tragedy, if you only look deep enough into it," and who recorded in his journal that "if you look beneath the surface of any farce you see a tragedy" – Conrad was throughout his life interested in the tendency of genres to blur into one another, and specifically in the sorrow that lies embedded in jest.[54] In his 1912 *Personal Record* he writes: "it is very difficult to be wholly joyous or wholly sad on this earth. The comic, when it is human, soon takes upon itself a face of pain."[55] An aphorism like this could just as easily have sprung from the pen of Hardy. And it is notably applicable to "The Idiots," "An Outpost of Progress," and *The Secret Agent*: narratives where the grotesque and the ironic yield a profound melancholy.

Thomas Mann, in his essay on *The Secret Agent*, reaches a similar verdict about this very Conradian tendency:

The striking feature of modern art is that it has ceased to recognise the categories of tragic and comic, or the dramatic classifications, tragedy and comedy. It sees life as tragi-comedy, with the result that the grotesque is its most genuine style – to the extent, indeed, that to-day that is the only guise in which the sublime may appear.[56]

Mann's definition of modern art through the grotesque is striking, especially since it does not seem very obviously to describe his own fiction. It does, though, correctly identify the dissolution of categories and certainties that defines *The Secret Agent* and indeed so much of the satirical realism that emerged so forcefully at the threshold of modernism. If we can understand Mann's "grotesque" to mean a mostly realist grotesque, a distortedness that is not ultimately fantastical, then *The Secret Agent* does indeed seem representative of its era. It is a fusion of comic detail and tragic sensibility, a fictional mode that reaches what Mann calls sublimity only by passing through the ugliness of the city and its foolish denizens. We are reminded here of the closing image of "An Outpost of Progress," where the gruesome face of Kayerts, who has gone mad and hanged himself, greets the crew of the Great Civilizing Company that has finally arrived on the island: "his toes were only a couple of inches above the ground; his arms hung stiffly down; he seemed to be standing rigidly at attention, but with one purple cheek playfully posed on the shoulder. And, irreverently, he was putting out a swollen tongue at his Managing Director."[57] This posture of disgust is as emblematic an image of Conrad's grotesque as any other in his fiction. Kayerts's purple expression – tongue wagging contemptuously, wavering terribly between the comic and the tragic – is a perfectly literalized icon of the Conradian "face of pain."

This idea of the pain inherent in all comedy also makes us think again about all the references in *The Secret Agent* to elaborate jokes, ferocious jokes, and the colossal fooling of everybody all around. In Conrad's 1906 story "The Informer" – set among anarchists, with a Professor-like figure working on detonators, and therefore an important companion-piece to *The Secret Agent* – the narrator concludes by responding to a remark about a character who "likes to have his little joke sometimes": "I fail to understand the connection of this last remark. I have been utterly unable to discover where in all this the joke comes in."[58] These final lines would not be entirely out of place at the conclusion of *The Secret Agent*. If Conrad's corrosive irony begins by arresting us with its consistency, and if it continues by unnerving us with the pain that it inflicts, then it ends by confounding us altogether in our quest to know exactly where the joke comes in. It is an irony beyond any identifiable ethics: as Geoffrey Galt Harpham writes, the parallels Conrad draws "between the anarchism and official society" – parallels that create what I call the novel's uniform and absolute satire – "have a corrosive effect on any kind of ethical resolve or conviction."[59] Irony can be ethical when it is stable enough to propose any kind of dialectic or choice, not when it works to destroy variation and scale.

This kind of irony is not simply Booth's unstable irony; it is an irony that leads to a zone beyond irony: in Mark Wollaeger's phrase, an irony that "verges on vituperation and revulsion."[60] In this zone it is no longer really an important question whether a statement can be trusted or even a novel's fundamental attitude understood. Instead it becomes clear that fooling is so widespread, and negativity so supreme, that it is simply impossible to know where the joke lies. This zone is where we find ourselves when we apprehend something so grotesque that we cannot know whether to laugh or to grimace in agony – when the comic, because (in Conrad's formulation) it is "human," takes the face of pain. Irony seems an inadequate term for this experience. Is Conrad being ironic when he writes, apropos of the Assistant Commissioner, "We can never cease to be ourselves" (92)? Or is this the most sincere statement that *The Secret Agent* can make – and indeed, because it is so true of the unchangingly abject specimens of this novel, also its saddest? This is no longer irony; it is simply fact, and therefore a malediction. One of the enduring achievements of *The Secret Agent* is that it consistently makes us ask what lies on the other side of irony.

This audacious perversity – to push irony until it begins to dissolve – is perhaps Conrad's purest Flaubertian quality. In Flaubert's late works especially, the oddity and grotesqueness of image and story give the impression of a writer trying to push fictional representation past satire, past realism, and even beyond irony. Flaubert insisted that *Un coeur simple* was not meant to be taken ironically; his intention was not to mock Félicité but, in some sense, to honor and pity her.[61] And in *Bouvard et Pécuchet* and its appended *Dictionnaire des idées reçues* we are faced with a mode of representation that refuses to distinguish between irony and its opposite. Bouvard and Pécuchet are undoubtedly being held up for ridicule, but Flaubert's matter-of-fact narration lets his pseudo-reportage do all the work for him. The extreme, naïve simplicity of the novel's style pretends to relate things exactly as they happen; nowhere in Flaubert's fiction is the editorializing voice of the author less audible (though, of course, it is never absent). This is the same method as in the *Dictionnaire des idées reçues*, where Flaubert wanted only to ape the sayings of others, never to add a word or phrase of his own. The late Flaubert, that is to say, flirts with a sort of hyperrealism, the appearance of a radical and severe quasi-documentary method, in order to allow satirical exposure to emerge organically and (despite his extreme labors) to seem effortless. Flaubert himself seemed to conceive of *Bouvard et Pécuchet* as a kind of exercise in radical realism. In July 1874, as he was writing it, his correspondent, Turgenev, tried to convince him that – given its satiric subject – the novel should take the form of something "*quick*, as in Swift or Voltaire." In his extraordinarily revealing response, Flaubert objected stridently:

I don't agree with you about the manner in which one should handle this subject. If it were treated briefly, in a concise and light way, it would be a more or less witty fantasy, but without range and without verisimilitude, whereas in detailing and developing I will appear to believe in my story, and I can do something serious and even terrifying.[62]

Probably nowhere does Flaubert come so close to defining the mode I call satirical realism, of which he was the most instinctive practitioner. Wit and fantasy are the enemy: they guard against "belief" in the story; they foster a lightness that comes at the expense of seriousness and indeed credibility. The more realistic or infused with verisimilitude, says Flaubert, the more severely satirical (and therefore the more compulsory). There is no need to scorn the world when the world holds itself up for scorn all on its own.

But the oddest consequence of this satirical hyperrealism is how, paradoxically, it can yield a strange and unexpected sympathy. To read *Un coeur simple* is to vacillate between finding Félicité's love of Loulou utterly ridiculous and to experience a profound compassion for a woman in possession of such devotion and love. Such is our experience reading nearly all of Flaubert: mockery and empathy are compatible and concomitant reactions to Emma Bovary, to Frédéric Moreau, to Bouvard and Pécuchet. And this disarming sensation, of scorn and compassion interpenetrating, also defines our reading of *The Secret Agent*. Conrad makes use of a bizarre *style indirect libre* in the novel: he might enter into and mimic the consciousness of his characters, only to swerve abruptly away and distance himself from them. Here is just one example: after Michaelis, Yundt, and Ossipon leave a meeting at the Verloc house early in the novel, we are invited to enter Verloc's thoughts as he descends "into the abyss of moral reflections." He mulls over the personalities and failings of the various anarchists, and the conclusions he reaches seem basically accurate: Yundt is unhappily involved with a "bleary-eyed old woman"; Michaelis is idle; Ossipon is louche. This train of thought then expands into a larger criticism of the "majority of revolutionists" and their feeble philosophies. We are, in this sequence, lured into thinking that Verloc's thought process closely mirrors the narrator's; but suddenly we are jarred out of such an illusion: "Lost for a minute in the abyss of meditation, Mr Verloc did not reach the depth of these abstract considerations. Perhaps he was not able. In any case he had not the time" (45–6).

Conrad often enjoys such violent swings between identification and repudiation. In the case above it progresses mostly linearly: first we seem to be aligned with Verloc, then we are told that he is thoroughly incapable of complex thought. In general these two modes fundamentally coexist. Certain scenes – the cab ride through London, or the episode of Winnie's murder of her husband – are astonishing for the way they weave together the depiction of inanity with the traces of real affect. In the cab scene, for instance, we are exposed to the cruelty of animal suffering and the bizarre cries of Stevie, but we are also reminded that the cabdriver, too, is to be viewed with sympathy: he whips the horse "not because his soul was cruel and his heart evil, but because he had to earn his fare" (122). Suffering, Conrad seems to say here – and in what might be considered a departure from his often cosmic satire – is sometimes simply the product of quotidian circumstance. It is realistic and banal. The lesson of the cabdriver is entirely consistent with the image of Stevie in this same scene: there is foolishness, and there is ugly caricature, but there is also a very real occasion for sympathy that emerges from the dramatization of toil and pain.

In an important sense this uneasy coexistence of satire and sympathy lies at the very core of *The Secret Agent*, in the portrait of Adolf and Winnie Verloc. We should not discount as disingenuous Conrad's claim in the Author's Note that the novel is "Winnie Verloc's story"; nor should we forget the Assistant Commissioner's remark in conversation with Sir Ethelred, as he is piecing together the case, that "from a certain point of view we are here in the presence of a domestic drama" (8, 168). *The Secret Agent*, much like *Jude the Obscure* and *New Grub Street*, encompasses both extreme satire and nuanced conjugal portraiture. The Verlocs' final scene together – in which the husband cavalierly explains away Stevie's death, while the wife lurks in silence and finally kills him with the carving knife – contains a stunning variety of emotions and sensations. The scene is ridiculous (Verloc's feeble rationalizations); hyperrealistic (the meticulously traced parabola of Winnie as she moves across the room, the close detail of Verloc's blood dripping onto the floor); and, at times, deeply moving, as a portrait of a woman in despair. It is meanwhile all narrated as coolly as any other scene in the novel. To read of the last moments of Verloc's life is to ask oneself once again where the joke comes in; the simultaneity of so many impressions and moods renders that puzzle finally unsolvable.

But if this scene of domestic drama is one of profound uncertainty, it cannot be said to differ from any other episode in *The Secret Agent*. This book, after all, is not quite a novel but a "roman (?)". We cannot be faulted for suspecting that Conrad's question mark may, in fact, be necessary, or for wondering whether this generic murkiness is a result of *The Secret Agent*'s consistent breach of the relatively comforting boundaries of irony, its insistence on always pushing beyond those boundaries. The book does ultimately exist in the realm of "beyond": past the margin between disdain and forgiveness, where satire cannot be dissociated from a rigorous and vigilant realism. The truth is that Conrad saw unities where most others would see binary divisions. In his allusion to the London rain's oppression of "mankind" he writes that man's colossal and hopeless vanity is "deserving of scorn, wonder, and compassion" – as if these terms were not at all in contradiction (80). And in the Author's Note he would claim that "the whole treatment of the tale" is based on "its inspiring indignation and underlying pity and contempt"; three pages later comes his explanation that "ironic treatment alone would enable me to say all I felt I would have to say in scorn as well as in pity" (4, 7). Pity and contempt, scorn and pity: these are terms that in the imagination of some writers would be in steadfast and natural opposition. But in the Conradian equation they are fused, much like truth and caricature, until they form a strange cohesion, a dark and very luminous whole.

Epilogue

Retrospect in literary criticism allows us certain neat symmetries and clear panoramas: it lets us call *The Pickwick Papers* the first Victorian novel and *Jude the Obscure* the last, and it encourages us to use the arbitrary divisions of decades and centuries to chart the history of literature. Sometimes retrospect affords too suspiciously precise a literary-historical calendar. But sometimes it lets us see how literature may have been confronting the problem of its chronology – of its own existence in time – all along. At certain points in literary history, for example, we can sense the novel's sharp awareness of having reached some kind of new territory. We feel its exhilaration that a new kind of expression or representation is suddenly possible. But at other times we can feel the novel's anxiety that those same things have become no longer possible or sustainable. A certain kind of writing might be aware of its own expiration – it might even be the conscious agent of its own demise.

New Grub Street is a fine example of this kind of destructive self-consciousness: Gissing's novel emerges from a culture of realist fiction and even sets its scene there, all the while enacting that very movement's death. It comes not to praise realism but to bury it. In a sense the wider scene of late Victorian fiction was doing something quite similar: testing the far limits of realism, describing what they were like, and releasing the satirical vapors native to those reaches. The late Victorian novel was at once interested in the possibilities of realism and intent on exposing its boundaries. The archetypal scene of this literary endgame probably comes not from Gissing but from Hardy. The sight of the three hanging children in *Jude the Obscure*, described with a meticulous realism but saturated in satirical precedent, is an image of such conclusive horror that it effectively signals the end of a sequence of English fiction. Jude's terrible view in that small Christminster room is a vista that leads ultimately nowhere. There would, of course, be other English novels later in the 1890s, but by then Hardy had essentially surveyed the landscape of possibility within the realist idiom he had inherited. *Jude the Obscure* is terminal not only for Hardy but for a larger population of English writers.

This is obviously not to say that twentieth-century fiction abandoned or discarded realism in any way. *The Secret Agent* may look backward from its Edwardian perch – back at an earlier period of London history, and at a different kind of fiction from Conrad's other novels from that decade – but it doesn't, of course, shut the door on any realist principle or method in fiction. There would always be new realisms, and eras in which the term and its partisans would come back into vogue: the late 1950s and early 1960s in British theater, for example, or the 1980s in American fiction. In many ways we are living today in an age once again obsessed with the reproduction of lived experience, with all its promises and implications: documentary film, the memoir, journalistic fiction. The novel, in particular, is always staking out and then colonizing its own new terrain of the real. Critics from Erich Auerbach and Ian Watt to James Wood have always understood the real to be the standard, the default, the normal mode of fiction, from which all others deviate. Realism did not, of course, pass with the nineteenth century; it regrouped, shifted, adopted new forms.

Still, the Edwardian years mark a genuine turning point in the development of English fiction and our expectations of it. In the subsequent two decades, the reviews where the great modernists would publish their work, and the critics with whom they would be in dialogue, no longer seemed quite as interested in the question so persistently asked of Hardy and Gissing in the 1880s and 1890s: the question of the place of realism in fiction. Novels – *Sons and Lovers, Mrs Dalloway* – could still be singled out for their fidelity toward a certain verisimilitude in representation. But an era of fixation on the subject had undoubtedly passed. The word itself no longer held the same purchase on the critical vocabulary: most modernists were not busy staking out – in essays or within their fiction – their positions on that school or movement, as Hardy and Gissing had done before them. Critical attention mostly shifted elsewhere: to particular kinds of formal innovation, and to the intricate psychological investigations that such innovation permitted. Much of the modernist fiction thought to embody a great realism, and a realism characteristic of its era – *Ulysses* most prominently – in many ways owes only a small debt to late Victorian fiction. *Ulysses* can surely be praised for immense accomplishments of realist narrative; but in the aggregate its temper and its formal self-awareness owe far more to Fielding or Sterne than to Hardy or Gissing. The "scrupulous meanness" of *Dubliners* perhaps comes closer to the austerity of the late Victorian novel.

It has been my conviction throughout this book that nineteenth-century realism reached its limit when it blurred irrevocably into satire, when the task of representing the human in its natural habitat could no longer be distinguished from the act of scorning the entire category of human, and that entire habitat known as the world. In my first chapter I attested to the longstanding kinship and affinities of realism and satire. But the main period I have been studying, the fin-de-siècle years, marks surely the most remarkable convergence of these two modes. This convergence could not be sustained forever: just as they had once fused so notably in the second half of the nineteenth century, English realism and satire largely diverged in the subsequent years. The passing of Victorian realism resulted in the flight of much satire to non-realist territory. This did not mean any extinction of English satire; in fact, satire may be said to have enjoyed a golden age in 1930s England especially, with Evelyn Waugh and Wyndham Lewis at the height of their powers. But the farcical excesses of *Decline and Fall* and *Vile Bodies*, or the angular caricatures of *The Apes of God*, are significant precisely for their retreat from verisimilitude, for the distance they insisted on keeping from the earnestness of other contemporary novels. They were written at a time when satirists no longer had much interest in the possibilities of realist representation.

This seems true, at least, of English fiction. Other major English satirists of the period, and just after, wrote in a dystopian mode, equally far from familiar realist norms: the Huxley of *Brave New World*, the Orwell of *Animal Farm* and *Nineteen Eighty-Four*. To probe existing conditions by displacing them onto an allegorical future tense is to reject one of the principal tenets of most realist fiction: that it should be essentially contemporary. It's possible that this divergence of realism and satire was an English trend specifically. In France in the 1930s, at precisely the time these satirists were all active in England, Louis-Ferdinand Céline published two masterpieces, *Voyage au bout de la nuit* and *Mort à crédit*, in which an entirely new form of realism channeled a furious satirical energy. Céline's fiction is unlike anything in late Victorian fiction; it is virtually without precedent at all. But we are faced in his novels with the same barrage of anger and despair we know from *Jude the Obscure* and *The Nether World* and *The Secret Agent* – just as we are met with a similar immersion in the odious details of everyday low life. Céline's postwar fiction (*Féerie pour une autre fois*, and the trilogy of *D'un château l'autre*, *Nord*, and *Rigodon*) developed such a hallucinatory idiom that Célinian hyperrealism blurred into an intermittently fantastical mode.

But his prewar novels unquestionably belong to the class of fiction that I have been delineating. In the terms I have devised and adhered to throughout this book, *Voyage au bout de la nuit*, not *Ulysses*, is an authentic twentieth-century work of satirical realism. Joyce's novel pokes fun at many things, and its energies are boundless, but it does not rail against present circumstances, through their lifelike evocation in narrative, the way that Gissing's or Céline's novels do.

The Joyce of *Ulysses* belongs to a different tradition of satire, if he belongs to satire at all. This is the encyclopedic or Menippean tradition, which tackles everything voraciously, and which packs vast erudition within its pages, often through rowdy juxtaposition: this is the mode of Rabelais, and consequently the focus of Bakhtin's theories of the novel, and perhaps the genre of the Pynchon of *Gravity's Rainbow*. It is probably also the mode that James Wood argues is so characteristic of contemporary fiction, and which he calls "hysterical realism." This kind of satire does not care much for austerity. And in this respect it not only differs from satirical realism; it seems innately at odds with it. But some satire will always be channeled through the punishing severity of realism. Indeed the history of the novel suggests that the tendency of late Victorian fiction was not a nineteenth-century phenomenon only: the pursuit of the real in fiction seems often to lead, as if compulsively, to that satirical zone at the margins of realism. The realist austerity and supreme satirical detachment of Naipaul's *A House for Mr Biswas* are simultaneous and interlocking in a way that can sometimes recall *Jude the Obscure*. In contemporary fiction, satirical realism can take the form of extreme black comedy (Martin Amis's *Money*) or operate through a kind of detached and bleak perspective on the panorama of human degradation (Michel Houellebecq's *Les particules élémentaires*). Philip Roth's *Sabbath's Theater* is a recent masterpiece of an intense and concentrated realism driven by a relentless satirical force.

But it does sometimes seem that novels like these are the exception. More commonly there exists in our contemporary fiction a pallid realism with none of the energies of satire, just as there is endless contemporary satire – in fiction, in film, in television – that is decidedly non-realist and even anti-realist. (Farcical parody, in particular, is enjoying its own renaissance.) It's hard not to feel that both modes today lack the same moral rigor and intensity of those central works of nineteenth-century satirical realism. This is not to say that contemporary realism and satire are complacent, only that the reading public is less likely to be shocked by the outrage of the real through its fictional representation, less likely to understand realism as protest, in large part because very few people still turn to fiction – or write fiction – for that kind of experience. The fiction of the late nineteenth century could still lay claim to some of that authority. This authority is what could generate a kind of writing like satirical realism in the first place: as a preeminent literary form, the novel could claim both a representational advantage and a superlative moral seriousness. It was precisely the novel's union of two long-proximate modes that enabled such a superior kind of art, a mode of fiction that would disarm us with its verisimilitude, only to overwhelm us with its polemical drive and indignation. It was the most moral kind of literature. But its achievement, its forging of so absolute an image of the world, was in the end a necessarily Pyrrhic victory. For in pursuing realism's most extreme prospects it also discovered realism's limits; and in making so many things in fiction possible it immediately rendered so much else obsolete.

Notes

CHAPTER I AUGUSTAN SATIRE AND
VICTORIAN REALISM

1 Edmund Gosse, "The Limits of Realism in Fiction," in *Questions at Issue* (New York: D. Appleton and Company, 1893), 143–51.

2 Oscar Wilde, "The Critic as Artist," in *The Artist as Critic: Critical Writings of Oscar Wilde*, ed. Richard Ellmann (New York: Random House, 1968), 390, 397; *The Picture of Dorian Gray* (Oxford: Oxford University Press, 2006), 163.

3 Arthur Waugh, "Reticence in Literature," *The Yellow Book* 1 (April 1894), 204–12.

4 In formulating a definition of realism, it will be clear throughout this book that I follow Raymond Williams's plain and essential two-fold point: "realism in art and literature is both a method and a general attitude." *Keywords* (New York: Oxford University Press, 1985), 260.

5 See Ronald Paulson, *Satire and the Novel in Eighteenth-Century England* (New Haven: Yale University Press, 1967), 8–11.

6 John Lawlor, "Radical Satire and the Realistic Novel," *Essays and Studies* 8 (1955), 67–73. See also Claude Rawson's two-part essay "Cannibalism and Fiction: Reflections on Narrative Form and 'Extreme' Situations," *Genre* 10:4 (Winter 1977), 667–711, and 11:2 (Summer 1978), 227–313. Another rare consideration of the subject is the first chapter of Ronald Paulson's *Satire and the Novel in Eighteenth-Century England* (see note 5). Paulson even uses the phrase "satiric realism," but his canvas is markedly different from my own: like Ian Watt, he is focusing on the emergence of the novel in eighteenth-century England, rather than on the place of satire in nineteenth-century realist fiction. In a different book, *The Fictions of Satire* (Baltimore: Johns Hopkins University Press, 1967), Paulson also stresses the mimetic (in addition to the rhetorical) quality of satire: see pages 3–9.

7 James Wood's recent book on laughter and the novel, *The Irresponsible Self,* is one of the finest studies of the moral implications of satirical writing, though his interest doesn't lie in satire's relation to realism. Wood depends on a division between two kinds of comedy: the comedy of correction, identified with Momus, where we laugh *at*; and the tragicomedy of forgiveness, Wood's main subject, where we laugh *with*. My category *satirical realism* is, in essence, a third kind. It is too harsh to be Wood's forgiving

178

tragicomedy – and yet it has rejected the whole notion of correction. I revisit this theme later: if satirical realism is simply representing "the truth," it has transcended that basic margin between correction and forgiveness. It is ultimately neither of these things. See *The Irresponsible Self* (New York: Farrar, Straus and Giroux, 2004), 5–6.

8   For the kinship of Swift and Flaubert (and some differences between them), see also Claude Rawson, *Satire and Sentiment, 1660–1830* (New Haven: Yale University Press, 2000), 51–2, 71–2, 76–7, and 201–7; and *Gulliver and the Gentle Reader: Studies in Swift and Our Time* (London: Routledge & Kegan Paul, 1973), 97–9.

9   Alvin Kernan, *The Plot of Satire* (New Haven: Yale University Press, 1965), 221. This is true, too, of Northrop Frye's theory of genres: the blurring of satire (winter) into tragedy (autumn), on one side, and comedy (spring), on the other, is a similar way of imagining this tendency. See *Anatomy of Criticism* (Princeton: Princeton University Press, 1957), especially 224 and 237. See also 162: the words "irony and satire" are "elements of the literature of experience" which Frye adopts "in place of 'realism.'"

10 On satire's relation to epic – notably in the form of mock-heroic – see Rawson, *Satire and Sentiment*, 29–97.

11 In this respect the scope of my study differs from that of George Levine, who sees English realism embodied not in the aggressive fin-de-siècle fiction I emphasize, but rather in the "much more affable and moderate tradition" earlier in the century. See *The Realistic Imagination: English Fiction from Frankenstein to Lady Chatterley* (Chicago: University of Chicago Press, 1981), 4–6.

12 See, for example, Gordon Haight, *George Eliot: A Biography* (New York: Oxford University Press, 1968), 259; Rosemarie Bodenheimer, *The Real Life of Mary Ann Evans: George Eliot, Her Letters and Fiction* (Ithaca: Cornell University Press, 1994), 51; and especially Ruth Bernard Yeazell, *Art of the Everyday: Dutch Painting and the Realist Novel* (Princeton: Princeton University Press, 2007), 91–101, 116–21.

13 George Eliot, *Adam Bede* (Oxford: Clarendon Press, 2001), 165–7. Eliot's ars poetica is remarkably similar to Gogol's at the beginning of chapter 7 of *Dead Souls*, where he proclaims himself to be the rare writer willing to pursue the ugliness of reality, "all the terrible, stupendous mire of trivia in which our life is entangled, the whole depth of cold, fragmented, everyday characters that swarm over our often bitter and boring earthly path." See Nikolai Gogol, *Dead Souls*, trans. Richard Pevear and Larissa Volokhonsky (New York: Vintage, 1997), 133–5.

14 George Eliot, *Scenes of Clerical Life* (Oxford: Clarendon Press, 1985), 169 ("Mr Gilfil's Love Story") and 217 ("Janet's Repentance").

15 George Eliot, *Felix Holt, The Radical* (Oxford: Clarendon Press, 1980), 22.

16 George Eliot, *Middlemarch* (Oxford: Clarendon Press, 1986), 22.

17 John Ruskin, "Fiction, Fair and Foul – V," in *The Works of John Ruskin*, ed. E.T. Cook and Alexander Wedderburn (London: George Allen, 1908), 34: 377. See also Levine, *The Realistic Imagination*, 208.

18 Gustave Flaubert, *Madame Bovary*, in *Oeuvres* (Paris: Gallimard, 1951), I: 311, 593.

19 Jonathan Swift, *Gulliver's Travels*, in *Prose Works of Jonathan Swift*, ed. Herbert Davis (Oxford: Basil Blackwell, 1941), II: 75–6.

20 Kernan, *The Plot of Satire*, 37; Erich Auerbach, *Mimesis: The Representation of Reality in Western Literature* (Princeton: Princeton University Press, 1953), 404. Ronald Paulson similarly writes that "part of the pleasure of reading satire derives from its microscopic imitation of the topically and immediately commonplace" (*Satire and the Novel in Eighteenth-Century England*, 22).

21 On the importance of the technology of the microscope to Swift's grotesque-optical imagination, see Marjorie Nicolson, *Science and Imagination* (Ithaca: Cornell University Press, 1956), 193–9. *Gulliver's Travels*, according to Nicolson, "would not be what it is had Swift not looked through a microscope – perhaps the one he bought for Stella – and felt the fascination and repulsion of grossly magnified nature" (157). Nicolson's discussion of Swift is part of a larger chapter on the microscope and English literature (especially satire) of the seventeenth and eighteenth centuries generally.

22 Swift, *A Tale of a Tub With Other Early Works, 1696–1707*, in *Prose Works of Jonathan Swift*, I: 109; *A Modest Proposal*, in *Prose Works of Jonathan Swift: Irish Tracts, 1728–1733*, 12: 112.

23 Steven Connor, *The Book of Skin* (Ithaca: Cornell University Press, 2004), 50–1, 48, 107. Connor opens his book by looking specifically at the word "complexion" itself: since the seventeenth century, its meaning has evolved from only the color of the skin to the "texture and condition of the skin … indicators of more general conditions of health, vigour, and age" (19–21).

24 Alexander Pope, *The Dunciad*, in *The Poems of Alexander Pope*, John Butt (gen. ed.) (New Haven: Yale University Press, 1953), 5: 365–6.

25 Pope, *An Essay on Man*, in *The Poems of Alexander Pope*, 3: 38–40. See also Pope's "To Mr Addison, Occasioned by his Dialogues on Medals," lines 19–22: "Ambition sigh'd; She found it vain to trust/ The faithless Column and the crumbling Bust;/ Huge moles, whose shadow stretch'd from shore to shore,/ Their ruins ruin'd, and their place no more!" (6: 203) On the cultural fascination with the microscope in eighteenth-century literature, see Ann Jessie Van Sant, *Eighteenth-Century Sensibility and the Novel* (Cambridge: Cambridge University Press, 1993), 102–4.

26 François Rabelais, *Pantagruel*, in *Oeuvres complètes* (Paris: Gallimard, 1994), 219.

27 Horace, *Satires and Epistles* (London: Penguin, 1997), 68. See also Connor's discussion of the "divinatory function" and "reading" of moles in *The Book of Skin*, 96–101. For his discussion of pores, see 111–12.

28 George Meredith, *An Essay on Comedy and the Uses of the Comic Spirit* (Westminster: Archibald Constable and Co., 1897), 33–4.

29 Marcel Proust, *Du côté de chez Swann*, in *A la recherche du temps perdu* (Paris: Gallimard, 1954) 1: 175. ("Les autres arbitrairement formées par moi … ce petit bouton qui s'enflammait au coin du nez.")

30 Swift, *A Tale of a Tub,* in *Prose Works of Jonathan Swift*, 1: 110.

31 Wyndham Lewis, *Men Without Art* (London: Cassell & Co., 1934), 118–26.

32 Gustave Flaubert, *L'Éducation sentimentale*, in *Oeuvres* (Paris: Gallimard, 1952), 2: 47.

33 Roland Barthes, "The Reality Effect," in *The Rustle of Language*, trans. Richard Howard (Berkeley and Los Angeles: University of California Press, 1989), 141–2, 148.

34 Gustave Flaubert, *Correspondance* (Paris: Gallimard, 1980), 2: 209. ("Ce qui nous reste, c'est l'extérieur de l'homme.")

35 Henry James, "Charles de Bernard and Gustave Flaubert: The Minor French Novelists," in *Literary Criticism* (New York: Library of America, 1984), 2: 170.

36 George Eliot, *The Lifted Veil and Brother Jacob* (London: Penguin, 2001), 3.

37 Sandra M. Gilbert and Susan Gubar, *The Madwoman in the Attic: The Woman Writer and the Nineteenth-Century Literary Imagination* (New Haven: Yale University Press, 2000), 443–77. See also Kate Flint, *The Victorians and the Visual Imagination* (Cambridge: Cambridge University Press, 2000), 96; David Carroll, *George Eliot and the Conflict of Interpretations* (Cambridge: Cambridge University Press, 1992), 30–4; and Neil Hertz, *George Eliot's Pulse* (Stanford: Stanford University Press, 2003), 53–6.

38 Gilbert and Gubar do mention Swift and Pope, but only in passing.

39 See Haight, *George Eliot: A Biography*, 277–92; and Eliot's letter to John Blackwood, July 30, 1859, in George Eliot, *The George Eliot Letters*, ed. Gordon S. Haight (New Haven: Yale University Press, 1954) 3: 124–5.

40 U.C. Knoepflmacher, *George Eliot's Early Novels: The Limits of Realism* (Berkeley and Los Angeles: University of California Press, 1968), 138.

41 George Henry Lewes, *Lewes Ms Journals*, Journal X, entry for March 22, 1859. Unpublished manuscript, Beinecke Rare Book and Manuscript Library, Yale University. See also Sally Shuttleworth's introduction in the Penguin edition of *The Lifted Veil and Brother Jacob*.

42 In April 1860, George Eliot visited Keats's grave in Rome and wrote in a letter to Maria Congreve: "Poor Keats's tombstone, with that despairing inscription, is almost as painful to think of as Swift's" (*The George Eliot Letters*, 3: 288).

43 Christopher Lane, *Hatred and Civility: The Antisocial Life in Victorian England* (New York: Columbia University Press, 2004).

44 Eliot, *Middlemarch*, 219. On a similar tendency in "The Lifted Veil," Lane writes: "Finding no limit to perfidy, [the story] is doubtless Eliot's bleakest work ... An impasse arises here between Eliot's rhetoric of fellow feeling and the elements of revulsion that seem to cancel it in her fiction." *Hatred and Civility*, 108, 117.

45 George Eliot, *Impressions of Theophrastus Such* (Iowa City: University of Iowa Press, 1994), xliv. ("Neque enim notare singulos mens est mihi,/ Verum ipsam vitam et mores hominum ostendere.")

46 Jean-Jacques Rousseau, *Les Confessions*, in *Oeuvres complètes* (Paris: Gallimard, 1959), 1: 5.

47 Eliot, *The George Eliot Letters*, 1: 276.
48 On this latter point see Alex Woloch, *The One Vs. the Many: Minor Characters and the Space of the Protagonist in the Novel* (Princeton: Princeton University Press, 2003), 12–42.
49 Jonathan Swift, *The Correspondence of Jonathan Swift*, ed. Harold Williams (Oxford: Clarendon Press, 1963), 3: 103.
50 See Carroll, *George Eliot and the Conflict of Interpretations*, 29: much of Theophrastus's task is to "establish the point of view from which the impressions are to be delivered ... How can the interpreter of society interpret himself?"; but also Bodenheimer: "the intense and circular introspection of Such certainly goes far beyond anything that would have been necessary to make the official point of fellowship in folly" (*The Real Life of Mary Ann Evans*, 158).
51 Juvenal, *The Sixteen Satires*, trans. Peter Green (London: Penguin, 1998), 106 (lines 38–41).
52 Philip Larkin, "This Be the Verse," in *High Windows* (London: Faber and Faber, 1974), 30.
53 In this respect *Impressions of Theophrastus Such* bears some similarity to a book written only about five years earlier: Trollope's *The Way We Live Now*. Trollope is, of course, also interested in whether the present age is more corrupt than earlier eras. Roger Carbury represents that conservative view; one of his interlocutors disagrees: "I think, too, that they who grumble at the times, as Horace did, and declare that each age is worse than its forerunner, look only at the small things beneath their eyes, and ignore the course of the world at large" (*The Way We Live Now* (London: Penguin, 1994), 425). More often than not, though, Trollope seems to side with Carbury. See also Eliot's own epigraph to chapter 45 of *Middlemarch*, from Sir Thomas Browne: "It is the humour of many heads to extol the days of their forefathers, and declaim against the wickedness of times present. Which notwithstanding they cannot handsomely do, without the borrowed help and satire of times past; condemning the vices of their own times, by the expression of vices in times which they commend, which cannot but argue the community of vice in both. Horace, therefore, Juvenal, and Persius, were no prophets, although their lines did seem to indigitate and point at our times." *Middlemarch*, 433.
54 On perspective and perception in realism, see Elizabeth Deeds Ermarth, *Realism and Consensus in the English Novel* (Princeton: Princeton University Press, 1983), 16–37.
55 Theophrastus's emphasis on wit recalls Eliot's 1856 *Westminster Review* essay on Heinrich Heine, in which she distinguishes between that same category ("allied to the ratiocinative intellect") and the competing category "humour," which is "diffuse, and flows along without any other law than its own fantastic will." See "German Wit: Heinrich Heine," in *Selected Essays, Poems and Other Writings* (London: Penguin, 1990), 70.
56 These lines, from the first edition of 1859, are not included in the main text of the Clarendon edition.

57 In this respect Juvenal echoes Horace, who explains in satire II.i that he would be simply unable to write heroic verses about Caesar or "lines of battle bristling with lances" when he could write satire instead (*Satires and Epistles*, 85–6). Pope's famous rendition of this Horatian apologia – "Fools rush into my Head, and so I write" – is a close cousin of Juvenal's "difficile est saturam non scribere."

58 Juvenal, *The Sixteen Satires*, 4–5 (lines 30–1, 52–4, 63–70).

59 Henry Fielding, *Joseph Andrews* (Oxford: Clarendon Press, 1967), 4–7.

60 Fielding, *Tom Jones* (London: Penguin, 1985), 67, 307, 730. Fielding's self-consciousness, though purportedly all about "facts," is really an aspect of what Ian Watt called the novelist's "realism of assessment" (as opposed to only a "realism of presentation"): see Ian Watt, *The Rise of the Novel: Studies in Defoe, Richardson and Fielding* (Berkeley and Los Angeles: University of California Press, 1957), especially 288.

61 William Hazlitt, *Lectures on the English Comic Writers* (London: Taylor and Hessey, 1819), 32–3.

62 The axiom "Ridicule is the test of truth" has often been attributed to Shaftesbury, but most scholars believe this to be apocryphal. See Alfred Owen Aldridge, "Shaftesbury and the Test of Truth," *PMLA* 60:1 (March 1945), 129–56.

63 See Peter Gay, *The Cultivation of Hatred* (New York: W.W. Norton, 1993), 382.

64 Anthony Trollope, *An Autobiography* (Oxford: Oxford University Press, 1999), 95.

65 Theodor Adorno, "Reconciliation Under Duress," in Adorno et al., *Aesthetics and Politics* (London: Verso, 2007), 157.

66 Lewis, *Men Without Art*, 121.

67 William Makepeace Thackeray, "Charity and Humour," in *The Works of William Makepeace Thackeray* (New York: Scribner's, 1903–1904), 26: 417.

68 Levine, *The Realistic Imagination*, 134.

69 This habit also surfaces in art-historical criticism: artists celebrated chiefly for their satirical genius, for their skill in caricature, have often been praised for their preternatural sense of the real. To take two examples: Hazlitt, in *Lectures on the English Comic Writers*, included a chapter on Hogarth, whose tableaux "bear all the marks, and carry all the conviction of reality with them" (278). And Baudelaire, in his essay "Quelques caricaturistes français," argued that "les images triviales, les croquis de la foule et de la rue, les caricatures, sont souvent le miroir le plus fidèle de la vie" ("mundane images, sketches of the crowd and the street, caricatures, are often the most faithful mirror of life"). Vernet's work is praised for its "accent véridique" ("ring of truth"), Pigal's scenes for their "vérités vulgaires" ("common truths"), and Charlet's figures for their "caractère réel" ("real nature"); as for Daumier, "ce n'est pas précisément de la caricature, c'est de l'histoire, de la triviale et terrible réalité" ("it's not exactly caricature, it's history, mundane and fearsome reality"). Charles Baudelaire, *Oeuvres complètes* (Paris: Gallimard, 1976), 2: 544–52.

70 Lewis, *Men Without Art*, 109.

71 "Le bourgeois (c'est-à-dire l'humanité entière maintenant, y compris le peuple)"; "les bourgeois, c'est-à-dire tout le monde." Flaubert, *Correspondance*, 2: 179 (letter of November 22, 1852) and 3: 170 (letter of August 17, 1861).

72 See, for instance, Nabokov's *Lectures on Literature* (San Diego: Harcourt Brace, 1980), 126–7.

73 Gay, *The Cultivation of Hatred*, 391.

74 On Céline, see Julia Kristeva's similar point: "His novels are realistic out of social constraint and, to some extent, out of hatred." *Powers of Horror: An Essay on Abjection*, trans. Leon S. Roudiez (New York: Columbia University Press, 1982), 137.

75 Meredith, *An Essay on Comedy*, 62. See also Erich Auerbach, writing about Flaubert in *Mimesis*: "like so many important nineteenth-century artists, he hates his period" (487).

76 Watt, *The Rise of the Novel*, 48, 59.

77 For Lukács's antipathy toward naturalism, see especially *Studies in European Realism: A Sociological Survey of the Writings of Balzac, Stendhal, Zola, Tolstoy, Gorky*, trans. Edith Bone (New York: Grosset & Dunlap, 1964), 6–12, 85–96, and 140–3; and "Narrate or Describe?" in *Writer and Critic and Other Essays*, trans. Arthur D. Kahn (New York: Grosset & Dunlap, 1974), 110–48. For his aversion to the avant-garde, expressionism, and modernism, see especially "Realism in the Balance" in Adorno et al., *Aesthetics and Politics*, 28–59.

78 Lukács, "Narrate or Describe?", 127.

79 Lukács, *Studies in European Realism*, 189; Georg Lukács, *Essays on Realism*, trans. David Fernbach (Cambridge, MA: MIT Press, 1980), 51–2; and "Realism in the Balance," in Adorno et al., *Aesthetics and Politics*, 38. On Lukács's emphasis on type and the typical, see, for instance, *Studies in European Realism*, 6, 88, 154, and 168.

80 Brecht, "Against Georg Lukács," in Adorno et al., *Aesthetics and Politics*, 69.

81 Adorno, "Reconciliation under Duress," in *Aesthetics and Politics*, 159, 162.

82 See Terry Lovell, *Pictures of Reality: Aesthetics, Politics, and Pleasure* (London: BFI, 1980); Paulson, *The Fictions of Satire*, 18 (where Paulson mentions "the conservatism that underlies even revolutionary satire"); and Christopher Yu, *Nothing to Admire: The Politics of Poetic Satire from Dryden to Merrill* (Oxford: Oxford University Press, 2003), which complicates the notion of satirical conservatism (Pope's, for instance) by emphasizing liberalism. See also Robert C. Elliott, *The Power of Satire: Magic, Ritual, Art* (Princeton: Princeton University Press, 1960), 266 ("The satirist claims, with much justification, to be a true conservative"); P.K. Elkin, *The Augustan Defence of Satire* (Oxford: Clarendon Press, 1973), 189 ("satire, by tradition at least, safeguards existing boundaries ... the satirist [is] guardian of the commonweal"); and Rawson, *Satire and Sentiment*, 180 ("The main feeling of a large-scale threat to the civilised order was itself a commonplace among Augustan writers of conservative cast for almost a century").

83 Lukács, *Studies in European Realism*, 19; "Realism in the Balance," in *Aesthetics and Politics*, 56.
84 "Sainte ... Elle est l'indignation des coeurs forts et puissants, le dédain militant de ceux que fâchent la médiocrité et la sottise ... Je n'ai pu faire deux pas dans la vie sans rencontrer trois imbéciles, et c'est pourquoi je suis triste." Emile Zola, "Mes haines," in *Ecrits sur l'art* (Paris: Gallimard, 1991), 35.
85 G.K. Chesterton, *George Bernard Shaw* (New York: Hill and Wang, 1956), 175.
86 Flaubert, *Correspondance*, 2: 85; Lewis, *Men Without Art*, 113. See also Hazlitt: "Comedy naturally wears itself out – destroys the very food on which it lives; and by constantly and successfully exposing the follies and weaknesses of mankind to ridicule, in the end leaves itself nothing worth laughing at" (*Lectures on the English Comic Writers*, 302).
87 Mikhail Bakhtin, *Problems of Dostoevsky's Poetics* (Minneapolis: University of Minnesota Press, 1984). On polyphony, see especially 6–8; on the open-endedness of the polyphonic novel, 39, 63; on the freedom of characters, 51–3, 64–5; on the incorporation of many genres and styles, especially the fantastic, 114–18. See also Frye, *Anatomy of Criticism*, 309–12.
88 Bakhtin, *Rabelais and His World* (Bloomington: Indiana University Press, 1984), 19–21, 122–3. Bakhtin repeatedly draws a distinction between Rabelais's grotesque realism or carnivalesque and later "solely negative" forms of satire, which he holds in low esteem: see 21, 38–9, 51, 62, 67, 120, 306.
89 See Wood, *The Irresponsible Self*, 178–94.

CHAPTER 2 TERMINAL SATIRE AND 'JUDE
THE OBSCURE'

1 Thomas Hardy, *Jude the Obscure* (London: Macmillan, 1912), 203.
2 Thomas Hardy, *Tess of the d'Urbervilles* (London: Macmillan, 1912), 508; *The Mayor of Casterbridge* (London: Macmillan, 1912), 144.
3 The second passage, Jude's reaction to the clergymen, appeared only in the serial version. Thomas Hardy, *Jude the Obscure*, ed. Dennis Taylor (London: Penguin, 1988), 456.
4 Florence Emily Hardy, *The Early Life of Thomas Hardy, 1840–1891* (New York: Macmillan, 1928), 272.
5 This list is strikingly similar to the catalog of authors that Sue, describing to Jude her extensive reading, says that she has read: Martial, Lucian, and Smollett appear there too, alongside Juvenal, Scarron, Sterne, Fielding, and others (*Jude the Obscure*, 176).
6 Thomas Hardy, *The Literary Notebooks of Thomas Hardy*, ed. Lennart A. Björk (London: Macmillan, 1985), I: 9, 213–16.
7 Hardy, *Literary Notebooks*, I: 214.
8 Thomas Hardy, "The Science of Fiction," in *Thomas Hardy's Personal Writings*, ed. Harold Orel (Lawrence: University of Kansas Press, 1966), 136.

9 John Addington Symonds, *Essays Speculative and Suggestive* (London: Chapman and Hall, 1890), 1: 189; Hardy, *Literary Notebooks*, 2: 36. See also Hardy's long notebook citation from Eugène-Melchior de Vogüé's 1886 *Revue des Deux Mondes* essay, "De la Littérature Réaliste," which casts a similarly skeptical eye on the later realism and naturalism of the period (*Literary Notebooks*, 1: 219–23).

10 Edmund Gosse, "The Limits of Realism in Fiction," in *Questions at Issue* (New York: D. Appleton and Company, 1893), 145.

11 Hardy, *Two on a Tower* (London: Macmillan, 1912), 1; *The Woodlanders* (London: Macmillan, 1912), 1.

12 Hardy, *The Return of the Native* (London: Macmillan, 1912), 3.

13 In this respect, as in so many others, Hardy had an immense influence on D.H. Lawrence. See, for example, *Women in Love*, where Birkin imagines the "beautiful clean thought" of "a world empty of people"; Ursula thinks about "how stupid anthropomorphism is! ... The universe is non-human, thank God"; and Birkin concludes: "whatever the mystery which has brought forth man and the universe, it is a non-human mystery ... man is not the criterion." *Women in Love* (Cambridge: Cambridge University Press, 1987), 127, 264, 478.

14 This is also similar to Hardy's first conception of the verse epic that would become *The Dynasts*: in 1891 he foresaw it as "A Bird's Eye View of Europe at the Beginning of the Nineteenth Century." See Florence Emily Hardy, *The Early Life of Thomas Hardy*, 306.

15 Gustave Flaubert, *Correspondance* (Paris: Gallimard, 1980), 2: 204. "L'auteur, dans son oeuvre, doit être comme Dieu dans l'univers, présent partout, et visible nulle part."

16 James Wood, *The Broken Estate: Essays on Literature and Belief* (New York: Random House, 1999), 48.

17 "Quand est-ce qu'on écrira les faits au point de vue *d'une blague supérieure*, c'est-à-dire comme le bon Dieu les voit, d'en haut?" (Flaubert, *Correspondance*, 2: 168).

18 H.G. Wells, in his review of *Jude* in the February 8, 1896, *Saturday Review*, praised this scene for its "pitiless irony" and pronounced it "one of the most grimly magnificent passages in English fiction." Hardy's scene, with its ironic juxtapositions, recalls the *comices agricoles* episode of *Madame Bovary*, which relies on a very similar technique.

19 Hardy, *The Mayor of Casterbridge*, 386.

20 See Michael Millgate, *Thomas Hardy: A Biography* (New York: Random House, 1982), 353.

21 Thomas Hardy, *Collected Letters*, ed. Richard Little Purdy and Michael Millgate (Oxford: Clarendon Press, 1978–1988), 2: 93.

22 On "folly" see Jude's remark to the curate Mr. Highbridge at the end of part II: "'Now I know I have been a fool, and that folly is with me'" (148).

23 Hardy's reference to Jude as a "puppet" may signal the influence of Thackeray, one of the "satirists" he was reading in the early 1890s. "Puppet" is an essential word in *Vanity Fair*. In the prelude to that novel, "Before the

Curtain," Thackeray calls his heroine "the famous little Becky Puppet"; and the final chapter concludes with an invitation to the reader: "Come children, let us shut up the box and the puppets, for our play is played out." See *Vanity Fair* (London: Penguin, 2003), 6, 809.

24 G.K. Chesterton, *The Victorian Age in Literature* (London: Williams and Norgate, 1913), 144.

25 This theme of the anthropomorphism of God also appeared in a major study of paranoia from the same era: Freud's 1911 case study of Dr. Schreber, or "Psycho-analytic Notes on an Autobiographical Account of a Case of Paranoia (Dementia Paranoides)." Freud, who writes that his patient "could not avoid the thought that God Himself had played the part of accessory, if not of instigator, in the plot against him," reminds the reader that this paranoid attitude towards God is predicated on a certain understanding that He is somewhat human. See *The Standard Edition of the Complete Psychological Works of Sigmund Freud*, trans. James Strachey (London: Hogarth Press, 1958), 12: 39 and especially 51–2.

26 William Wordsworth, *The Poetical Works of William Wordsworth*, ed. E. de Selincourt and Helen Darbishire (Oxford: Clarendon Press, 1947), 4: 281 (lines 63–4).

27 Florence Emily Hardy, *The Early Life of Thomas Hardy*, 63.

28 Florence Emily Hardy, *The Later Years of Thomas Hardy, 1892–1928* (New York: Macmillan, 1930), 179.

29 Joss Marsh, *Word Crimes: Blasphemy, Culture, and Literature in Nineteenth-Century England* (Chicago: University of Chicago Press, 1998). See pages 269–327.

30 Gosse, "Mr Hardy's New Novel," *Cosmopolis* 1 (January 1896), 68. See also Marsh, *Word Crimes*, 269, 278.

31 T.S. Eliot, *After Strange Gods: A Primer of Modern Heresy* (London: Faber and Faber, 1934), 54.

32 G.W. Foote, preface to *Satires and Profanities* by James Thomson (London: Progressive Publishing Company, 1884), v.

33 Thomas Hardy, *Thomas Hardy: The Complete Poems*, ed. James Gibson (London: Palgrave, 2001), 417.

34 The idea that the satiric source is not identified seems to lie behind what was probably Hardy's first use of the phrase "satire of circumstance," in his 1876 novel *The Hand of Ethelberta*. His character Christopher Julian is "unable, like many other people, to enjoy being satirised in words, because of the irritation it caused him as aimed-at-victim," but "he sometimes had philosophy enough to appreciate a satire of circumstance, because nobody intended it." *The Hand of Ethelberta* (London: Macmillan, 1912), 97.

35 On this point see Peter Widdowson's *On Thomas Hardy: Late Essays and Earlier* (Houndmills: Macmillan, 1998). Widdowson's collection includes an essay on Arabella and "satirical discourse" in *Jude*; he sees "satire" as inherently antithetical to "tragedy" as a means of interpreting Hardy's fiction. See especially pages 173–4.

36 J. Hillis Miller, *Fiction and Repetition: Seven English Novels* (Cambridge, MA: Harvard University Press, 1982), 13, 140.

37 D.H. Lawrence, *Study of Thomas Hardy and Other Essays* (Cambridge: Cambridge University Press, 1985), 120.

38 Irving Howe, *Thomas Hardy* (New York: Macmillan, 1967), 145–6.

39 Mrs. Oliphant, "The Anti-Marriage League," *Blackwood's Magazine*, January 1896, 141.

40 "Mr Hardy's New Novel," *The Illustrated London News*, January 11, 1896, 50.

41 Havelock Ellis, "Concerning *Jude the Obscure*," *The Savoy*, October 1896, 40, 41–2.

42 See Gillian Beer, *Darwin's Plots: Evolutionary Narrative in Darwin, George Eliot, and Nineteenth-Century Fiction* (Cambridge: Cambridge University Press, 1983), 240.

43 Jonathan Swift, *A Modest Proposal* in *Prose Works of Jonathan Swift: Irish Tracts, 1728–1733*, ed. Herbert Davis (Oxford: Basil Blackwell, 1955), 12: 109–10.

44 The most notorious such misreading is recounted by Wayne Booth in *The Rhetoric of Irony* (Chicago: University of Chicago Press, 1974), 105. There was a similar occurrence in the Victorian period upon the 1840 publication of a tract called "On the Possibility of Limiting Populousness" that promoted the idea of gassing children. It was taken by many to be a serious proposal but is now assumed to have been an imitation of Swift. See R. Sauer, "Infanticide and Abortion in Nineteenth Century Britain," *Population Studies* 32 (1978): 81–93.

45 John Bayley, *An Essay on Hardy* (Cambridge: Cambridge University Press, 1978), 16.

46 Florence Emily Hardy, *The Later Years of Thomas Hardy*, 80.

47 See especially Hardy, *Collected Letters*, 2: 97–106.

48 This is also evidence of a larger Hardyan technique in the representation of violence and death. Such cool specificity of detail recalls the similarly after-the-fact report of Tess's murder of Alec in *Tess of the d'Urbervilles*. In that novel it is the householder, Mrs. Brooks, who comes across the first evidence of death. She looks up at the ceiling and notices a spot on the white surface: "It was about the size of a wafer when she first observed it, but it speedily grew as large as the palm of her hand, and then she could perceive that it was red" (488).

49 Such violently hyperrealistic narration unsettles many readers of Hardy. Philip Larkin, for instance, observed upon rereading him: "I am more conscious than I was, too, of an undercurrent of sensual cruelty in the writing – this seems an extraordinary thing to say of Hardy, but for all his gentleness he had a strong awareness of, and even relish for, both the macabre and the cruel." "Wanted: Good Hardy Critic," in *Required Writing: Miscellaneous Pieces, 1955–1982* (New York: Farrar, Straus, and Giroux, 1984), 171.

50 For more on Arabella in this context, see Widdowson, *On Thomas Hardy*, 179–87.

51 Thomas Hardy, *Jude the Obscure*, ed. Dennis Taylor (London: Penguin, 1998), 463.

52 Hardy, *Collected Letters*, 1: 190.

53 Arthur Schopenhauer, *The World as Will and Representation*, trans. E.F.J. Payne (New York: Dover, 1969), 1: 322.

54 Hardy, *Personal Writings*, 49.

55 Hardy, *Personal Writings*, 44–5.

56 Lionel Johnson, *The Art of Thomas Hardy* (New York: Russell & Russell, 1928), 37.

57 Johnson, *The Art of Thomas Hardy*, 38. For *The Hand of Ethelberta*, see also Hardy's letter to Leslie Stephen on May 21, 1875, in which he responded to Stephen's objection to the subtitle "A Comedy in Chapters": "My meaning was simply, as you know, that the story would concern the follies of life rather than the passions, & be told in something of a comedy form, all the people having weaknesses at which the superior lookers-on smile, instead of being ideal characters. I should certainly deplore being thought to have set up in the large joke line – the genteelest of genteel comedy being as far as ever I should think it safe to go at any time" (*Collected Letters*, 1: 37). Hardy's last line here attests to the great distance from *Ethelberta*'s essentially well-mannered comedy to *Jude*'s radically bleak satire.

58 Florence Emily Hardy, *The Early Life of Thomas Hardy*, 272.

59 Hardy, *The Complete Poems*, 168.

60 Florence Emily Hardy, *The Early Life of Thomas Hardy*, 294. This article, by Oswald Crawfurd, appeared in *The Fortnightly Review*, April 1, 1890. "Then again," Crawfurd wrote, "it may be said of the drama as it may be said of fiction, that it is not for edification. A play with a purpose is considered by the best critics to be as great a mistake as a novel with a purpose" (316).

61 Hardy, *Collected Letters*, 2: 126.

62 See, for example, the unsigned review in the *Athenaeum*, November 25, 1895.

63 See especially his November 24, 1898, letter to William Archer (Hardy, *Collected Letters*, 2: 206).

64 Miller, *Thomas Hardy: Distance and Desire* (Cambridge, MA: Harvard University Press, 1970), 71.

65 Hardy, *The Complete Poems*, 929.

66 On *Jude the Obscure* and the notion of an absolute silence, see also D.H. Lawrence, writing in a somewhat different register: "After Sue [Bridehead], after Dostoievsky's *Idiot*, after Turner's late pictures, after the Symbolist poetry of Mallarmé and the others, after the music of Debussy, there is no further possible utterance of the peace that passeth all understanding, the peace of God which is Perfect Knowledge. There is only silence beyond this." *Study of Thomas Hardy*, 125.

67 Swift, *A Tale of a Tub* in *Prose Works of Jonathan Swift*, 1: 135.

68 Louis-Ferdinand Céline, *Voyage au bout de la nuit*, in *Romans* (Paris: Gallimard, 1981), 1: 505.

CHAPTER 3 GEORGE GISSING'S AMBIVALENT REALISM

1 George Gissing, *New Grub Street* (Oxford: Oxford University Press, 1998), 208, 148, 377, 337.

2 "Our One English Realist," *Daily Chronicle*, May 26, 1892. See Gissing's letter to Eduard Bertz, June 18, 1892, where he calls this anonymous review (of *Born in Exile*) "a very fair & full account of my book. I believe this is as yet the only favourable notice." George Gissing, *The Collected Letters of George Gissing*, ed. Paul F. Mattheisen, Arthur C. Young, and Pierre Coustillas (Athens, OH: Ohio University Press, 1994), 5: 43.

3 Henry James, "London Notes," in *Literary Criticism* (New York: Library of America, 1984), 1: 1405. H.G. Wells, "George Gissing: An Impression," *The Living Age*, 25: 3143 (1904), 38.

4 *Whitehall Review*, April 18, 1891, 19–20; *Athenaeum*, May 9, 1891, 601.

5 *Saturday Review*, 71 (May 2, 1891), 524–5; and 71 (May 9, 1891), 572.

6 Walter Besant, "Notes and News," *Author* 2:1 (June 1, 1891), 15; and Andrew Lang, "Realism in Grub Street," *Author* 2:2 (July 1, 1891), 43–4.

7 Thomas Hardy, "The Science of Fiction," in *Thomas Hardy's Personal Writings*, ed. Harold Orel (Lawrence: University of Kansas Press, 1966), 136.

8 Gustave Flaubert and George Sand, *Correspondance*, ed. Alphonse Jacobs (Paris: Flammarion, 1981), 521. Letter of February 6, 1876 ("j'exècre ce qu'on est convenu d'appeler le *réalisme*, bien qu'on m'en fasse un des pontifes"). Twenty years earlier, Flaubert had written to a friend about *Madame Bovary*: "I am believed to be smitten with the real, even though I loathe it. It's in hatred of realism that I began this novel." ("On me croit épris du réel, tandis que je l'exècre. Car c'est en haine du réalisme que j'ai entrepris ce roman.") Letter to Edma Roger des Genettes, October 30, 1856: Gustave Flaubert, *Correspondance* (Paris: Gallimard, 1980), 2: 643.

9 Even Arthur Morrison – famed documentarian of the London slums – wrote against the label, in the preface to the third edition of *A Child of the Jago*: "it is a fact that I have never called myself a 'realist,' and I have never put forth any work as 'realism.'" (Chicago: Academy Chicago Publishers, 1995), ix.

10 George Gissing, "The Place of Realism in Fiction," *Humanitarian* 7:1 (July 1895) 14–16.

11 It is interesting, nonetheless, that Gissing does not once mention Zola by name in the essay.

12 Linda Nochlin, *Realism* (London: Penguin, 1990), 28, 103–6.

13 Q.D. Leavis, "Gissing and the English Novel," *Scrutiny* 7:1 (June 1938), 73–81. See especially 79.

14 Gissing, *Collected Letters*, 4: 289.

15 Pat Rogers, *Grub Street: Studies in a Subculture* (London: Methuen, 1972), 76, 183, 211, 220.

16 Adrian Poole proposes these real-life models, while John Halperin emphasizes the autobiographical interpretation. See Poole, *Gissing in Context*

(London: Macmillan, 1975), 141; and Halperin, *Gissing: A Life in Books* (Oxford: Oxford University Press, 1982), 142.

17 Alexander Pope, *The Dunciad* (1742 version), in *The Poems of Alexander Pope*, ed. John Sutherland (New Haven: Yale University Press, 1953), 5: 301, 274 (Book II, l. 123 and Book I, l. 44).

18 For more on the relation of literature to the "literary world," see Gissing's 1886 letter to Hardy, where he wrote of the need "to pursue literature as distinct from the profession of letters." Florence Emily Hardy, *The Early Life of Thomas Hardy, 1840–1891* (New York: Macmillan, 1928), 239.

19 See, for instance, Gissing's disconsolate letter to Eduard Bertz on September 6, 1890, just before he began *New Grub Street* (*Collected Letters*, 4: 235).

20 George Gissing, *In the Year of Jubilee* (London: Everyman/J.M. Dent, 1994), 356. For more on Nancy's ill-fated ambition to be a writer see pages 262–3.

21 Thackeray proposes this same idea in *Pendennis*. After recounting the title character's long effort in publishing his own novel, the narrator refuses to name the price Pendennis's book fetched from his publisher, "lest other young literary aspirants should expect to be as lucky as he was, and unprofessional persons forsake their own callings, whatever they may be, for the sake of supplying the world with novels, whereof there is already a sufficiency." See *Pendennis* (Harmondsworth: Penguin, 1972), 439.

22 Pope, *The Dunciad Variorum*, in *The Poems of Alexander Pope*, 5: 49.

23 Ian Watt, *The Rise of the Novel: Studies in Defoe, Richardson and Fielding* (Berkeley and Los Angeles: University of California Press, 1957), especially 48, 59. Watt also, however, takes note of the demands and debasements of Grub Street, though he tends to focus on booksellers rather than paper manufacturers (see 53–6).

24 See Gissing, *New Grub Street*, 90, 103, 304, 398. See also David Grylls, "The Annual Return to Old Grub Street: What Samuel Johnson Meant to Gissing," *Gissing Newsletter* 20:1 (January, 1984), 1–27.

25 Pope, *The Dunciad* (1742 version), in *The Poems of Alexander Pope*, 5: 315 (Book II, ll. 361–2); *Epistle to Dr. Arbuthnot*, in *The Poems of Alexander Pope*, 4: 109 (l. 188).

26 Jonathan Swift, *A Tale of a Tub With Other Early Works, 1696–1707*, in *Prose Works of Jonathan Swift*, ed. Herbert Davis (Oxford: Basil Blackwell, 1957), 1: 58.

27 George Gordon, Lord Byron, "English Bards and Scottish Reviews," in *The Complete Poetical Works of Byron*, ed. Paul Elmer More (Boston: Houghton Mifflin, 1933), 247 (lines 385–6).

28 Walter Benjamin, "Karl Kraus," in *Reflections*, trans. Edmund Jephcott (New York: Schocken, 1978), 245.

29 "Il jugea qu'il n'y avait point de métier au monde dont ou dût être plus dégoûté." Voltaire, *Candide*, in *Romans et contes*, ed. René Groos (Paris: Gallimard, 1954), 200.

30 Honoré de Balzac, *Illusions perdues*, in *La Comédie humaine*, Pierre-Georges Castex (gen. ed.) (Paris: Gallimard, 1977), 5: 327, 442–5, and especially

457–62. It is also interesting to recall Balzac's novel in light of *New Grub Street*'s Popeian satire on the surplus of paper: *Illusions perdues* begins with the Séchard printing business, which similarly sets the stage for Balzac's investigations into the suspicious uses of paper later in the novel.

31 Balzac, *Illusions perdues*, in *La Comédie humaine*, 5: 408. Posthumous appraisals of Gissing made much of his resemblance to Balzac. See, for instance, H.G. Wells's evaluation in *The Living Age*, 40, 43.

32 Thackeray, *Pendennis*, 354.

33 Gissing, *Collected Letters*, 2: 360; 4: 100, 221; 5: 229.

34 Gissing, *Collected Letters*, 4: 277. It is also worth noting that his most sustained reading during these years, as he frequently told his correspondents, was in Aristophanes.

35 On the parallel between Gissing and the mostly foolish Whelpdale, see this jovial character's long narrative about his experiences in America, which are based very closely on Gissing's own: 390–5.

36 Letter to Eduard Bertz, May 20, 1892 (Gissing, *Collected Letters*, 5: 36).

37 George Gissing, *Born in Exile* (London: Everyman/J.M. Dent, 1993), 105.

38 In his correspondence Gissing often voices complaint in a way that would suggest a considerable identification with Peak. See, for example, his June 21, 1887, letter to his sister Ellen, where he rails against the "fatuity, vulgarity & blatant blackguardism" of the Jubilee celebrations: "the vulgarity of the mass of mankind passes all utterance." *Collected Letters*, 3: 125.

39 John Carey, *The Intellectuals and the Masses: Pride and Prejudice Among the Literary Intelligentsia, 1880–1939* (London: Faber and Faber, 1992), 93–4.

40 Fredric Jameson, *The Political Unconscious: Narrative as a Socially Symbolic Act* (Ithaca: Cornell University Press, 1981), 185–205.

41 Patrick Brantlinger, *The Reading Lesson: The Threat of Mass Literacy in Nineteenth-Century British Fiction* (Bloomington: Indiana University Press, 1998), 183. See also Brantlinger's *Bread and Circuses: Theories of Mass Culture as Social Decay* (Ithaca: Cornell University Press, 1983), especially 130–4, for a related discussion of the "masses" in relation to Malthusianism.

42 On this point see also Ian Watt in *The Rise of the Novel*, writing about a similar tendency in an earlier era: "There was in any case no general agreement that [the growth of the reading public] would be desirable. Throughout the eighteenth century utilitarian and mercantilist objections to giving the poor a literate education increased" (39).

43 Carey, *The Intellectuals and the Masses*, 15.

44 George Gissing, *The Whirlpool* (London: Everyman/J.M. Dent, 1997), 16.

45 George Gissing, *The Nether World* (Oxford: Oxford University Press, 1999), 57, 74, 280.

46 Juvenal, *The Sixteen Satires*, trans. Peter Green (London: Penguin, 1998), 18. ("nil habet infelix paupertas durius in se,/ quam quod ridiculos homines facit.")

47 Gissing was quite interested in Ibsen, especially in the early 1890s. In 1891 he wrote to Eduard Bertz of his admiration for Ibsen but expressed regret that

he was a playwright: "For my own part, I grieve that they are *plays*. More & more I dislike the conditions of theatrical exhibition. It is of necessity an appeal to the mob; consequently there is much of degradation in it … I much wish Ibsen had put his thoughts into narrative form." *Collected Letters*, 4: 275–6.

48 Jonathan Swift, *The Correspondence of Jonathan Swift*, ed. Harold Williams (Oxford: Clarendon Press, 1963), 3: 103.

49 Pope addresses essentially the same theme in the second dialogue of the *Epilogue to the Satires*: "Spare then the Person, and expose the Vice." *The Poems of Alexander Pope*, 4: 314 (lines 10–21).

50 The same theme recurs later in Gissing's career, in both his 1901 novel *Our Friend the Charlatan* and his thinly veiled 1903 memoir *The Private Papers of Henry Ryecroft*, the last of his books published during his lifetime. In *Our Friend the Charlatan*, one character admires Nietzsche's "frank contempt of the average man," and another confesses "I don't know that I have much faith in leagues … I am a lost individualist." See *Our Friend the Charlatan* (New York: Henry Holt, 1901), 211, 271. In *Ryecroft*, the title figure (a Gissing-like author) writes: "I am no friend of the people. As a force, by which the tenor of the time is conditioned, they inspire me with distrust, with fear; as a visible multitude, they make me shrink aloof, and often move me to abhorrence. For the greater part of my life, the people signified to me the London crowd, and no phrase of temperate meaning would utter my thoughts of them under that aspect … Right or wrong, this is my temper. But he who should argue from it that I am intolerant of all persons belonging to a lower social rank than my own would go far astray. Nothing is more rooted in my mind than the vast distinction between the individual and the class. Take a man by himself, and there is generally some reason to be found in him, some disposition for good; mass him with his fellows in the social organism, and ten to one he becomes a blatant creature, without a thought of his own, ready for any evil to which contagion prompts him. It is because nations tend to stupidity and baseness that mankind moves so slowly; it is because individuals have a capacity for better things that it moves at all." Like so many characters in *New Grub Street*, Ryecroft also voices a disdain for the vulgar and ignorant public specifically in relation to reading: "the public which would feel no lack if all book-printing ceased to-morrow, is enormous." See *The Private Papers of Henry Ryecroft* (Westminster: Archibald Constable and Co., 1903), 47–8 and 67.

51 On Gissing's debt to Dickens, see John Goode, *George Gissing: Ideology and Fiction* (New York: Barnes and Noble, 1979), 13–40. See also my essay "Some Versions of Vitriol (The Novel Circa 1890)," *Novel: A Forum on Fiction* 42:1 (Spring 2009), 23–39, which discusses Gissing, Dickens, and realism.

52 George Gissing, *The Immortal Dickens* (London: Cecil Palmer, 1925), 13.

53 George Gissing, *Charles Dickens: A Critical Study* (New York: Haskell House, 1974), 64.

54 Raymond Williams, *The Country and the City* (New York: Oxford University Press, 1973), 222.

55 Arnold Bennett, "Mr George Gissing: An Inquiry," *Academy*, 57 (1899), 725. George Orwell saw this homogenizing tendency – what Bennett called the "vast wholes" – to be one of Gissing's greatest qualities, especially in terms of the pessimism that allowed him to avoid scenes of improbable humor, and which usually covers the novels like a total blanket: "Very few English novels exist throughout on the same plane of probability. Gissing solves this problem without apparent difficulty, and it may be that his native pessimism was a help to him." George Orwell, "Not Enough Money: A Sketch of George Gissing," in *Essays*, ed. John Carey (New York: Alfred A. Knopf, 2002), 469.

56 See George Gissing, *London and the Life of Literature in Late Victorian England: The Diary of George Gissing, Novelist*, ed. Pierre Coustillas (Hassocks: Harvester, 1978), 185. Bertz's essay originally appeared as "George Gissing: Ein Realist-Idealist" in three installments in the weekly *Deutsche Presse* in November 1889.

57 *Spectator*, February 9, 1895, 206.

58 "An Idealistic Realist," *Atlantic Monthly* 93: 556 (February 1904), 280.

59 Arthur Waugh, "George Gissing," *Fortnightly Review* 75: 446 (February 1904), 244, 251, 253.

60 George Gissing, "The Hope of Pessimism," in *George Gissing: Essays and Fiction*, ed. Pierre Coustillas (Baltimore: Johns Hopkins Press, 1970), 80.

61 Gissing, *Collected Letters*, 1: 307. (Letter to Algernon Gissing, November 3, 1880.)

62 Florence Emily Hardy, *The Early Life of Thomas Hardy, 1840–1891* (New York: Macmillan, 1928), 272.

63 Virginia Woolf, "An Impression of Gissing," in *The Essays of Virginia Woolf*, ed. Andrew McNeillie (San Diego: Harcourt Brace Jovanovich, 1988), 3: 373.

64 Holbrook Jackson, *The Eighteen Nineties* (New York: Alfred A. Knopf, 1922), 27.

65 "George Gissing," in George Orwell, *Collected Essays, Journalism and Letters of George Orwell*, ed. Sonia Orwell and Ian Angus (New York: Harcourt Brace & World, 1968), 4: 433, 435.

66 On this point see also Michael Collie, who writes of Gissing's "ruthless or logically unremitting reluctance to resort to a panacea of any kind." *The Alien Art: A Critical Study of George Gissing's Novels* (Folkestone: Dawson, 1979), 167.

67 Edith Sichel, "Two Philanthropic Novelists: Mr Walter Besant and Mr George Gissing," *Murray's Magazine* 3: 16 (April 1888), 516; Edward Clodd, *Memories* (London: Chapman and Hall, 1916), 174.

68 Edmund Gosse, "The Limits of Realism in Fiction," in *Questions at Issue* (New York: D. Appleton and Company, 1893), 152, 154, 145.

CHAPTER 4 THE ENGLISH CRITICS AND THE
NORWEGIAN SATIRIST

1   William Archer, "Ibsen and English Criticism," *Fortnightly Review* 46: 271 (July 1889), 30.
2   There had been a one-night performance of *The Pillars of Society* in 1880 and an obscure staging of *A Doll's House* by amateur actors in 1885, but neither can be considered a full Ibsen production. See Miriam Frank, *Ibsen in England* (Boston: Four Seas Company, 1919), 168–9.
3   Edmund Gosse, "Ibsen's Social Dramas," *Fortnightly Review* 45: 265 (January 1889), 108, 110.
4   Pascale Casanova, *The World Republic of Letters*, trans. M.B. DeBevoise (Cambridge, MA: Harvard University Press, 2004), 157–63.
5   Henrik Ibsen, *Ibsen: Letters and Speeches*, ed. Evert Sprinchorn (New York: Hill and Wang, 1964), 119. See page 318 for the June 27, 1895, letter to Archer.
6   London newspapers nevertheless reported in 1891 that the Norwegian was rumored to be arriving on English shores. See *Athenaeum*, May 23, 1891; Michael Meyer, *Ibsen: A Biography* (Garden City, NY: Doubleday, 1971), 736.
7   See Kirsten Shepherd-Barr, *Ibsen and Early Modernist Theatre, 1890–1900* (Westport, CT: Greenwood Press, 1997), 25.
8   Henry James, "Henrik Ibsen: On the Occasion of *Hedda Gabler*," in *Essays in London and Elsewhere* (New York: Harper & Brothers, 1893), 231.
9   George Bernard Shaw, *The Quintessence of Ibsenism*, in *The Works of Bernard Shaw* (London: Constable & Co., 1930), 19: 18.
10 Shaw, *Our Theatres in the Nineties* in *The Works of Bernard Shaw*, 23: 77–8 and 24: 269.
11 Shaw, *Heartbreak House*, in *The Works of Bernard Shaw*, 15: 3–4.
12 William Archer, "The Real Ibsen," *International Monthly* 3 (February 1901), 182.
13 Edmund Gosse, "A Norwegian Drama," *Spectator*, July 20, 1872, 922–3. An earlier *Spectator* article (from March 16, 1872), "Ibsen's New Poems," called the Norwegian's early verse "brilliant satire in sonnets, sparkling with wit and polemical zeal" (344–5). Gosse's final Ibsen article for the *Spectator* (March 27, 1875), entitled "Ibsen's Jubilee," concluded that "it is in his satirical dramas, with their brilliant, lyrical form, that his genius shows itself to the greatest advantage" (401–2).
14 Edmund Gosse, "Ibsen, the Norwegian Satirist," *Fortnightly Review* 13: 731 (January 1873), 74–5. This essay would later be incorporated into Gosse's 1879 collection *Studies in the Literature of Northern Europe*.
15 Ibsen, *Letters and Speeches*, 134–5.
16 All translations from Ibsen here are by Michael Meyer. Henrik Ibsen, *Brand*, in *Plays: Five*, trans. and ed. Michael Meyer (London: Methuen, 2000), 24.
17 Ibsen, *Peer Gynt* in *Plays: Six*, 11, 173.
18 Edmund Gosse, *Ibsen* (London: Hodder and Stoughton, 1907), vii.

19 A small rivalry developed between Gosse and Archer on the question of who deserved primary credit for discovering and introducing Ibsen. See Ann Thwaite, *Edmund Gosse: A Literary Landscape, 1849–1928* (London: Secker & Warburg, 1984), 339–43.

20 Charles Augustin Sainte-Beuve, "Madame Bovary, par M. Gustave Flaubert," in *Causeries du lundi* (Paris: Garnier Frères, 1912), 13: 363. ("Fils et frère de médecins distingués, M. Gustave Flaubert tient la plume comme d'autres le scalpel. Anatomistes et physiologistes, je vous trouve partout!") For the cartoon, see F.W.J. Hemmings, *Culture and Society in France, 1848–1898* (New York: Scribner's, 1971), 116.

21 In this respect Ibsen's rebuff of the idea that he was comparable to Zola – "Zola descends into the sewer to bathe in it, I to cleanse it" – is somewhat misleading. Even if "bathing in it" would suggest a celebration of the squalid that Ibsen indeed never manifested, "cleansing it" would – at first – suggest a clear program of reform that, despite Shaw's insistence, never really animated Ibsen's writing. Ibsen was certainly referring to a less political sewer-cleansing, a thorough scouring of the dirt of naïve idealism that had accumulated on nineteenth-century society. See Michael Meyer's introduction to *Ghosts* in *Plays: One*, 22.

22 See Beer, *Darwin's Plots*; and George Levine, *Darwin and the Novelists: Patterns of Science in Victorian Fiction* (Cambridge, MA: Harvard University Press, 1988) and *Dying to Know: Scientific Epistemology and Narrative in Victorian England* (Chicago: University of Chicago Press, 2002).

23 Toril Moi, *Henrik Ibsen and the Birth of Modernism: Art, Theater, Philosophy* (New York: Oxford University Press, 2006), 9.

24 Ibsen, *Letters and Speeches*, 75, 84.

25 Moi gives greater prominence to *Emperor and Galilean*, seeing in it the genesis of Ibsen's modernism (and following the playwright's own remark that it was his "*hovedverk*" – main or most important work). See Moi, *Henrik Ibsen*, 188.

26 On this point see Bjørn Hemmer's emphasis on the coexistence of realism with "caricature types" in *The Pillars of Society*: the coastal town where the play is set is "bathed in the light of ridicule." "Ibsen and the Realistic Problem Drama," in *The Cambridge Companion to Ibsen*, ed. James McFarlane (Cambridge: Cambridge University Press, 2004), 76.

27 It is conventionally understood that in the 1890s, in plays like *John Gabriel Borkman* and *When We Dead Awaken*, Ibsen's theater restrained its aggressive realist impulse in favor of a rather more mystical, symbolist mood.

28 James Joyce, "Ibsen's New Drama," in *On Ibsen*, ed. Dennis Phillips (Copenhagen and Los Angeles: Green Integer, 1999), 61.

29 Clement Scott, *The Theatre* 14 (July 1, 1889), 19.

30 Nym Crinkle, "The Foolishness of the Ibsenites," *The Theatre Magazine* 5: 9 (January 4, 1890), 165–6.

31 W.B. Yeats, *The Autobiography of W. B. Yeats* (New York: Macmillan, 1953), 167.

32 George Moore, "Note on 'Ghosts,'" in *Impressions and Opinions* (London: David Nutt, 1891), 224.

33 James, "Henrik Ibsen: On the Occasion of *Hedda Gabler*," in *Essays in London and Elsewhere*, 238. Toril Moi points out that such banal materials and things in Ibsen – sandwiches in *The Wild Duck*, for instance – belong not only to the everyday sphere of realism but also to the low genres of farce or folk comedy (*Henrik Ibsen*, 253).

34 Meyer, *Ibsen: A Biography*, 455.

35 One of the finest contemporary writers on Ibsen, Michael Goldman, identifies "constraint" as the essential quality of Ibsen's realism: constraint of the "realism from *Madame Bovary* on ... a source of confinement, limitation, failure." And Goldman emphasizes the performance of this constraint as the necessary element: "the sense of constraint does not come about simply because Ibsen's characters find or feel themselves trapped as the play reaches its climax. It is much more a question of how Ibsen's actors are constrained to perform this discovery." The point here is similar to Joyce's: Ibsen's plays need to be performed. See *Ibsen: The Dramaturgy of Fear* (New York: Columbia University Press, 1999), 38–9.

36 Stephen Lacey, *British Realist Theatre: The New Wave in its Context, 1956–1965* (London: Routledge, 1995), 64–70. For Lacey's discussion of Brecht, see 102–3 and 154–9. See also Raymond Williams, "A Lecture on Realism," *Screen* 18:1 (Spring 1977), 61–74.

37 Brecht's resistance to naturalism is, in this respect, similar to that of his usual antagonist, Lukács. In the essay "Narrate or Describe?" Lukács rails against the fixation on description – rather than the "narration" of novelists like Tolstoy – that he associates with Flaubert and especially Zola. Stylized and therefore detached description makes such writers "aloof as observers and critics of capitalist society": they have capitulated to what they wrongly see as the inevitability of stultifying bourgeois life, rather than forging an ideology of resistance to it. The omnipresent description that defines their fiction, meanwhile, "debases characters to the level of inanimate objects." See Georg Lukács, *Writer and Critic and Other Essays*, trans. Arthur D. Kahn (New York: Grosset & Dunlap, 1971), 110–48. The veneration of Balzac and antipathy toward Zola are, of course, central to Lukács's *Studies in European Realism*: see especially 5–8 and 21–96.

38 Brecht, *The Messingkauf Dialogues*, trans. John Willett (London: Methuen, 1965), 27.

39 J.L. Styan, *Modern Drama in Theory and Practice, Volume I: Realism and Naturalism* (Cambridge: Cambridge University Press, 1981), 9.

40 Virginia Woolf, "The Novels of E.M. Forster," in *The Death of the Moth and Other Essays* (New York: Harcourt Brace, 1942), 168.

41 Ibsen, *Letters and Speeches*, 200, 211, 218, 222.

42 Florence Emily Hardy, *The Early Life of Thomas Hardy, 1840–1891* (New York: Macmillan, 1928), 272; George Gissing, *The Collected Letters of George Gissing*, ed. Pierre Coustillas, Paul F. Matthiesen, and Arthur C. Young (Athens, OH: Ohio University Press, 1990), 1: 307.

43 Ibsen's phrasing is similar to Dr. Stockmann's in *An Enemy of the People*: Stockmann praises the few brave individuals who "stand at the outposts" against the majority. See Ibsen, *Plays: Two*, 193.

44 Ibsen's notes in Meyer's introduction to *Ghosts* in Ibsen, *Plays: One*, 20–1. Ibsen's emphasis on the general failure of "mankind" underscores his theater's roots in the satiric tradition and especially in satire's interest in the passing on of vice to subsequent generations (one of the central themes of *Ghosts* in particular). Raymond Williams sees this idea of "inherited debt" as one of the essential themes of all Ibsen dramas: see *Drama from Ibsen to Brecht* (New York: Oxford University Press, 1969), 36, 50–1, 58.

45 Auguste Ehrhard, *Henrik Ibsen et le théatre contemporain* (Paris: Lecène, Oudin, et Cie., 1892), 237, 238, 332, 307–8. ("Parce qu'il est réaliste, Ibsen est pessimiste … L'expérience de la vie le confirme dans cette opinion désolante que les infirmités de l'âme sont incurables et que le vice, la bêtise, le mensonge continueront à triompher dans le monde … l'horreur du monde tel qu'il existe est exprimée avec plus de passion, et, malgré cette ardeur, Ibsen envisage les êtres et les choses du regard le plus lucide … Idéaliste par sa thèse, Ibsen est un admirable réaliste par la manière dont il la présente.")

46 Hjalmar Hjorth Boyesen, *A Commentary on the Works of Henrik Ibsen* (New York: Russell & Russell, 1894), 201.

47 Georg Brandes, *Henrik Ibsen, Björnstjerne Björnson: Critical Studies* (New York: Macmillan, 1899), 3–4.

48 William Archer, "'Ghosts' and Gibberings," *Pall Mall Gazette*, April 8, 1891, 3.

49 James, "Henrik Ibsen: On the Occasion of Hedda Gabler," in *Essays in London and Elsewhere*, 237.

50 For a discussion of the continuities between early Ibsen comedies like *Love's Comedy, St John's Night*, and even the transitional work *The League of Youth* and the darker later works, see Robin Young, "Ibsen and Comedy," in McFarlane (ed.), *The Cambridge Companion to Ibsen*, 58–67. The emphasis in the essay, however, falls on comedy rather than satire: Young does not address the way in which the specifically satirical quality of plays like *Peer Gynt* inform the censorious austerity of the later realist dramas, which is, of course, my interest here. A brief essay on the more satirical elements of Ibsen's humor is Brian W. Downs's "*Love's Comedy* and Ibsen's Humour," in *Discussions of Henrik Ibsen*, ed. James McFarlane (Boston: D.C. Heath and Company, 1962), 28–34.

51 Henry James, "John Gabriel Borkman," in *The Scenic Art* (New Brunswick: Rutgers University Press, 1948), 292.

52 Oswald Crawfurd, "The London Stage," *Fortnightly Review* 47: 280 (April 1, 1890), 515.

53 On Ibsen and the Scribean "well-made play," see, for example, Williams, *Drama from Ibsen to Brecht*, 28–32.

54 William Archer, *William Archer on Ibsen: The Major Essays, 1889–1919*, ed. Thomas Postlewait (Westport, CT: Greenwood Press, 1984), 262.

55   Clement Scott, "Terry's Theatre," *Daily Telegraph*, January 28, 1891, 3.

56   Oswald Crawfurd, "The Ibsen Question," *Fortnightly Review* 49: 293 (May 1891), 734–5.

57   Ibsen, *An Enemy of the People* in *Plays: Two*, 165, 192.

58   Crawfurd, "The Ibsen Question," 740.

59   Max Nordau, *Degeneration* (New York: D. Appleton and Company, 1895), 475, 479, 481.

60   Shaw, "The Sanity of Art," in *The Works of Bernard Shaw*, 19: 303.

61   Anon. (Egmont Hake?), *Regeneration: A Reply to Max Nordau* (New York: G.B. Putnam's Sons, 1896), 157.

62   See Moi, *Henrik Ibsen*, 2, 13, 30–2, 67–70, and especially 216–17.

63   For a summary of this view see Michael Holroyd, *Bernard Shaw: The Search for Love, 1856–1898* (New York: Random House, 1988), 199–200.

64   Shaw, *The Quintessence of Ibsenism*, in *The Works of Bernard Shaw*, 19: 30.

65   Shaw, *Music in London*, vol. 2, in *The Works of Bernard Shaw*, 27: 136 (July 6, 1892).

66   G.K. Chesterton, *George Bernard Shaw* (New York: Hill and Wang, 1956), 80–1.

67   See, for example, Williams, *Drama from Ibsen to Eliot*, 41.

68   Keith M. May, *Ibsen and Shaw* (London: Macmillan, 1985), 124.

69   Shaw, *Works of Bernard Shaw*, 24: 251–2, 288.

70   George Bernard Shaw, "Ibsen's New Play," *Academy* 51: 1289 (January 16, 1897), 67–8.

71   *An Unsocial Socialist* in *Works of Bernard Shaw*, 5: 71.

72   In an 1896 letter to Golding Bright, Shaw wrote: "My first three plays, 'Widowers' Houses,' 'The Philanderer,' and 'Mrs Warren's Profession' were what people would call realistic. They were dramatic pictures of middle class society from the point of view of a Socialist who regards the basis of that society as thoroughly rotten economically and morally." *Collected Letters, 1874–1897*, ed. Dan H. Laurence (New York: Viking, 1985), 1: 632.

73   Shaw, *Cashel Byron's Profession*, in *The Works of Bernard Shaw*, 4: vii, 231, vii, ix.

74   Thomas Hardy, "Why I Don't Write Plays," in *Thomas Hardy's Personal Writings*, ed. Harold Orel (Lawrence: University of Kansas Press, 1966), 139; Gissing, *Collected Letters*, 4: 275–6. On the subject of Gissing's wish that Ibsen had written fiction rather than drama, see Lukács's point (in *The Historical Novel*) that a play like *Rosmersholm* "could not become a real drama" since it is "as far as subject matter, structure, action and psychology are concerned, really a novel, the last chapter of which Ibsen has clothed in the outward form of drama ... the basis of the play is still, of course, that of a novel, full of the undramatic drama of modern bourgeois life." Lukács's point relates to his larger argument that dramatic realism arises from the centrality of the "world historical individual," while novelistic realism, like epic, arises instead from the "totality of objects." See the chapter "Historical Novel and Historical Drama" in *The Historical Novel*, trans. Hannah and

Stanley Mitchell (London: Merlin Press, 1962), 125. With regard to Lukács on drama and epic, see also *The Theory of the Novel: A Historico-Philosophical Essay on the Forms of Great Epic Literature*, trans. Anna Bostock (Cambridge, MA: MIT Press, 1971), 40–55.

75 Shaw, *Plays Unpleasant*, in *The Works of Bernard Shaw*, 7: viii. One of these plays, *Widowers' Houses*, was originally begun as a collaboration (titled *Rhinegold*) with William Archer in the 1880s.

76 On Shaw's "intellectual comedy of manners," see, for instance, Pericles Lewis, *The Cambridge Introduction to Modernism* (Cambridge: Cambridge University Press, 2007), 45.

77 Shaw, *The Philanderer*, in *Plays Unpleasant*, in *The Works of Bernard Shaw*, 7:68.

78 F. Anstey, *Mr Punch's Pocket Ibsen* (London: Macmillan, 1893).

79 In recent years there seems to have been a renaissance of Ibsen burlesques similar to those of the late nineteenth century. In 2002 Lee Breuer adapted *A Doll's House* into *Dollhouse*, in which the male characters are all played by dwarves. In 2005 the Chicago-based Neo-Futurists staged *The Last Two Minutes of the Complete Works of Henrik Ibsen*, which condenses all the spectacular finales into two hours. The following year Les Frères Corbusier presented *Heddatron*, in which robots in Ypsilanti, Michigan, recite the dialogue from *Hedda Gabler*.

CHAPTER 5 TRUTH AND CARICATURE IN 'THE SECRET AGENT'

1 Joseph Conrad, *Collected Letters*, ed. Frederick R. Karl and Laurence Davies (Cambridge: Cambridge University Press, 1988), 3: 446, 461.

2 "I have just finished a novel (?) where there is not a drop of water – except for the rain, which is natural given that everything takes place in London. It contains a half-dozen anarchists, two women and an idiot. In any case, they're all imbeciles."

3 Joseph Conrad, *The Secret Agent* (Cambridge: Cambridge University Press, 1990), 4.

4 Conrad, *Collected Letters*, 3: 365; *The Secret Agent*, 7.

5 Joseph Conrad, *The Nigger of the 'Narcissus,'* in *Tales of Land and Sea* (Garden City, NY: Hanover House, 1953), 108.

6 Joseph Conrad, "Books," in *Notes on Life and Letters*, ed. J.H. Stape (Cambridge: Cambridge University Press, 2002), 12.

7 Joseph Conrad, *Conrad's Polish Background: Letters to and from Polish Friends*, ed. Zdzislaw Nadjer; trans. Halina Carroll (London: Oxford University Press, 1964), 228; Frederick Karl, *Joseph Conrad: The Three Lives* (New York: Farrar, Straus, and Giroux, 1979), 605; Edward Said, *Joseph Conrad and the Fiction of Autobiography* (Cambridge, MA: Harvard University Press, 1966), 40.

8 Norman Sherry, *Conrad's Western World* (Cambridge: Cambridge University Press, 1971), 205–334.

9   Albert J. Guerard, *Conrad the Novelist* (Cambridge, MA: Harvard University Press, 1958), 218.

10 Ian Watt, *Essays on Conrad* (Cambridge: Cambridge University Press, 2000), 122.

11 Joseph Conrad, *Heart of Darkness* (London: Penguin, 2007), 3.

12 Conrad's "enormous town" anticipates by a few years the masterpiece of his dedicatee, H.G. Wells, who in *Tono-Bungay* described the "huge dingy immensity of London port" and compared the city to "the unorganized, abundant substance of some tumourous growth-process" (*Tono-Bungay* (London: Macmillan, 1909), 121). Both novels recall Henry James's version of the teeming capital in *The Princess Casamassima* – like *The Secret Agent*, a novel concerned with terrorism – where James always emphasizes the alarming enormity of London, and where his hero, Hyacinth Robinson, "seemed to see, immensely magnified, the monstrosity of the great ulcers and sores of London." *The Princess Casamassima* (New York: Scribner's, 1908), 355–6.

13 Martin Price, "Conrad: Satire and Fiction," in *English Satire and the Satiric Tradition*, ed. Claude Rawson (Oxford: Basil Blackwell, 1984), 227–8.

14 Juvenal, *The Sixteen Satires*, trans. Peter Green (London: Penguin, 1998), 14 (lines 5–9).

15 See Walter Jackson Bate, *Samuel Johnson* (Washington: Counterpoint, 1998), 172.

16 Samuel Johnson, "London," in *Selected Poetry and Prose*, ed. Frank Brady and W.K. Wimsatt (Berkeley and Los Angeles: University of California Press, 1977), 47 (lines 9–10).

17 James Boswell, *Life of Johnson* (Oxford: Oxford University Press, 1998), 86.

18 Rebecca Walkowitz, in *Cosmopolitan Style: Modernism Beyond the Nation* (New York: Columbia University Press, 2006), sees *The Secret Agent*'s international London more for its cosmopolitanism – and for both Conrad's characters' and his own resulting "cultivated naturalness" and "adaptability" within an English context – than for this kind of contaminated darkness (see 38–53). In a sense I am interested in the way that Conrad's satiric rendering of London as a totality suggests the limits of cosmopolitanism, even if that subject is of great relevance to Conrad: the very question of national identity is crushed by our shared participation and imprisonment in the category he calls "mankind."

19 Joseph Conrad, *Under Western Eyes* (London: Penguin, 1999), 201.

20 Kate Flint, *The Victorians and the Visual Imagination* (Cambridge: Cambridge University Press, 2000), 9, 164; Linda Nochlin, *Realism* (London: Penguin, 1990), 168, 175; Alexander Welsh, *The City of Dickens* (Oxford: Clarendon Press, 1971), 9–10; Peter Brooks, *Realist Vision* (New Haven: Yale University Press, 2005), 3–4.

21 Conrad, *The Secret Agent*, 15.

22 J. Hillis Miller, *Poets of Reality: Six Twentieth-Century Writers* (Cambridge, MA: Belknap Press, 1966), 50.

23 Irving Howe, *Politics and the Novel* (New York: Horizon, 1957), 97; Sherry, *Conrad's Western World*, 323.

24 Conrad, *The Secret Agent*, 12, 125; Charles Dickens, *Our Mutual Friend* (Oxford: Oxford University Press, 1998), 6.

25 Verloc himself is described in exactly this way midway through the novel, when his wife tells him to answer the shop door: "Mr Verloc obeyed woodenly, stony-eyed, and like an automaton whose face had been painted red. And this resemblance to a mechanical figure went so far that he had an automaton's absurd air of being aware of the machinery inside of him" (149).

26 Conrad, *Collected Letters*, 3: 367, 374, 448.

27 Gustave Flaubert, *Correspondance* (Paris: Gallimard, 1980), 2: 416. ("La *Bovary*, qui aura été pour moi un exercice excellent, me sera peut-être funeste ensuite comme *réaction*, car j'en aurai pris (ceci est faible et imbécile) un dégoût extrême des sujets à milieu commun. C'est pour cela que j'ai tant de mal à l'écrire, ce livre. Il me faut de grands efforts pour m'imaginer mes personnages et puis pour les faire parler, car ils me répugnent profondément.")

28 It is likely that Conrad was familiar with Flaubert's own torturous experience writing fiction. In his book on Conrad, Ford Madox Ford recalls that the two of them read the *Correspondance* "daily together over a space of years." *Joseph Conrad: A Personal Remembrance* (Boston: Little, Brown, 1924), 57.

29 Robert Louis Stevenson, "A Note on Realism," in *The Works of Robert Louis Stevenson* (New York: Scribner's, 1925), 27: 79.

30 Robert Louis Stevenson, *The Letters of Robert Louis Stevenson*, ed. Sidney Colvin (New York: Scribner's, 1911), 4: 58, 153, 194, 209–10.

31 Conrad's imbeciles echo even more directly Flaubert's reference, in an 1853 letter to Louis Bouilhet, to "mon trio d'imbéciles," referring to Emma, Charles, and Homais in *Madame Bovary* (*Correspondance*, 2: 360).

32 For more on Stevenson, *The Ebb-Tide*, and realism, see Aaron Matz, "Some Versions of Vitriol (The Novel Circa 1890)," *Novel: A Forum on Fiction* 42:1 (Spring 2009), 23–39.

33 Conrad, *The Secret Agent*, 16, 67, 80, 115, 127, 132, 231.

34 Joseph Conrad, "An Outpost of Progress," in *Tales of Unrest* (London: Penguin, 1977), 108.

35 Conrad, *The Secret Agent*, 8, 3.

36 Joseph Conrad, *Almayer's Folly* (London: Penguin, 1976), 17, 159–64.

37 Aristotle, *On the Parts of Animals*, trans. with a commentary by James G. Lennox (Oxford: Clarendon Press, 2001), 69, III.10.

38 As should be clear from this chapter, I do not agree with Fredric Jameson that we "must indeed take Conrad seriously when he tells us that the only thing that interested him in Flaubert was the latter's style" (Fredric Jameson, *The Political Unconscious: Narrative as a Socially Symbolic Act* (Ithaca: Cornell University Press, 1981), 212). Conrad's protestation to this effect has the same ring of disingenuousness (or, at best, repression) that marks some of his defensive claims in the Author's Note to *The Secret Agent*.

39 Félicité's parrot, Loulou, looks ahead not only to *The Secret Agent*'s player piano – they both make noise perfunctorily, programmatically – but also to the Goulds' parrot in *Nostromo*, which mimics human sound just as Loulou does. Dickens made use of the same device: Mrs. Merdle's shrieking parrot in *Little Dorrit*.

40 Ian Watt notes that in *Almayer's Folly* Conrad could have been thinking of the French etymology (*folie*) of the English "folly": Almayer's folly is not "mere foolishness" but something approaching "mania or madness." See *Conrad in the Nineteenth Century* (Berkeley and Los Angeles: University of California Press, 1979), 65–6.

41 Conrad, "Books," in *Notes on Life and Letters*, 10.

42 H.G. Wells, *Kipps* (London: Macmillan, 1905), 392.

43 Conrad had written "The Black Mate" when he was still a seaman, but critics like Frederick Karl generally consider "The Idiots" to be his first story. See Karl, *Joseph Conrad: The Three Lives*, 374.

44 Conrad, "The Idiots," in *Tales of Unrest*, 59.

45 Jonathan Swift, *Gulliver's Travels* in *Prose Works of Jonathan Swift*, ed. Herbert Davis (Oxford: Basil Blackwell, 1941), 11: 273.

46 Philip Larkin, *High Windows* (London: Faber and Faber, 1974), 30. See also the beginning of Pope and Arbuthnot's *Scriblerus*, where Dr. Cornelius Scriblerus affirms to his wife that "it was better to be childless than to become the parent of a fool." Alexander Pope and John Arbuthnot, *Memoirs of the Extraordinary Life, Works and Discoveries of Martinus Scriblerus* (London: Hesperus Press, 2002), 8.

47 Joseph Conrad, *Lord Jim* (London: Penguin, 1989), 120, 123.

48 Miller, *Poets of Reality*, 19.

49 Ian Watt, *Conrad: The Secret Agent: A Casebook* (London: Macmillan, 1973), 80.

50 F.R. Leavis, *The Great Tradition: George Eliot, Henry James, Joseph Conrad* (London: Chatto & Windus, 1948), 210.

51 Karl, *Joseph Conrad: The Three Lives*, 587; R.A. Gekoski, *Conrad: The Moral World of the Novelist* (London: Paul Elek, 1978), 150–1.

52 Wayne Booth, *The Rhetoric of Irony* (Chicago: University of Chicago Press, 1974), 10, 240, 30.

53 Conrad, *Collected Letters*, 3: 491, 365.

54 Thomas Hardy, *Collected Letters*, ed. Richard Little Purdy and Michael Millgate (Oxford: Clarendon Press, 1978), 1: 190; Florence Emily Hardy, *The Early Life of Thomas Hardy, 1840–1891* (New York: Macmillan, 1928), 282.

55 Joseph Conrad, *A Personal Record* (London: J.M. Dent & Sons, 1919), 14.

56 Thomas Mann, "Joseph Conrad's 'The Secret Agent'" in *Past Masters and Other Papers*, trans. H.T. Lowe-Porter (New York: Alfred A. Knopf, 1933), 240–1.

57 Conrad, "An Outpost of Progress," in *Tales of Unrest*, 110.

58 Joseph Conrad, "The Informer: An Ironic Tale" in *The Complete Short Fiction of Joseph Conrad*, ed. Samuel Hynes (Hopewell, NJ: Ecco Press, 1992), 2: 42.

59 Geoffrey Galt Harpham, *One of Us: The Mastery of Joseph Conrad* (Chicago: University of Chicago Press, 1996), 65.

60 Mark Wollaeger, *Joseph Conrad and the Fictions of Skepticism* (Stanford: Stanford University Press, 1990), 145–6.

61 See Flaubert's letter to Madame Roger des Genettes about *Un coeur simple*, June 19, 1876: "Cela n'est nullement ironique comme vous le supposez, mais au contraire très sérieux et très triste. Je veux apitoyer, faire pleurer les âmes sensibles – en étant une moi-même." *Correspondance*, 5: 57.

62 For Turgenev's letter, see Gustave Flaubert, *Lettres inédites à Tourgueneff* (Monaco: Editions du Rocher, 1946), 80 ("c'est un sujet à traiter *presto*, à la Swift, à la Voltaire"). For Flaubert's response, see *Correspondance*, 4: 843. ("Je ne suis point de votre avis sur la manière dont il faut prendre ce sujet-là. S'il est traité brièvement, d'une façon concise et légère, ce sera une fantaisie plus ou [moins] spirituelle, mais sans portée et sans vraisemblance, tandis qu'en détaillant et développant, j'aurai l'air de croire à mon histoire, et on peut faire une chose sérieuse et même effrayante.")

Bibliography

Adorno, Theodor, Walter Benjamin, Ernst Bloch, Bertolt Brecht, and Georg Lukács. *Aesthetics and Politics*. London: Verso, 2007.

Anon. (Hake, Egmont?) *Regeneration: A Reply to Max Nordau*. New York: G.B. Putnam's Sons, 1896.

Anstey, F. *Mr Punch's Pocket Ibsen*. London: Macmillan, 1893.

Archer, William. "Ibsen and English Criticism." *Fortnightly Review* 46: 271 (July 1889): 30–7.

"'Ghosts' and Gibberings." *Pall Mall Gazette*, April 8, 1891: 3.

"The Real Ibsen." *International Monthly* 3 (February 1901): 182.

William Archer on Ibsen: The Major Essays, 1889–1919. Ed. Thomas Postlewait. Westport, CT: Greenwood Press, 1984.

Athenaeum, May 9, 1891: 601.

Atlantic Monthly. "An Idealistic Realist." 93: 556 (February 1904): 280.

Auerbach, Erich. *Mimesis: The Representation of Reality in Western Literature*. Princeton: Princeton University Press, 1953.

Bakhtin, Mikhail. *Problems of Dostoevsky's Poetics*. Minneapolis: University of Minnesota Press, 1984.

Rabelais and His World. Bloomington: Indiana University Press, 1984.

Balzac, Honoré de. *La Comédie humaine*. Pierre-Georges Cartex (gen. ed.). 12 vols. Paris: Gallimard, 1976–1981.

Barthes, Roland. *The Rustle of Language*. Trans. Richard Howard. Berkeley and Los Angeles: University of California Press, 1989.

Bate, Walter Jackson. *Samuel Johnson*. Washington: Counterpoint, 1998.

Baudelaire, Charles. *Oeuvres complètes*. 2 vols. Paris: Gallimard, 1975–1976.

Bayley, John. *An Essay on Hardy*. Cambridge: Cambridge University Press, 1978.

Beer, Gillian. *Darwin's Plots: Evolutionary Narrative in Darwin, George Eliot, and Nineteenth-Century Fiction*. Cambridge: Cambridge University Press, 1983.

Beerbohm, Max. *The Happy Hypocrite*. London: John Lane, 1897.

Benjamin, Walter. *Reflections*. Trans. Edmund Jephcott. New York: Schocken, 1978.

Bennett, Arnold. *Fame and Fiction*. London: Grant Richards, 1901.

Besant, Walter. "Mr George Gissing: An Inquiry." *Academy* 57 (1899): 724–6.

"Notes and News." *Author* 2:1 (June 1, 1891): 15.

Bodenheimer, Rosemarie. *The Real Life of Mary Ann Evans: George Eliot, Her Letters and Fiction.* Ithaca: Cornell University Press, 1994.

Booth, Wayne. *The Rhetoric of Irony.* Chicago: University of Chicago Press, 1974.

Boswell, James. *Life of Johnson.* 1791. Oxford: Oxford University Press, 1998.

Boyesen, Hjalmar Hjorth. *A Commentary on the Works of Henrik Ibsen.* New York: Russell & Russell, 1894.

Brandes, Georg. *Henrik Ibsen, Björnstjerne Björnson: Critical Studies.* New York: Macmillan, 1899.

Brantlinger, Patrick. *Bread and Circuses: Theories of Mass Culture as Social Decay.* Ithaca: Cornell University Press, 1983.

   The Reading Lesson: The Threat of Mass Literacy in Nineteenth-Century British Fiction. Bloomington: Indiana University Press, 1998.

Brecht, Bertolt. *The Messingkauf Dialogues.* Trans. John Willett. London: Methuen, 1965.

Brooks, Peter. *Realist Vision.* New Haven: Yale University Press, 2005.

Byron, George Gordon, Lord. *The Complete Poetical Works of Byron.* Ed. Paul Elmer More. Boston: Houghton Mifflin, 1933.

Carey, John. *The Intellectuals and the Masses: Pride and Prejudice Among the Literary Intelligentsia, 1880–1939.* London: Faber and Faber, 1992.

Carroll, David. *George Eliot and the Conflict of Interpretations.* Cambridge: Cambridge University Press, 1992.

Casanova, Pascale. *The World Republic of Letters.* Trans. M.B. DeBevoise. Cambridge, MA: Harvard University Press, 2004.

Céline, Louis-Ferdinand. *Romans.* 4 vols. Paris: Gallimard, 1981–1993.

Chesterton, G.K. *George Bernard Shaw.* New York: Hill and Wang, 1956.

   The Victorian Age in Literature. London: Williams and Norgate, 1913.

Clodd, Edward. *Memories.* London: Chapman and Hall, 1916.

Collie, Michael. *The Alien Art: A Critical Study of George Gissing's Novels.* Folkestone: Dawson, 1979.

Connor, Steven. *The Book of Skin.* Ithaca: Cornell University Press, 2004.

Conrad, Joseph. *Almayer's Folly.* 1895. London: Penguin, 1976.

   Collected Letters. Ed. Frederick R. Karl and Laurence Davies. 6 vols. Cambridge: Cambridge University Press, 1983.

   The Complete Short Fiction of Joseph Conrad. 4 vols. Ed. Samuel Hynes. Hopewell, NJ: Ecco Press, 1991–1992.

   Conrad's Polish Background: Letters to and from Polish Friends. Ed. Zdzislaw Nadjer. Trans. Halina Carroll. London: Oxford University Press, 1964.

   Heart of Darkness. 1899. London: Penguin, 2007.

   Lord Jim. 1900. London: Penguin, 1989.

   The Nigger of the "*Narcissus,*" in *Tales of Land and Sea.* Garden City, NY: Hanover House, 1953.

   Nostromo. 1904. London: Penguin, 1990.

   Notes on Life and Letters. Ed. J.H. Stape. Cambridge: Cambridge University Press, 2002.

A Personal Record. 1912. London: J.M. Dent & Sons, 1919.

Tales of Unrest. 1898. London: Penguin, 1977.

The Secret Agent. 1907. Cambridge: Cambridge University Press, 1990.

Under Western Eyes. 1911. London: Penguin, 1999.

Crawfurd, Oswald. "The Ibsen Question." *Fortnightly Review* 49:293 (May 1891): 725–40.

"The London Stage." *Fortnightly Review* 47:280 (April 1, 1890): 499–516.

Crinkle, Nym. "The Foolishness of the Ibsenites." *The Theatre Magazine* 5:9 (January 4, 1890): 165–6.

Dickens, Charles. *Bleak House.* 1853. Oxford: Oxford University Press, 1998.

Hard Times. 1854. Oxford: Oxford University Press, 1998.

Little Dorrit. 1857. Oxford: Oxford University Press, 1999.

Our Mutual Friend. 1865. Oxford: Oxford University Press, 1998.

Ehrhard, Auguste. *Henrik Ibsen et le théatre contemporain.* Paris: Lecène, Oudin, et Cie., 1892.

Eliot, George. *Adam Bede.* 1859. Oxford: Clarendon Press, 2001.

Daniel Deronda. 1876. Oxford: Clarendon Press, 1984.

Felix Holt, The Radical. 1866. Oxford: Clarendon Press, 1980.

The George Eliot Letters. Ed. Gordon S. Haight. 9 vols. New Haven: Yale University Press, 1954–1978.

Impressions of Theophrastus Such. 1879. Iowa City: University of Iowa Press, 1994.

The Journals of George Eliot. Ed. Margaret Harris and Judith Johnston. Cambridge: Cambridge University Press, 1998.

The Lifted Veil and Brother Jacob. London: Penguin, 2001.

Middlemarch. 1871–1872. Oxford: Clarendon Press, 1986.

The Mill on the Floss. 1860. Oxford: Clarendon Press, 1980.

Scenes of Clerical Life. 1858. Oxford: Clarendon Press, 1985.

Selected Essays, Poems and Other Writings. London: Penguin, 1990.

Eliot, T.S. *After Strange Gods: A Primer of Modern Heresy.* London: Faber and Faber, 1934.

Elkin, P.K. *The Augustan Defence of Satire.* Oxford: Clarendon Press, 1973.

Elliott, Robert C. *The Power of Satire: Magic, Ritual, Art.* Princeton: Princeton University Press, 1960.

Ellis, Havelock. "Concerning *Jude the Obscure*." *The Savoy* 6 (October 1896): 40–2.

Ermarth, Elizabeth Deeds. *Realism and Consensus in the English Novel.* Princeton: Princeton University Press, 1983.

Fielding, Henry. *Joseph Andrews.* 1742. Oxford: Clarendon Press, 1967.

Tom Jones. 1749. London: Penguin, 1985.

Flaubert, Gustave. *Correspondance.* 5 vols. Paris: Gallimard, 1980–2007.

Lettres inédites à Tourgueneff. Monaco: Editions du Rocher, 1946.

Oeuvres. 2 vols. Paris: Gallimard, 1951–1952.

and George Sand. *Correspondance.* Ed. Alphonse Jacobs. Paris: Flammarion, 1981.

Flint, Kate. *The Victorians and the Visual Imagination.* Cambridge: Cambridge University Press, 2000.

Ford, Ford Madox. *Joseph Conrad: A Personal Remembrance.* Boston: Little, Brown, 1924.

Frank, Miriam. *Ibsen in England.* Boston: Four Seas Company, 1919.

Freud, Sigmund. *The Standard Edition of the Complete Psychological Works of Sigmund Freud.* Trans. James Strachey. 24 vols. London: Hogarth Press, 1953–1974.

Frye, Northrop. *Anatomy of Criticism.* Princeton: Princeton University Press, 1957.

Gay, Peter. *The Cultivation of Hatred.* New York: W.W. Norton, 1993.

Gekoski, R.A. *Conrad: The Moral World of the Novelist.* London: Paul Elek, 1978.

Gilbert, Sandra M., and Susan Gubar. *The Madwoman in the Attic: The Woman Writer and the Nineteenth-Century Literary Imagination.* New Haven: Yale University Press, 2000.

Gissing, George. *Born in Exile.* 1892. London: Everyman/J.M. Dent, 1993.

Charles Dickens: A Critical Study. 1898. New York: Haskell House, 1974.

The Collected Letters of George Gissing. Ed. Paul F. Matthiesen, Arthur C. Young, and Pierre Coustillas. 9 vols. Athens, OH: Ohio University Press, 1990–1997.

George Gissing: Essays and Fiction. Ed. Pierre Coustillas. Baltimore: Johns Hopkins Press, 1970.

The Immortal Dickens. London: Cecil Palmer, 1925.

In the Year of Jubilee. 1894. London: Everyman/J.M. Dent, 1994.

London and the Life of Literature in Late Victorian England: The Diary of George Gissing, Novelist. Ed. Pierre Coustillas. Hassocks: Harvester, 1978.

New Grub Street. 1891. Oxford: Oxford University Press, 1998.

The Nether World. 1889. Oxford: Oxford University Press, 1999.

The Odd Women. 1893. London: Penguin, 1983.

Our Friend the Charlatan. New York: Henry Holt, 1901.

"The Place of Realism in Fiction." *Humanitarian* 7:1 (July 1895): 14–16.

The Private Papers of Henry Ryecroft. Westminster: Archibald Constable and Co., 1903.

The Whirlpool. 1897. London: Everyman/J.M. Dent, 1997.

Gogol, Nikolai. *Dead Souls.* Trans. Richard Pevear and Larissa Volokhonsky. New York: Vintage, 1997.

Goldman, Michael. *Ibsen: The Dramaturgy of Fear.* New York: Columbia University Press, 1999.

Goode, John. *George Gissing: Ideology and Fiction.* New York: Barnes and Noble, 1979.

Gosse, Edmund. *A History of Eighteenth Century Literature.* London: Macmillan, 1889.

Ibsen. London: Hodder and Stoughton, 1907.

"Ibsen, the Norwegian Satirist." *Fortnightly Review* 13:731 (January 1873): 74–88.

"Ibsen's Jubilee." *Spectator* 2439 (March 27, 1875): 401–2.

"Ibsen's New Poems." *Spectator* 2281 (March 16, 1872): 344–5.

"Ibsen's Social Dramas." *Fortnightly Review* 45:265 (January 1889): 107–21.

"Mr Hardy's New Novel." *Cosmopolis* 1 (January 1896): 60–9.

"A Norwegian Drama." *Spectator* 2299 (July 20, 1872): 922–3.

Questions at Issue. New York: D. Appleton and Company, 1893.

Grylls, David. "The Annual Return to Old Grub Street: What Samuel Johnson Meant to Gissing." *Gissing Newsletter* 20:1 (January, 1984), 1–27.

Guerard, Albert J. *Conrad the Novelist.* Cambridge, MA: Harvard University Press, 1958.

Haight, Gordon S. *George Eliot: A Biography.* New York: Oxford University Press, 1968.

Halperin, John. *Gissing: A Life in Books.* Oxford: Oxford University Press, 1982.

Hardy, Florence Emily. *The Early Life of Thomas Hardy, 1840–1891.* New York: Macmillan, 1928.

The Later Years of Thomas Hardy, 1892–1928. New York: Macmillan, 1930.

Hardy, Thomas. *Collected Letters.* Ed. Richard Little Purdy and Michael Millgate. 7 vols. Oxford: Clarendon Press, 1978–1988.

The Complete Poems. Ed. James Gibson. London: Palgrave, 2001.

The Hand of Ethelberta. 1876. London: Macmillan, 1912.

Jude the Obscure. 1895. London: Macmillan, 1912.

The Literary Notebooks of Thomas Hardy. Ed. Lennart A. Björk. 2 vols. London: Macmillan, 1985.

The Mayor of Casterbridge. 1886. London: Macmillan, 1912.

The Return of the Native. 1878. London: Macmillan, 1912.

Tess of the d'Urbervilles. 1891. London: Macmillan, 1912.

Thomas Hardy's Personal Writings. Ed. Harold Orel. Lawrence: University of Kansas Press, 1966.

Two on a Tower. 1882. London: Macmillan, 1912.

The Woodlanders. 1887. London: Macmillan, 1912.

Harpham, Geoffrey Galt. *One of Us: The Mastery of Joseph Conrad.* Chicago: University of Chicago Press, 1996.

Hazlitt, William. *Lectures on the English Comic Writers.* London: Taylor and Hessey, 1819.

Hemmings, F.W.J. *Culture and Society in France, 1848–1898.* New York: Scribner's, 1971.

Hertz, Neil. *George Eliot's Pulse.* Stanford: Stanford University Press, 2003.

Holroyd, Michael. *Bernard Shaw: The Search for Love, 1856–1898.* New York: Random House, 1988.

Horace. *Satires and Epistles.* Trans. Niall Rudd. London: Penguin, 1997.

Howe, Irving. *Politics and the Novel.* New York: Horizon, 1957.

Thomas Hardy. New York: Macmillan, 1967.

Ibsen, Henrik. *Ibsen: Letters and Speeches.* Ed. Evert Sprinchorn. New York: Hill and Wang, 1964.

Plays. Trans. and ed. Michael Meyer. 6 vols. London: Methuen, 2000.

Illustrated London News. "Mr Hardy's New Novel." January 11, 1896: 50.

Jackson, Holbrook. *The Eighteen Nineties.* 1913. New York: Alfred A. Knopf, 1922.

James, Henry. *Essays in London and Elsewhere.* New York: Harper & Brothers, 1893.
   Literary Criticism. 2 vols. New York: Library of America, 1984.
   The Princess Casamassima. 1886. New York: Scribner's, 1908.
   The Scenic Art. New Brunswick: Rutgers University Press, 1948.

Jameson, Fredric. *The Political Unconscious: Narrative as a Socially Symbolic Act.*
   Ithaca: Cornell University Press, 1981.

Johnson, Lionel. *The Art of Thomas Hardy.* 1894. New York: Russell & Russell, 1928.

Johnson, Samuel. *Selected Poetry and Prose.* Ed. Frank Brady and W.K. Wimsatt.
   Berkeley and Los Angeles: University of California Press, 1977.

Joyce, James. *On Ibsen.* Ed. Dennis Phillips. Copenhagen and Los Angeles:
   Green Integer, 1999.

Juvenal. *The Sixteen Satires.* Trans. Peter Green. London: Penguin, 1998.

Karl, Frederick. *Joseph Conrad: The Three Lives.* New York: Farrar, Straus, and
   Giroux, 1979.

Kernan, Alvin. *The Plot of Satire.* New Haven: Yale University Press, 1965.

Knoepflmacher, U.C. *George Eliot's Early Novels: The Limits of Realism.* Berkeley
   and Los Angeles: University of California Press, 1968.

Kristeva, Julia. *Powers of Horror: An Essay on Abjection.* Trans. Leon S. Roudiez.
   New York: Columbia University Press, 1982.

Lacey, Stephen. *British Realist Theatre: The New Wave in its Context, 1956–1965.*
   London: Routledge, 1995.

Lane, Christopher. *Hatred and Civility: The Antisocial Life in Victorian England.*
   New York: Columbia University Press, 2004.

Lang, Andrew. "Realism in Grub Street." *Author* 2:2 (July 1, 1891): 43–4.

Larkin, Philip. *High Windows.* London: Faber and Faber, 1974.
   Required Writing: Miscellaneous Pieces, 1955–1982. New York: Farrar, Straus,
   and Giroux, 1984.

Lawlor, John. "Radical Satire and the Realistic Novel." *Essays and Studies* 8 (1955):
   67–73.

Lawrence, D.H. *Study of Thomas Hardy and Other Essays.* Ed. Bruce Steele.
   Cambridge: Cambridge University Press, 1985.
   Women in Love. 1920. Cambridge: Cambridge University Press, 1987.

Leavis, F.R. *The Great Tradition: George Eliot, Henry James, Joseph Conrad.*
   London: Chatto & Windus, 1948.

Leavis, Q.D. "Gissing and the English Novel." *Scrutiny* 7:1 (June 1938): 73–81.

Levine, George. *Darwin and the Novelists: Patterns of Science in Victorian Fiction.*
   Cambridge, MA: Harvard University Press, 1988.
   Dying to Know: Scientific Epistemology and Narrative in Victorian England.
   Chicago: University of Chicago Press, 2002.
   The Realistic Imagination: English Fiction from Frankenstein to Lady Chatterley.
   Chicago: University of Chicago Press, 1981.

Lewes, George Henry. *Lewes Ms Journals.* Journal X, March 22, 1859. Unpublished
   Manuscript, Beinecke Rare Book and Manuscript Library, Yale University.

Lewis, Pericles. *The Cambridge Introduction to Modernism.* Cambridge: Cambridge University Press, 2007.

Lewis, Wyndham. *Men Without Art.* London: Cassell & Co., 1934.

The Apes of God. London: Arthur Press, 1930.

Lovell, Terry. *Pictures of Reality: Aesthetics, Politics, and Pleasure.* London: BFI, 1980.

Lukács, Georg. *Essays on Realism.* Trans. David Fernbach. Cambridge, MA: MIT Press, 1980.

The Historical Novel. Trans. Hannah and Stanley Mitchell. London: Merlin Press, 1962.

Studies in European Realism: A Sociological Survey of the Writings of Balzac, Stendhal, Zola, Tolstoy, Gorky. Trans. Edith Bone. New York: Grosset & Dunlap, 1964.

The Theory of the Novel: A Historico-Philosophical Essay on the Forms of Great Epic Literature. Trans. Anna Bostock. Cambridge, MA: MIT Press, 1971.

Writer and Critic and Other Essays. Trans. Arthur D. Kahn. New York: Grosset & Dunlap, 1974.

Mann, Thomas. *Past Masters and Other Papers.* Trans. H.T. Lowe-Porter. New York: Alfred A. Knopf, 1933.

Marsh, Joss. *Word Crimes: Blasphemy, Culture, and Literature in Nineteenth-Century England.* Chicago: University of Chicago Press, 1998.

Matz, Aaron. "Some Versions of Vitriol (The Novel Circa 1890)." *Novel: A Forum on Fiction* 42:1 (Spring 2009), 23–39.

May, Keith M. *Ibsen and Shaw.* London: Macmillan, 1985.

McFarlane, James (ed.). *The Cambridge Companion to Ibsen.* Cambridge: Cambridge University Press, 1994.

(ed.). *Discussions of Henrik Ibsen.* Boston: D.C. Heath and Company, 1962.

Meredith, George. *An Essay on Comedy and the Uses of the Comic Spirit.* Westminster: Archibald Constable and Co., 1897.

Meyer, Michael. *Ibsen: A Biography.* Garden City, NY: Doubleday, 1971.

Miller, J. Hillis. *Fiction and Repetition: Seven English Novels.* Cambridge, MA: Harvard University Press, 1982.

Poets of Reality: Six Twentieth-Century Writers. Cambridge, MA: Belknap Press, 1966.

Thomas Hardy: Distance and Desire. Cambridge, MA: Harvard University Press, 1970.

Millgate, Michael. *Thomas Hardy: A Biography.* New York: Random House, 1982.

Moi, Toril. *Henrik Ibsen and the Birth of Modernism: Art, Theater, Philosophy.* New York: Oxford University Press, 2006.

Moore, George. *Impressions and Opinions.* London: David Nutt, 1891.

Morrison, Arthur. *A Child of the Jago.* Chicago: Academy Chicago Publishers, 1995.

Nabokov, Vladimir. *Lectures on Literature.* San Diego: Harcourt Brace, 1980.

Nicolson, Marjorie. *Science and Imagination.* Ithaca: Cornell University Press, 1956.

Nochlin, Linda. *Realism.* London: Penguin, 1990.

Nordau, Max. *Degeneration.* New York: D. Appleton and Company, 1895.

Oliphant, Mrs. (Margaret). "The Anti-Marriage League." *Blackwood's Magazine* 159 (January 1896): 135–49.

Orwell, George. *Collected Essays, Journalism and Letters of George Orwell.* Ed. Sonia Orwell and Ian Angus. 4 vols. New York: Harcourt Brace & World, 1968.

Essays. Ed. John Carey. New York: Alfred A. Knopf. 2002.

Nineteen Eighty-Four. London: Secker & Warburg, 1949.

Paulson, Ronald. *The Fictions of Satire.* Baltimore: Johns Hopkins University Press, 1967.

Satire and the Novel in Eighteenth-Century England. New Haven: Yale University Press, 1967.

Poole, Adrian. *Gissing in Context.* London: Macmillan, 1975.

Pope, Alexander. *The Poems of Alexander Pope.* John Butt (gen. ed.). 11 vols. New Haven: Yale University Press, 1951–1969.

and John Arbuthnot. *Memoirs of the Extraordinary Life, Works and Discoveries of Martinus Scriblerus.* 1741. London: Hesperus Press, 2002.

Price, Martin. "Conrad: Satire and Fiction." In *English Satire and the Satiric Tradition.* Ed. Claude Rawson. Oxford: Basil Blackwell, 1984.

Proust, Marcel. *A la recherche du temps perdu.* 3 vols. Paris: Gallimard, 1954.

Rabelais, François. *Oeuvres complètes.* Paris: Gallimard, 1994.

Rawson, Claude. "Cannibalism and Fiction: Reflections on Narrative Form and 'Extreme' Situations." *Genre* 10:4 (Winter 1977): 667–711 and 11:2 (Summer 1978): 227–313.

Gulliver and the Gentle Reader: Studies in Swift and Our Time. London: Routledge & Kegan Paul, 1973.

Satire and Sentiment, 1660–1830. New Haven: Yale University Press, 2000.

Rogers, Pat. *Grub Street: Studies in a Subculture.* London: Methuen, 1972.

Rousseau, Jean-Jacques. *Oeuvres complètes.* 5 vols. Paris: Gallimard, 1959–1995.

Ruskin, John. *The Works of John Ruskin.* Ed. E.T. Cook and Alexander Wedderburn. 39 vols. London: George Allen, 1903–1912.

Said, Edward. *Joseph Conrad and the Fiction of Autobiography.* Cambridge, MA: Harvard University Press, 1966.

Sainte-Beuve, Charles Augustin. *Causeries du lundi.* 15 vols. Paris: Garnier Frères, 1912.

Saturday Review 71 (May 2, 1891): 19–20.

Sauer, R. "Infanticide and Abortion in Nineteenth Century Britain." *Population Studies* 32 (1978): 81–93.

Scarry, Elaine. *The Body in Pain: The Making and Unmaking of the World.* New York: Oxford University Press, 1985.

Schopenhauer, Arthur. *The World as Will and Representation.* Trans. E.F.J. Payne. 2 vols. New York: Dover, 1969.

Scott, Clement. "Terry's Theatre." *Daily Telegraph,* January 28, 1891: 3.

The Theatre 14 (July 1, 1889): 19.

Shaw, George Bernard. *Collected Letters.* Ed. Dan H. Laurence. 4 vols. New York: Viking, 1985–1988.

"Ibsen's New Play." *Academy* 51:1289 (January 16, 1897): 67–8.

The Works of Bernard Shaw. 31 vols. London: Constable & Co., 1930–1934.

Shaw, Harry E. *Narrating Reality: Austen, Scott, Eliot.* Ithaca: Cornell University Press, 1999.

Shepherd-Barr, Kirsten. *Ibsen and Early Modernist Theatre, 1890–1900.* Westport, CT: Greenwood Press, 1997.

Sherry, Norman. *Conrad's Western World.* Cambridge: Cambridge University Press, 1971.

Sichel, Edith. "Two Philanthropic Novelists: Mr Walter Besant and Mr George Gissing." *Murray's Magazine* 3:16 (April 1888): 506–18.

Spectator, February 9, 1885: 206.

Stevenson, Robert Louis. *The Letters of Robert Louis Stevenson.* Ed. Sidney Colvin. 4 vols. New York: Scribner's, 1911.

The Works of Robert Louis Stevenson. 32 vols. New York: Scribner's, 1925.

Styan, J.L. *Modern Drama in Theory and Practice, Volume I: Realism and Naturalism.* Cambridge: Cambridge University Press, 1981.

Swift, Jonathan. *The Correspondence of Jonathan Swift.* Ed. Harold Williams. 5 vols. Oxford: Clarendon Press, 1963–1965.

Prose Works of Jonathan Swift. Ed. Herbert Davis. 14 vols. Oxford: Basil Blackwell, 1939–1968.

Symonds, John Addington. *Essays Speculative and Suggestive.* 2 vols. London: Chapman and Hall, 1890.

Thackeray, William Makepeace. *The English Humourists of the Eighteenth Century.* New York: Henry Holt, 1900.

Pendennis. 1850. Harmondsworth: Penguin, 1972.

Vanity Fair. 1847–1848. London: Penguin, 2003.

Works of William Makepeace Thackeray. 32 vols. New York: Scribner's, 1903–1904.

Thomson, James. *Satires and Profanities.* London: Progressive Publishing Company, 1884.

Thwaite, Ann. *Edmund Gosse: A Literary Landscape, 1849–1928.* London: Secker & Warburg, 1984.

Trollope, Anthony. *An Autobiography.* 1883. Oxford: Oxford University Press, 1999.

The Way We Live Now. 1875. London: Penguin, 1994.

Van Sant, Ann Jessie. *Eighteenth-Century Sensibility and the Novel.* Cambridge: Cambridge University Press, 1993.

Voltaire. *Romans et contes.* Ed. René Groos. Paris: Gallimard, 1954.

Walkowitz, Rebecca L. *Cosmopolitan Style: Modernism Beyond the Nation.* New York: Columbia University Press, 2006.

Watt, Ian. *Conrad in the Nineteenth Century.* Berkeley and Los Angeles: University of California Press, 1979.

(ed.). *Conrad: The Secret Agent: A Casebook.* London: Macmillan, 1973.

Essays on Conrad. Cambridge: Cambridge University Press, 2000.

The Rise of the Novel: Studies in Defoe, Richardson and Fielding. Berkeley and Los Angeles: University of California Press, 1957.

Waugh, Arthur. "George Gissing." *Fortnightly Review* 75: 446 (February 1904): 244–56.

"Reticence in Literature." *The Yellow Book* 1 (April 1894): 204–12.

Waugh, Evelyn. *Decline and Fall.* London: Chapman & Hall, 1928.

Vile Bodies. London: Chapman & Hall, 1930.

Wells, H.G. *Kipps.* London: Macmillan, 1905.

Tono-Bungay. London: Macmillan, 1909.

"Jude the Obscure." *Saturday Review*, February 8, 1896: 153–4.

"George Gissing: An Impression." *The Living Age* 25:3143 (October 1904): 38–45.

Welsh, Alexander. *The City of Dickens.* Oxford: Clarendon Press, 1971.

Whitehall Review, April 18, 1891: 19–20.

Widdowson, Peter. *On Thomas Hardy: Late Essays and Earlier.* Houndmills: Macmillan, 1998.

Wilde, Oscar. *The Artist as Critic: Critical Writings of Oscar Wilde.* Ed. Richard Ellmann. New York: Random House, 1968.

The Picture of Dorian Gray. 1891. Oxford: Oxford University Press, 2006.

Williams, Raymond. *The Country and the City.* New York: Oxford University Press, 1973.

Culture and Society, 1780–1950. New York: Columbia University Press, 1983.

Drama from Ibsen to Brecht. New York: Oxford University Press, 1969.

The English Novel from Dickens to Lawrence. London: Chatto & Windus, 1970.

Keywords. New York: Oxford University Press, 1985.

"A Lecture on Realism." *Screen* 18:1 (Spring 1977), 61–74.

Wollaeger, Mark. *Joseph Conrad and the Fictions of Skepticism.* Stanford: Stanford University Press, 1990.

Woloch, Alex. *The One Vs. the Many: Minor Characters and the Space of the Protagonist in the Novel.* Princeton: Princeton University Press, 2003.

Wood, James. *The Broken Estate: Essays on Literature and Belief.* New York: Random House, 1999.

The Irresponsible Self: On Laughter and the Novel. New York: Farrar, Straus, and Giroux, 2004.

Woolf, Virginia. *The Death of the Moth and Other Essays.* New York: Harcourt Brace, 1942.

The Essays of Virginia Woolf. Ed. Andrew McNeillie. 3 vols. San Diego: Harcourt Brace Jovanovich, 1986–1988.

Wordsworth, William. *The Poetical Works of William Wordsworth.* Ed. E. de Selincourt and Helen Darbishire. 5 vols. Oxford: Clarendon Press, 1940–1949.

Yeats, W.B. *The Autobiography of W. B. Yeats.* New York: Macmillan, 1953.

Yeazell, Ruth Bernard. *Art of the Everyday: Dutch Painting and the Realist Novel.* Princeton: Princeton University Press, 2007.

Yu, Christopher. *Nothing to Admire: The Politics of Poetic Satire from Dryden to Merrill.* Oxford: Oxford University Press, 2003.

Zola, Emile. *Ecrits sur l'art.* Paris: Gallimard, 1991.

Index

CAMBRIDGE STUDIES IN NINETEENTH-CENTURY
LITERATURE AND CULTURE

General Editor
Gillian Beer, *University of Cambridge*

Titles published

1. The Sickroom in Victorian Fiction: The Art of Being Ill
   Miriam Bailin, Washington University

2. Muscular Christianity: Embodying the Victorian Age
   edited by Donald E. Hall, California State University, Northridge

3. Victorian Masculinities: Manhood and Masculine Poetics in
   Early Victorian Literature and Art
   Herbert Sussman, Northeastern University, Boston

4. Byron and the Victorians
   Andrew Elfenbein, University of Minnesota

5. Literature in the Marketplace: Nineteenth-Century British
   Publishing and the Circulation of Books
   edited by John O. Jordan, University of California,
   Santa Cruz and Robert L. Patten, Rice University, Houston

6. Victorian Photography, Painting and Poetry
   Lindsay Smith, University of Sussex

7. Charlotte Brontë and Victorian Psychology
   Sally Shuttleworth, University of Sheffield

8. The Gothic Body: Sexuality, Materialism and Degeneration at the
   Fin de Siècle
   Kelly Hurley, University of Colorado at Boulder

9. Rereading Walter Pater
   William F. Shuter, Eastern Michigan University

10. Remaking Queen Victoria
    edited by Margaret Homans, Yale University and Adrienne Munich,
    State University of New York, Stony Brook

11. Disease, Desire, and the Body in Victorian Women's
    Popular Novels
    Pamela K. Gilbert, University of Florida